THE GRAYWOLF ANNUAL EIGHT:
THE NEW FAMILY

1 9 9 1

Previous *Graywolf Annuals*

THE GRAYWOLF

ANNUAL EIGHT

THE NEW

FAMILY

Edited by Scott Walker

GRAYWOLF PRESS: SAINT PAUL

Publication of this volume is made possible in part by grants from the National
Endowment for the Arts and the Minnesota State Arts Board. Graywolf Press
receives generous contributions from corporations, foundations, and
individuals, and is a member agency of United Arts, Saint Paul.

ISBN 1-55597-152-0
ISSN 0743-7471

9 8 7 6 5 4 3 2
First Printing, 1991

Published by Graywolf Press, 2402 University Avenue, Suite 203,
Saint Paul, Minnesota 55114. All rights reserved.

Cover art: Keith Haring, *Untitled* (exhibition poster), 1984
Screenprint on paper, © The Estate of Keith Haring, 1991
Photo: Joseph Coscia, Jr.

ACKNOWLEDGMENTS

Most of the stories collected in this *Graywolf Annual* have appeared previously in publications, as noted below. We gratefully acknowledge the cooperation of editors, agents, and authors for their permission to reprint the stories here.

Richard Bausch's "What Feels Like the World" is from *Spirits and Other Stories* (The Linden Press / Simon and Schuster, 1987). Copyright © 1987 by Richard Bausch.

Charles Baxter's "A Relative Stranger" is from *A Relative Stranger* (W. W. Norton & Company, Inc., 1990). Copyright © 1990 by Charles Baxter.

Kate Braverman's "Temporary Light" is from *Squandering the Blue* (Fawcett Columbine, 1990). Copyright © 1989 by Kate Braverman. Reprinted by permission of Ballantine Books, a Division of Random House, Inc.

Karen Brown's "Destiny" was first published in the *Georgia Review,* vol. XLIV, no. 3, Fall 1990. Copyright © by Karen Brown.

Dorothy Bryant's "Blood Relations" was first published in *Fiction Network,* 1987. Copyright © 1987 by Dorothy Bryant.

Kathleen Cambor's "Concessions" was first published in *American Short Fiction,* vol. 1, no. 1, Spring 1991 (University of Texas Press). Copyright © 1991 by Kathleen Cambor.

Ellen Hunnicutt's "Energy" was first published in the *Michigan Quarterly Review* and reprinted in *In the Music Library* (University of Pittsburgh Press, 1987). Copyright © 1987 by Ellen Hunnicutt. Reprinted here by permission of the University of Pittsburgh Press.

Maurice Kenny's "And Leave the Driving to Us" is from *Rain and Other Fictions* (White Pine Press, 1990). Copyright © 1990 by Maurice Kenny.

Nanci Kincaid's "Spittin' Image of a Baptist Boy" was first published in the *Carolina Quarterly* and was reprinted in *New Stories from the South: The Year's Best, 1990* (Algonquin Books of Chapel Hill, 1990). Copyright © 1989 by Nanci Kincaid.

Maxine Kumin's "Beginning with Gussie" was first published in the *American Voice,* no. 22, Spring 1991. Copyright © 1991 by Maxine Kumin.

Colleen J. McElroy's "How I Came to Dance with Queen Esther and the Dardanelles" is from *Driving Under the Cardboard Pines and Other Stories* (Creative Arts Book Company, 1990). Copyright © 1990 by Colleen J. McElroy.

Dennis McFarland's "Nothing to Ask For" was first published in the *New Yorker,* September 25, 1989. Copyright © 1989 by Dennis McFarland. Reprinted by permission of Brandt & Brandt Literary Agents, Inc.

Deborah Rose O'Neal's "Marguerite Marie" is from *Unholy Alliances* (Cleis Press, 1988). Copyright © 1988 by Deborah Rose O'Neal.

Pamela Painter's "New Family Car" was first published in *Story,* Winter 1991. Copyright © 1991 by Pamela Painter.

Annick Smith's "It's Come to This" was first published in *Story,* Winter 1991. Copyright © 1991 by Annick Smith.

CONTENTS

THE GRAYWOLF ANNUAL EIGHT:
THE NEW FAMILY

INTRODUCTION

"Happiness is having a large, loving, caring,
close-knit family in another city."
— George Burns

"If someone told me 20 years ago that I was
going to produce a whole week on divorce, I
never would have believed them."
— Mr. Rogers

IT MAY BE THAT the most tumultuous of revolutions are
the ones we hardly notice. In just one or two generations we
have seen radical change in the nature of the family, one of
the most deeply rooted human institutions. These transfor-
mations have occurred so quickly and with such stealth that
we've had no time to understand or to prepare for them.

The effects of these changes are so complex and intricate
that it will be years before we fully comprehend the magnitude of this revolution, perhaps years before it is generally
understood *to be* a revolution. The traditional family—
Ozzie and Harriet—is a myth, and has the resonant truth of
myth; as the family evolves and recreates itself, the mythic
power of the Ozzie and Harriet family continues to have a
forceful impact on our lives. Families have, in fact, changed.
The traditional nuclear family is now a minority in our culture. Many people in the current thirtysomething and
fortysomething generations were raised in that sort of family, and so suffer from equally vital conflicting visions of
how things ought to be—an entire generation has a
"Cinderella Complex." In this age of television and omni-
present saturation advertising, images of the traditional

family are perpetually before us, purposely inciting envy, and at times a withering sense of shame.

In this era of change we have to live our lives – divorcing, stepparenting, and buying birthday presents for our third husband's first cousin. There aren't many maps for this new territory. This anthology presents a range of short stories, each of which reflects some aspect of the New Family, in the hope that readers will find artful fiction to be a rough guide through thickets of choices and comparisons. Since we can't rely on the wisdom of tradition, we can perhaps listen to stories of others who are caught in the struggle and celebration of their new families.

THINK ABOUT ALL the ways families have been altered! Any one of the following could be regarded as the cause of fundamental change in the nature of families. What could have prepared us for:

- **Divorce**. Thousands of men and women who never considered the possibility of divorce now find themselves in their fifties facing painful and embarrassing issues: the dating scene, the possibility of spending the rest of their lives alone, the task of re-envisioning and remaking a family, and, for many women, first-time employment. Today, 50 percent of first marriages and 60 percent of second marriages end in divorce.
- **Single parents**. Twenty-five percent of families are headed by single parents, who must balance jobs, childrearing, housework, and the need for personal as well as family time.
- **Second and third marriages**. One-third of all children in the U.S. will live with a step-family by the time they are eighteen. Children and adults grapple with their relationships with half siblings, grandparents who are divorced and remarried, noncustodial

parents, and stepparents. These situations post troublesome questions: Who gets invited to the wedding? Are a stepmother's nieces and nephews her husband's son's cousins? Do they exchange birthday gifts? What about gifts for her husband's ex-wife's stepchildren, with whom her new stepchildren spend a good deal of time?

• **Two-career couples**. A profound change occurs in the way children are traditionally raised when both parents work. What are the long-term effects of day care? What *is* good day care? Fathers and mothers cope with the added pressure of balancing career and family time. Often two-career couples opt not to have children, consciously making the choice to build their "family" among friends. Also, career decisions often cause husbands and wives to live in separate parts of the country during the work week.

• **Geographical dispersion**. Our society is exceptionally mobile and families are often spread over great distances, a dramatic change from the past. Read the obituaries in any newspaper: more often than not, you'll note the survivors dispersed across the country. Does this mobility create or enhance a sense of rootlessness among people in our society? Does it give us a sense of abstraction from our communities? Or do we have stronger, more familial feelings about our communities? Who can we ask about parenting, if our parents aren't nearby?

• **Gay and lesbian couples**. Often cut off from their own families, gays and lesbians have become adept at building successful and supportive non-traditional families among friends. As our society has become more openly accepting of gay and lesbian lifestyles, more gays and lesbians (individually or as couples) have opted to include children in their

lives, through adoption or live birth, creating a very
new sort of family with very complex legal and social
issues to explore.

• **"Skip Generation" parenting**. It is now so common for children to be left to be raised by grandparents – left by unwed teenaged mothers or young
divorcees – that the sociologists have coined the
term "skip generation" to describe it.

• **"Biological clock" single parenting**. More and
more women who have been unable to find a suit-
able partner are deciding to bear or adopt and raise
children alone. Our culture seems to be surprisingly
accepting of what would have been scandalous a
generation ago.

The Graywolf Annual 8: The New Family contains contempo-
rary fiction about people coming to terms with these issues.
We hope our readers will enjoy them as fine stories which il-
lustrate how we are learning to live our lives, and how to better understand one another. Both established and new writ-
ers are featured, as in other *Annuals,* and we sought to offer
not a definitive range of stories but a context for further
reading and exploration.

The stories included here show many individuals struggling to establish themselves as families, often against a
background or undercurrent knowledge of the families
they are not.

In this *Graywolf Annual* stories by Karen Brown, Kate
Braverman, and Kathleen Cambor bring clearly into focus
the sense of isolation felt by single mothers, and the delicate
balances that must be maintained in their relationships with
their children and others.

The theme of many of these stories is a coming-to-grips
with that isolation – the uneasy feeling that all relationships
may be tentative. Isolation can provide impetus for trying to
reconstruct a family among friends, as in Dennis McFar-

land's beautiful story "Nothing to Ask For," a moving portrait of the friendship between two men, one of whom is dying of AIDS; and in Joan Wickersham's "Commuter Marriage," where a woman's live-in non-related family begins to seem more real than the family she has formed with her husband.

The same feeling of isolation can be an impediment to relationships. In Christopher Tilghman's "Mary in the Mountains," a divorcée chooses a life alone, and begins to make the best of it. Both the grandfather and granddaughter in Richard Bausch's "What Feels Like the World" desire a close relationship but feel distrustful, unsure of their proper roles, and locked into separate worlds.

Disconnections, dissonances, struggles to transform an old or failed life into a new one ... what an amazing task there is in front of us! We hope these stories celebrate the families that now are possible. They are good examples of people coping with important issues (and we regard them as *issues* and not *problems*).

A NUMBER OF PEOPLE contributed to the development of this anthology. I'd like to offer public acknowledgment to the Graywolf staff, helpful as always, and especially to Anne Czarniecki, Rosie O'Brien, and Martha Lee; and to Jennifer Regan, whose ideas and suggestions were generous and influential.

SCOTT WALKER
April 1991

RICHARD BAUSCH

✖

What Feels Like the World

Very early in the morning, too early, he hears her trying to jump rope out on the sidewalk below his bedroom window. He wakes to the sound of her shoes on the concrete, her breathless counting as she jumps—never more than three times in succession—and fails again to find the right rhythm, the proper spring in her legs to achieve the thing, to be a girl jumping rope. He gets up and moves to the window and, parting the curtain only slightly, peers out at her. For some reason he feels he must be stealthy, must not let her see him gazing at her from this window. He thinks of the heartless way children tease the imperfect among them, and then he closes the curtain.

She is his only granddaughter, the unfortunate inheritor of his big-boned genes, his tendency toward bulk, and she is on a self-induced program of exercise and dieting, to lose weight. This is in preparation for the last meeting of the PTA, during which children from the fifth and sixth grades will put on a gymnastics demonstration. There will be a vaulting horse and a minitrampoline, and everyone is to participate. She wants to be able to do at least as well as the other children in her class, and so she has been trying exercises to improve her coordination and lose the weight that keeps her rooted to the ground. For the past two weeks she has been eating only one meal a day, usually lunch, since that's the meal she eats at school, and swallowing cans of juice at other mealtimes. He's afraid of anorexia but trusts her calm determination to get ready for the event. There seems no desperation, none of the classic symptoms of the disease. Indeed, this project she's set for herself seems quite sane: to lose ten pounds, and to be able to get over the vaulting horse – in fact, she hopes that she'll be able to do a handstand on it and, curling her head and shoulders, flip over to stand upright on the other side. This, she has told him, is the outside hope. And in two weeks of very grown-up discipline and single-minded effort, that hope has mostly disappeared; she's still the only child in the fifth grade who has not even been able to propel herself over the horse, and this is the day of the event. She will have one last chance to practice at school today, and so she's up this early, out on the lawn, straining, pushing herself.

He dresses quickly and heads downstairs. The ritual in the mornings is simplified by the fact that neither of them is eating breakfast. He makes the orange juice, puts vitamins on a saucer for them both. When he glances out the living-room window, he sees that she is now doing somersaults in the dewy grass. She does three of them while he watches, and he isn't stealthy this time but stands in the window with what he hopes is an approving, unworried look on his face. After each somersault she pulls her sweat shirt down, takes a deep breath, and begins again, the arms coming down slowly, the head ducking slowly under; it's as if she falls on her back, sits up, and then stands up. Her cheeks are ruddy with effort. The moistness of the grass is on the sweat suit, and in the ends of her hair. It will rain this morning – there's thunder beyond the trees at the end of the street. He taps on the window, gestures, smiling, for her to come in. She waves at him, indicates that she wants him to watch her, so he watches her. He applauds when she's finished – three hard, slow tumbles. She claps her hands together as if to remove dust from them and comes trotting to the door. As she moves by him, he tells her she's asking for a bad cold, letting herself get wet so early in the morning. It's his place to nag. Her glance at him acknowledges this.

"I can't get the rest of me to follow my head," she says about the somersaults.

They go into the kitchen and she sits down, pops a vitamin into her mouth, and takes a swallow of the orange juice. "I guess I'm not going to make it over that vaulting horse after all," she says suddenly.

"Sure you will."

"I don't care." She seems to pout. This is the first sign of true discouragement she's shown.

He's been waiting for it. "Brenda—honey, sometimes people aren't good at these things. I mean, I was never any good at it."

"I bet you were," she says. "I bet you're just saying that to make me feel better."

"No," he says, "really."

He's been keeping to the diet with her, though there have been times during the day when he's cheated. He no longer has a job, and the days are long; he's hungry all the time. He pretends to her that he's still going on to work in the mornings after he walks her to school, because he wants to keep her sense of the daily balance of things, of a predictable and orderly routine, intact. He believes this is the best way to deal with grief—simply to go on with things, to keep them as much as possible as they have always been. Being out of work doesn't worry him, really: he has enough money in savings to last awhile. At sixty-one, he's almost eligible for Social Security, and he gets monthly checks from the girl's father, who lives with another woman, and other children, in Oregon. The father has been very good about keeping up the payments, though he never visits or calls. Probably he thinks the money buys him the privilege of remaining aloof, now that Brenda's mother is gone. Brenda's mother used to say he was the type of man who learned early that there was nothing of substance anywhere in his soul, and spent the rest of his life trying to hide this fact from himself. No one was more upright, she would say, no one more honorable, and God help you if you ever had to live with him. Brenda's father was the subject of bitter sarcasm and scorn. And yet, perhaps not so surprisingly, Brenda's mother would call him in those months just after the divorce, when Brenda was still only a toddler, and she would try to get the baby to say things to him over the phone. And she would sit there with Brenda on her lap and cry after she had hung up.

"I had a doughnut yesterday at school," Brenda says now.

"That's lunch. You're supposed to eat lunch."

"I had spaghetti, too. And three pieces of garlic bread. And pie. And a big salad."

"What's one doughnut?"

"Well, and I didn't eat anything the rest of the day."

"I know," her grandfather says. "See?"

They sit quiet for a little while. Sometimes they're shy with each other—more so lately. They're used to the absence of her mother by now—it's been almost a year—but they still find themselves missing a beat now and then, like a heart with a valve almost closed. She swallows the last of her juice and then gets up and moves to the living room, to stand gazing out at the yard. Big drops have begun to fall. It's a storm, with rising wind and, now, very loud thunder. Lightning branches across the sky, and the trees in the yard disappear in sheets of rain. He has come to her side, and he pretends an interest in the details of the weather, remarking on the heaviness of the rain, the strength of the wind. "Some storm," he says finally. "I'm glad we're not out in it." He wishes he could tell what she's thinking, where the pain is; he wishes he could be certain of the harmlessness of his every word. "Honey," he ventures, "we could play hooky today. If you want to."

"Don't you think I can do it?" she says.

"I know you can."

She stares at him a moment and then looks away, out at the storm.

"It's terrible out there, isn't it?" he says. "Look at that lightning."

"You don't think I can do it," she says.

"No. I know you can. Really."

"Well, I probably can't."

"Even if you can't. Lots of people—lots of people never do anything like that."

"I'm the only one who can't that *I* know."

"Well, there's lots of people. The whole thing is silly, Brenda. A year from now it won't mean anything at all—you'll see."

She says nothing.

"Is there some pressure at school to do it?"

"No." Her tone is simple, matter-of-fact, and she looks directly at him.

"You're sure?"

She's sure. And of course, he realizes, there *is* pressure; there's the pressure of being one among other children, and being the only one among them who can't do a thing.

"Honey," he says lamely, "it's not that important."

When she looks at him this time, he sees something scarily unchildlike in her expression, some perplexity that she seems to pull down into herself. "It is too important," she says.

He DRIVES HER TO school. The rain is still being blown along the street and above the low roofs of the houses. By the time they arrive, no more than five minutes from the house, it has begun to let up.

"If it's completely stopped after school," she says, "can we walk home?"

"Of course," he says. "Why wouldn't we?"

She gives him a quick wet kiss on the cheek. "Bye, Pops."

He knows she doesn't like it when he waits for her to get inside, and still he hesitates. There's always the apprehension that he'll look away or drive off just as she thinks of something she needs from him, or that she'll wave to him and he won't see her. So he sits here with the car engine idling, and she walks quickly up and into the building. In the few seconds before the door swings shut, she turns and gives him a wave, and he waves back. The door is closed now. Slowly he lets the car glide forward, still watching the door. Then he's down the driveway, and he heads back to the house.

It's HARD TO DECIDE what to do with his time. Mostly he stays in the house, watches television, reads the newspapers. There are household tasks, but he can't do anything she might notice, since he's supposed to be at work during these hours. Sometimes, just to please himself, he drives over to the bank and visits with his old co-workers, though there doesn't seem to be much to talk about anymore and he senses that he makes them all uneasy. Today he lies down on the sofa in the living room and rests awhile. At the windows the sun begins to show, and he thinks of driving into town, perhaps stopping somewhere to eat a light breakfast. He accuses himself with the thought and then gets up and turns on the television. There isn't anything of interest to watch, but he watches anyway. The sun is bright now out on the lawn, and the wind is the same, gusting and shaking the window frames. On television he sees feasts of incredible sumptuousness, almost nauseating in the impossible brightness and succulence of the food: advertisements from cheese companies, dairy associations, the makers of cookies and pizza, the sellers of seafood and steaks. He's angry with himself for wanting to cheat on the diet. He thinks of Brenda at school, thinks of crowds of children, and it comes to him

more painfully than ever that he can't protect her. Not any
more than he could ever protect her mother.

He goes outside and walks up the drying sidewalk to the
end of the block. The sun has already dried most of the
morning's rain, and the wind is warm. In the sky are great
stormy Matterhorns of cumulus and wide patches of the
deepest blue. It's a beautiful day, and he decides to walk
over to the school. Nothing in him voices this decision; he
simply begins to walk. He knows without having to think
about it that he can't allow her to see him, yet he feels com-
pelled to take the risk that she might; he feels a helpless wish
to watch over her, and, beyond this, he entertains the vague
notion that by seeing her in her world he might be better
able to be what she needs in his.

So he walks the four blocks to the school and stands just
beyond the playground, in a group of shading maples that
whisper and sigh in the wind. The playground is empty. A
bell rings somewhere in the building, but no one comes out.
It's not even eleven o'clock in the morning. He's too late for
morning recess and to early for the afternoon one. He feels
as though she watches him to make his way back down the
street.

His neighbor, Mrs. Eberhard, comes over for lunch. It's a
thing they planned, and he's forgotten about it. She knocks
on the door, and when he opens it she smiles and says, "I
knew you'd forget." She's on a diet too, and is carrying what
they'll eat: two apples, some celery and carrots. It's all in a
clear plastic bag, and she holds it toward him in the palms of
her hands as though it were piping hot from the oven. Jane
Eberhard is relatively new in the neighborhood. When
Brenda's mother died, Jane offered to cook meals and regu-
late things, and for a while she was like another member of
the family. She's moved into their lives now, and sometimes
they all forget the circumstances under which the friend-

ship began. She's a solid, large-hipped woman of fifty-eight, with clear, young blue eyes and gray hair. The thing she's good at is sympathy; there's something oddly unspecific about it, as if it were a beam she simply radiates.

"You look so worried," she says now, "I think you should be proud of her."

They're sitting in the living room, with the plastic bag on the coffee table before them. She's eating a stick of celery.

"I've never seen a child that age put such demands on herself," she says.

"I don't know what it's going to do to her if she doesn't make it over the damn thing," he says.

"It'll disappoint her. But she'll get over it."

"I don't guess you can make it tonight."

"Can't," she says. "Really. I promised my mother I'd take her to the ocean this weekend. I have to go pick her up tonight."

"I walked over to the school a little while ago."

"Are you sure you're not putting more into this than she is?"

"She was up at dawn this morning, Jane. Didn't you see her?"

Mrs. Eberhard nods. "I saw her."

"Well?" he says.

She pats his wrist. "I'm sure it won't matter a month from now."

"No," he says, "that's not true. I mean, I wish I could believe you. But I've never seen a kid work so hard."

"Maybe she'll make it."

"Yes," he says. "Maybe."

Mrs. Eberhard sits considering for a moment, tapping the stick of celery against her lower lip. "You think it's tied to the accident in some way, don't you?"

"I don't know," he says, standing, moving across the room. "I can't get through somehow. It's been all this time and I still don't know. She keeps it all to herself – all of it. All

I can do is try to be there when she wants me to be there. I don't know – I don't even know what to say to her."

"You're doing all you can do, then."

"Her mother and I..." he begins. "She – we never got along that well."

"You can't worry about that now."

Mrs. Eberhard's advice is always the kind of practical good advice that's impossible to follow.

He comes back to the sofa and tries to eat one of the apples, but his appetite is gone. This seems ironic to him. "I'm not hungry now," he says.

"Sometimes worry is the best thing for a diet."

"I've always worried. It never did me any good, but I worried."

"I'll tell you," Mrs. Eberhard says. "It's a terrific misfortune to have to be raised by a human being."

He doesn't feel like listening to this sort of thing, so he asks her about her husband, who is with the government in some capacity that requires him to be both secretive and mobile. He's always off to one country or another, and this week he's in India. It's strange to think of someone traveling as much as he does without getting hurt or killed. Mrs. Eberhard says she's so used to his being gone all the time that next year, when he retires, it'll take a while to get used to having him underfoot. In fact, he's not a very likable man; there's something murky and unpleasant about him. The one time Mrs. Eberhard brought him to visit, he sat in the living room and seemed to regard everyone with detached curiosity, as if they were all specimens on a dish under a lens. Brenda's grandfather had invited some old friends over from the bank – everyone was being careful not to let on that he wasn't still going there every day. It was an awkward two hours, and Mrs. Eberhard's husband sat with his hands folded over his rounded belly, his eyebrows arched. When he spoke, his voice was cultivated and quiet, full of self-satisfaction and haughtiness. They had been speaking in low tones about how Jane Eberhard had moved in to take over after the accident, and Mrs. Eberhard's husband cleared his throat, held his fist gingerly to his mouth, pursed his lips, and began a soft-spoken, lecturelike monologue about his belief that there's no such thing as an accident. His considered opinion was that there are subconscious explanations for everything. Apparently, he thought he was entertaining everyone. He sat with one leg crossed over the other and held forth in his calm, magisterial voice, explaining how everything can be reduced to a matter of conscious or subconscious will. Finally his wife asked him to let it alone, please, drop the subject.

"For example," he went on, "there are many collisions on the highway in which no one appears to have applied brakes before impact, as if something in the victims had decided on death. And of course there are the well-known cases of people stopped on railroad tracks, with plenty of time to get off, who simply do not move. Perhaps it isn't being frozen by the perception of one's fate but a matter of decision making, of will. The victim decides on his fate."

"I think we've had enough, now," Jane Eberhard said.

The inappropriateness of what he had said seemed to dawn on him then. He shifted in his seat and grew very quiet, and when the evening was over he took Brenda's grandfather by the elbow and apologized. But even in the apology there seemed to be a species of condescension, as if he were really only sorry for the harsh truth of what he had wrongly deemed it necessary to say. When everyone was gone, Brenda said, "I don't like that man."

"Is it because of what he said about accidents?" her grandfather asked.

She shook her head. "I just don't like him."

"It's not true, what he said, honey. An accident is an accident."

She said, "I know." But she would not return his gaze.

"Your mother wasn't very happy here, but she didn't want to leave us. Not even – you know, without. . . without knowing it or anything."

"He wears perfume," she said, still not looking at him.

"It's cologne. Yes, he does – too much of it."

"It smells," she said.

I N T H E A F T E R N O O N he walks over to the school. The sidewalks are crowded with children, and they all seem to recognize him. They carry their books and papers and their hair is windblown and they run and wrestle with each other in the yards. The sun's high and very hot, and most of the clouds have broken apart and scattered. There's still a fairly steady wind, but it's gentler now, and there's no coolness in it.

Brenda is standing at the first crossing street down the hill from the school. She's surrounded by other children yet seems separate from them somehow. She sees him and smiles. He waits on his side of the intersection for her to cross, and when she reaches him he's careful not to show any obvious affection, knowing it embarrasses her.

"How was your day?" he begins.

"Mr. Clayton tried to make me quit today."

He waits.

"I didn't get over," she says. "I didn't even get close."

"What did Mr. Clayton say?"

"Oh – you know. That it's not important. That kind of stuff."

"Well," he says gently, "*is* it so important?"

"I don't know." She kicks at something in the grass along the edge of the sidewalk – a piece of a pencil someone else had discarded. She bends, picks it up, examines it, and then drops it. This is exactly the kind of slow, daydreaming behavior that used to make him angry and impatient with her mother. They walk on. She's concentrating on the sidewalk before them, and they walk almost in step.

"I'm sure I could never do a thing like going over a vaulting horse when I was in school," he says.

"Did they have that when you were in school?"

He smiles. "It was hard getting everything into the caves. But sure, we had that sort of thing. We were an advanced tribe. We had fire, too."

"Okay," she's saying, "okay, okay."

"Actually, with me, it was pull-ups. We all had to do pull-ups. And I just couldn't do them. I don't think I ever accomplished a single one in my life."

"I can't do pull-ups," she says.

"They're hard to do."

"Everybody in the fifth and sixth grades can get over the vaulting horse," she says.

How much she reminds him of her mother. There's a certain mobility in her face, a certain willingness to assert herself in the smallest gesture of the eyes and mouth. She has her mother's green eyes, and now he tells her this. He's decided to try this. He's standing, quite shy, in her doorway, feeling like an intruder. She's sitting on the floor, one leg outstretched, the other bent at the knee. She tries to touch her forehead to the knee of the outstretched leg, straining, and he looks away.

"You know?" he says. "They're just the same color—just that shade of green."

"What was my grandmother like?" she asks, still straining.

"She was a lot like your mother."

"I'm never going to get married."

"Of course you will. Well, I mean—if you want to, you will."

"How come you didn't ever get married again?"

"Oh," he says, "I had a daughter to raise, you know."

She changes position, tries to touch her forehead to the other knee.

"I'll tell you, that mother of yours was enough to keep me busy. I mean, I called her double trouble, you know, because I always said she was double the trouble a son would have been. That was a regular joke around here."

"Mom was skinny and pretty."

He says nothing.

"Am I double trouble?"

"No," he says.

"Is that really why you never got married again?"

"Well, no one would have me, either."

"Mom said you liked it."

"Liked what?"

"Being a widow."

"Yes, well," he says.

"Did you?"

"All these questions," he says.

"Do you think about Grandmom a lot?"

"Yes," he says. "That's—you know, we remember our loved ones."

She stands and tries to touch her toes without bending her legs. "Sometimes I dream that Mom's yelling at you and you're yelling back."

"Oh, well," he says, hearing himself say it, feeling himself back down from something. "That's—that's just a dream. You know, it's nothing to think about at all. People who love each other don't agree sometimes—it's—it's nothing. And I'll bet these exercises are going to do the trick."

"I'm very smart, aren't I?"

He feels sick, very deep down. "You're the smartest little girl I ever saw."

"You don't have to come tonight if you don't want to," she says. "You can drop me off if you want, and come get me when it's over."

"Why would I do that?"

She mutters. "*I* would."

"Then why don't we skip it?"

"Lot of good *that* would do," she says.

FOR DINNER THEY DRINK apple juice, and he gets her to eat two slices of dry toast. The apple juice is for energy. She drinks it slowly and then goes into her room to lie down, to conserve her strength. She uses the word *conserve*, and he tells her he's so proud of her vocabulary. She thanks him. While she rests, he does a few household chores, trying really just to keep busy. The week's newspapers have been piling up on the coffee table in the living room, the carpets need to be vacuumed, and the whole house needs dusting. None of it takes long enough; none of it quite distracts him. For a while he sits in the living room with a newspaper in his lap and pretends to be reading it. She's restless too. She comes back through to the kitchen, drinks another glass of apple juice, and then joins him in the living room, turns the television on. The news is full of traffic deaths, and she turns to one of the local stations that shows reruns of old situation comedies. They both watch *M*A*S*H* without really taking it in. She bites the cuticles of her nails, and her gaze wanders around the room. It comes to him that he could speak to her now, could make his way through to her grief – and yet he knows that he will do no such thing; he can't even bring himself to speak at all. There are regions of his own sorrow that he simply lacks the strength to explore, and so he sits there watching her restlessness, and at last it's time to go over to the school. Jane Eberhard makes a surprise visit, bearing a handsome good-luck card she's fashioned herself. She kisses Brenda, behaves exactly as if Brenda were going off to some dangerous, faraway place. She stands in the street and waves at them as they pull away, and Brenda leans out the window to shout goodbye. A moment later, sitting back and staring out at the dusky light, she says she feels

a surge of energy, and he tells her she's way ahead of all the others in her class, knowing words like *conserve* and *surge*.

"I've always known them," she says.

It's beginning to rain again. Clouds have been rolling in from the east, and the wind shakes the trees. Lightning flickers on the other side of the clouds. Everything seems threatening, relentless. He slows down. There are many cars parked along both sides of the street. "Quite a turnout," he manages.

"Don't worry," she tells him brightly. "I still feel my surge of energy."

It begins to rain as they get out of the car, and he holds his sport coat like a cape to shield her from it. By the time they get to the open front doors, it's raining very hard. People are crowding into the cafeteria, which has been trans-formed into an arena for the event – chairs set up on four sides of the room as though for a wrestling match. In the center, at the end of the long bright-red mat, are the vault-ing horse and the minitrampoline. The physical-education teacher, Mr. Clayton, stands at the entrance. He's tall, thin, scraggly-looking, a boy really, no older than twenty-five.

"There's Mr. Clayton," Brenda says.

"I see him."

"Hello, Mr. Clayton."

Mr. Clayton is quite distracted, and he nods quickly, leans toward Brenda, and points to a doorway across the hall. "Go on ahead," he says. Then he nods at her grandfather.

"This is it," Brenda says.

Her grandfather squeezes her shoulder, means to find the best thing to tell her, but in the next confusing minute he's lost her; she's gone among the others and he's being swept along with the crowd entering the cafeteria. He makes his way along the walls behind the chairs, where a few other people have already gathered and are standing. At the other end of the room a man is speaking from a lectern about old business, new officers for the fall. Brenda's

grandfather recognizes some of the people in the crowd. A woman looks at him and nods, a familiar face he can't quite place. She turns to look at the speaker. She's holding a baby, and the baby's staring at him over her shoulder. A moment later, she steps back to stand beside him, hefting the baby higher and patting its bottom.

"What a crowd," she says.

He nods.

"It's not usually this crowded."

Again, he nods.

The baby protests, and he touches the miniature fingers of one hand – just a baby, he thinks, and everything still to go through.

"How is – um . . . Brenda?" she says.

"Oh," he says, "fine." And he remembers that she was Brenda's kindergarden teacher. She's heavier than she was then, and her hair is darker. She has a baby now.

"I don't remember all my students," she says, shifting the baby to the other shoulder. "I've been home now for eighteen months, and I'll tell you, it's being at the PTA meeting that makes me see how much I *don't* miss teaching."

He smiles at her and nods again. He's beginning to feel awkward. The man is still speaking from the lectern, a meeting is going on, and this woman's voice is carrying beyond them, though she says everything out of the side of her mouth.

"I remember the way you used to walk Brenda to school every morning. Do you still walk her to school?"

"Yes."

"That's so nice."

He pretends an interest in what the speaker is saying.

"I always thought it was so nice to see how you two got along together – I mean these days it's really rare for the kids even to know who their grandparents *are*, much less have one to walk them to school in the morning. I always

thought it was really something." She seems to watch the lectern for a moment, and then speaks to him again, this time in a near whisper. "I hope you won't take this the wrong way or anything, but I just wanted to say how sorry I was about your daughter. I saw it in the paper when Brenda's mother... well, you know, I just wanted to tell you how sorry. When I saw it in the paper, I thought of Brenda, and how you used to walk her to school. I lost my sister in an automobile accident, so I know how you feel—it's a terrible thing. Terrible. An awful thing to have happen. I mean it's much too sudden and final and everything. I'm afraid now every time I get into a car." She pauses, pats the baby's back, then takes something off its ear. "Anyway, I just wanted to say how sorry I was."

"You're very kind," he says.

"It seems so senseless," she murmurs. "There's something so senseless about it when it happens. My sister went through a stop sign. She just didn't see it, I guess. But it wasn't a busy road or anything. If she'd come along one second later or sooner nothing would've happened. So senseless. Two people driving two different cars coming along on two roads on a sunny afternoon and they come together like that. I mean—what're the chances, really?"

He doesn't say anything.

"How's Brenda handling it?"

"She's strong," he says.

"I would've said that," the woman tells him. "Sometimes I think the children take these things better than the adults do. I remember when she first came to my class. She told everyone in the first minute that she'd come from Oregon. That she was living with her grandfather, and her mother was divorced."

"She was a baby when the divorce—when she moved here from Oregon."

This seems to surprise the woman. "Really," she says, low.

"I got the impression it was recent for her. I mean, you know, that she had just come from it all. It was all very vivid for her, I remember that."

"She was a baby," he says. It's almost as if he were insisting on it. He's heard this in his voice, and he wonders if she has, too.

"Well," she says, "I always had a special place for Brenda. I always thought she was very special. A very special little girl."

The PTA meeting is over, and Mr. Clayton is now standing at the far door with the first of the charges. They're all lining up outside the door, and Mr. Clayton walks to the microphone to announce the program. The demonstration will commence with the minitrampoline and the vaulting horse: a performance by the fifth- and sixth-graders. There will also be a break-dancing demonstration by the fourth-grade class.

"Here we go," the woman says. "My nephew's afraid of the minitramp."

"They shouldn't make them do these things," Brenda's grandfather says, with a passion that surprises him. He draws in a breath. "It's too hard," he says, loudly. He can't believe himself. "They shouldn't have to go through a thing like this."

"I don't know," she says vaguely, turning from him a little. He has drawn attention to himself. Others in the crowd are regarding him now—one, a man with a sparse red beard and wild red hair, looking at him with something he takes for agreement.

"It's too much," he says, still louder. "Too much to put on a child. There's just so much a child can take."

Someone asks gently for quiet.

The first child is running down the long mat to the mini-trampoline; it's a girl, and she times her jump perfectly, soars over the horse. One by one, other children follow. Mr. Clayton and another man stand on either side of the horse and help those who go over on their hands. Two or three go over without any assistance at all, with remarkable effortlessness and grace.

"Well," Brenda's kindergarden teacher says, "there's my nephew."

The boy hits the minitramp and does a perfect forward flip in the air over the horse, landing upright and then rolling forward in a somersault.

"Yea, Jack!" she cheers. "No sweat! Yea, Jackie boy!"

The boy trots to the other end of the room and stands with the others; the crowd is applauding. The last of the sixth-graders goes over the horse, and Mr. Clayton says into the microphone that the fifth-graders are next. It's Brenda who's next. She stands in the doorway, her cheeks flushed, her legs looking too heavy in the tights. She's rocking back and forth on the balls of her feet, getting ready. It grows quiet. Her arms swing slightly, back and forth, and now, just for a moment, she's looking at the crowd, her face hiding whatever she's feeling. It's as if she were merely curious as to who is out there, but he knows she's looking for him, searching the crowd for her grandfather, who stands on his toes, unseen against the far wall, stands there thinking his heart might break, lifting his hand to wave.

A Relative Stranger

I WAS SEPARATED from my biological mother when I was four months old. Everything from that period goes through the wash of my memory and comes out clean, blank. The existing snapshots of my mother show this very young woman holding me, a baby, at arm's length, like a caught fish, outside in the blaring midday summer sunlight. She's got clothes up on the clothesline in the background, little cotton infant things. In one picture a spotted dog, a mongrel combination of Labrador and Dalmatian, is asleep beside the bassinet. I'd like to know what the dog's name was, but time has swallowed that information. In another picture, a half-empty bottle of Grain Belt beer stands on the lawn near a wading pool. My mother must have figured that if she could have me, at the age of seventeen, she could also have the beer.

My mother's face in these pictures is having a tough time with daylight. It's a struggle for her to bask in so much glare. She squints and smiles, but the smile is all on one side, the right. The left side stays level, except at the edge, where it slips down. Because of the sunlight and the black-and-white film, my mother's face in other respects is bleached without details, like a sketch for a face. She's a kid in these pictures and she has a kid's face, with hair pulled back with bobby pins and a slight puffiness in the cheeks, which I think must be bubble gum.

She doesn't look like she's ever been used to the outdoors, the poor kid. Sunlight doesn't become her. It's true she smiled, but then she did give me up. I was too much serious work, too much of a squalling load. Her girlish smile was unsteady and finally didn't include me. She gave me away – this is historical record – to my adoptive parents, Harold and Ethel Harris, who were older and more capable of parental love. She also gave them these photographs, the old kind, with soft sawtooth borders, so I'd be sure to know how she had looked when the unfamiliar sunlight hit her in a certain way. I think her teenaged boyfriend, my father, took these pictures. Harold and Ethel Harris were my parents in every respect, in love and in their care for me, except for the fact of these pictures. The other children in the family, also adopted, looked at the snapshots of this backyard lady with curiosity but not much else.

My biological father was never a particle of interest to me compared to my adoptive father, Harold Harris, a man who lived a life of miraculous calm. A piano tuner and occasional jazz saxophonist, Harold liked to sit at home, humming and tapping his fingers in the midst of uproar and riot, kids shouting and plaster falling. He could not be riled; he never made a fist. He was the parental hit of any childhood group, and could drive a car competently with children sitting on his shoulders and banging their hands on the side of his head. Genetic inheritance or not, he gave us all a feeling for pitch. Ask me for an F-sharp, I'll give you one. I get the talent from Harold.

I WENT TO HIGH SCHOOL, messed around here and there, did some time in the Navy, and when I was discharged I married my sweetheart of three years, the object of my shipboard love letters, Lynda Claire Norton. We had an apartment. I was clerking at Meijer's Thrifty Acres. I thought we were doing okay. Each night I was sleeping naked next to a sexual angel. At sunrise she would wake me with tender physical comfort, with hair and fingertips. I was working to get a degree from night school. Fourteen months after we were married, right on the day it was due, the baby came. A boy, this was. Jonathan Harold Harris. Then everything went to hell.

I was crazy. Don't ask me to account for it. I have no background or inclination to explain the human mind. Besides, I'm not proud of the way I acted. Lynda moved right out, baby and all, the way any sensible woman would have, and she left me two empty rooms in the apartment in which I could puzzle myself out.

I had turned into the damnedest thing. I was a human monster movie. I'd never seen my daddy shouting the way I had; he had never carried on or made a spectacle of himself. Where had I picked up this terrible craziness that made me yell at a woman who had taken me again and again into her arms? I wrote long letters to the world while I worked at home on my model ships, a dull expression on my face. You will say that liquor was the troublemaker here and you would be correct, but only so far. I had another bad ingredient I was trying to track down. I broke dishes. My mind, day and night, was muzzy with bad intentions. I threw a light bulb against a wall and did not sweep up the glass for days. Food burned on the stove and then I ate it. I was committing outrageous offenses against the spirit. Never, though, did I smash one of the model ships. Give me credit for that.

I love oceans and the ships that move across them. I believe in man-made objects that take their chances on the earth's expanses of water. And so it happened that one weekday afternoon I was watching a rerun of *The Caine Mutiny*, with my workboard set up in front of me with the tiny pieces of my model *Cutty Sark* in separated piles, when the phone rang. For a moment I believed that my wife had

had second thoughts about my behavior and was going to give me another chance. To tell the truth, whenever the phone rang, I thought it would be Lynda, announcing her terms for my parole.

"Hello? Is this Oliver Harris?" a man's voice asked.

"This is him," I said. "Who's this?"

"This is your brother." Just like that. Very matter-of-fact. This is your brother. Harold and Ethel Harris had had two other adopted sons, in addition to me, but I knew them. This voice was not them. I gripped the telephone.

Now—and I'm convinced of this—every adopted child fears and fantasizes getting a call like this announcing from out of the blue that someone in the world is a relative and has tracked you down. I know I am not alone in thinking that anyone in the world might be related to me. My biological mother and father were very busy, urgent lovers. Who knows how much procreation they were capable of, together and separately? And maybe they had brothers and sisters, too, as urgent in their own way as my mother and father had been in theirs, filling up the adoption agencies with their offspring. I could never go into a strange city without feeling that I had cousins in it.

Therefore I gripped the telephone, hoping for reason, for the everyday. "This is not my brother," I said.

"Oh yes, it is. Your mother was Alice Barton, right?"

"My mother was Ethel Harris," I said.

"Before that," the voice said, "your mother was Alice Barton. She was my mother, too. This is your brother, Kurt. I'm a couple of years younger than you." He waited. "I know this is a shock," he said.

"You can't find out about me," I said. The room wasn't spinning, but I had an idea that it might. My mouth was open halfway and I was taking short sweaty breaths through it. One shiver took its snaky way down and settled in the lumbar region. "The records are sealed. It's all private, completely secret."

"Not anymore, it isn't," he said. "Haven't you been keeping up? In this country you can find out anything. There are no secrets worth keeping anymore; nobody *wants* privacy, so there isn't any."

He was shoving this pile of ideas at me. *My* thoughts had left me in great flight, the whole sad flock of them. "Who are you?" I asked.

"Your brother Kurt," he said, repeating himself. "Listen, I won't bore you to explain what I had to do to find you. The fact is that it's possible. Easy, if you have money. You pay someone and someone pays someone and eventually you find out what you want to know. Big surprise, right?" He waited, and when I didn't agree with him, he started up again, this time with small talk. "So I hear that you're married and you have a kid yourself." He laughed. "And I'm an uncle."

"What? No. Now you're only partly right," I said, wanting very hard to correct this man who said he was my brother. "My wife left me. I'm living here alone now."

"Oh. I'm sorry about that." He offered his sympathies in a shallow, masculine way: the compassion offered by princes and salesmen. "But listen," he said, "you're not alone. It's happened before. Couples separate all the time. You'll get back. It's not the end of the world. Oliver?"

"What?"

"Would you be willing to get together and talk?"

"Talk? Talk about what?"

"Well, about being brothers. Or something else. You can talk about anything you please." He waited for me to respond, and I didn't. This was my only weapon – the terrible static of telephone silence. "Look," he said, "this is tough for me. *I'm not a bad person.* I've been sitting by this phone for an hour. I don't know if I'm doing the right thing. My wife . . . you'll meet her . . . she hasn't been exactly supportive. She thinks this is a mistake. She says I've gone too far this time. I dialed your number four times before I dialed it to the end.

I make hundreds of business calls but this one I could not do. It may be hard for you, also: I mean, I take a little getting used to. I can be obsessive about little things. That's how I found you."

"By being obsessive."

"Yeah. Lucille... that's my wife... she says it's one of my faults. Well, I always wanted a brother, you know, blood-related and everything, but I couldn't have one until I found you. But then I thought you might not like me. It's possible. Are you following me?"

"Yes, I am." I was thinking: here I am in my apartment, recently vacated by my wife, talking to a man who says he's my brother. Isn't there a law against this? Someone help me.

"You don't have to like me," he said, his brusque voice starting to stumble over the consonants. That made me feel better. "But that isn't the point, is it?" Another question I didn't have to answer, so I made him wait. "I can imagine what's in your head. But let's meet. Just once. Let's try it. Not at a house. I only live about twenty miles away. I can meet you in Ann Arbor. We can meet in a bar. I *know* where you live. I drove by your building. I believe I've even seen your car."

"Have you seen me?" This brother had been cruising past my house, taking an interest. Do brothers do that? What *do* they do?

"Well, no, but who cares about looks where brothers are concerned? We'll see each other. Listen, there's this place a couple of miles from you, the Wooden Keg. Could we meet there? Tomorrow at three? Are you off tomorrow?"

"That's a real problem for me," I said. "Booze is my special poison."

"Hell, that's all right," he said. "I'll watch out for you. I'm your brother. Oh. There's one other thing. I lied. I look like you. That's how you'll recognize me. I have seen you."

I held on to the telephone a long time after I hung up. I

turned my eyes to the television set. José Ferrer was getting
drunk and belligerent at a cocktail party. I switched off the
set.

I WAS IN THAT BAR one hour before I said I would be,
and my feelings were very grim. I wasn't humming. I didn't
want him to be stationed there when I came in. I didn't want
to be the one who sauntered in through the door and
walked the long distance to the bar stool. I didn't want some
strange sibling checking out the way I close the distance or
blink behind my glasses while my eyes adjust to the light. I
don't like people watching me when they think they're going to get a skeleton key to my character. I'm not a door and
I won't be opened that easily.

Going into a bar in the midsummer afternoon takes you
out of the steel heat and air-hammer sun; it softens you up
until you're all smoothed out. This was one of those wood-
sidewall bars with air that hasn't recirculated for fifty years,
with framed pictures of thoroughbreds and cars on the
walls next to the chrome decorator hubcaps. A man's bar,
smelling of cigarettes and hamburger grease and beer. The
brown padded light comes down on you from some re-
cessed source, and the leather cushions on those bar stools
are as soft as a woman's hand, and before long the bar is one
big bed, a bed on a barge eddying down a sluggish river
where you've got nothing but good friends lined up on the
banks. This is why I am an alcoholic. It wasn't easy drinking
Coca-Cola in that place, that dim halfway house between the
job and home, and I was about to slide off my wagon and order my first stiff one when the door cracked open behind
me, letting in a trumpet blast of light, and I saw, in the door-
frame outline, my brother coming toward me. He was taking his own time. He had on a hat. When the door closed
and my eyes adjusted, I got a better look at him, and I saw

what he said I would see: I saw instantly that this was my brother. The elves had stolen my shadow and given it to him. A version of my face was fixed on a stranger. From the outdoors came this example of me, wearing a coat and tie.

He took a bar stool next to mine and held out his hand. I held out mine and we shook like old friends, which we were a long way from becoming. "Hey," we both said. He had the eyes, the cheek, and the jaw in a combination I had seen only in the mirror. "Oliver," he said, refusing to let my hand go. "Good to meet you."

"Kurt," I said. "Likewise." Brother or no brother, I wasn't giving away anything too fast. This is America, after all.

"What're you drinking?" he asked.

"Coke."

"Oh. Right." He nodded. When he nodded, the hat nodded. After he saw me looking at it, he said, "Keeps the sun out of my eyes." He took it off and tried to put it on the bar, but there wasn't enough room for it next to the uncleared beer glasses and the ashtrays, so he stood up and dropped it on a hook over by the popcorn machine. There it was, the only hat. He said, "My eyes are sensitive to light. What about yours?" I nodded. Then he laughed, hit the bar with the broad flat of his hand, and said, "Isn't this great?" I wanted to say, yes, it's great, but the true heart of the secret was that no, it was not. It was horrifyingly strange without being eventful. You can't just get a brother off the street. But before I could stop him from doing it, he leaned over and put his right arm, not a large arm but an arm all the same, over my shoulders, and he dropped his head so that it came sliding in toward my chest just under the chin. Here was a man dead set on intimacy. When he straightened up, he said, "We're going to have ourselves a day today, that's for sure." His stutter took some of the certainty out of the words. "You don't have to work this afternoon, right?"

"No," I said. "I'm not scheduled."

"Great," he said. "Let me fill you in on myself."

INSTEAD OF GIVING ME his past, he gave me a résumé. He tried to explain his origins. My biological mother, for all the vagueness in her face, had been a demon for good times. She had been passionate and prophylactically carefree. Maybe she had had twenty kids, like old Mother Hubbard. She gave us away like presents to a world that wanted us. This one, this Kurt, she had kept for ten months before he was adopted by some people called Sykes. My brother said that he understood that we – he and I – had two other siblings in Laramie, Wyoming. There might be more he didn't know about. I had a sudden image of Alice Barton as a human stork, flying at tree level and dropping babies into the arms of waiting parents.

Did I relax as my brother's voice took me through his life? Were we related under the skin, and all the way around the block? He talked; I talked. The Sykes family had been bookish types, lawyers, both of them, and Kurt had gone to Michigan State University in East Lansing. He had had certain advantages. No falling plaster or piano tuning. By learning the mysterious dynamics of an orderly life, he had been turned out as a salesman, and now he ran a plastics factory in Southfield, north of Detroit. "A small business," he said in a friendly, smug way. "Just fifteen employees." I heard about his comfortably huge home. I heard about his children, my nephews. From the wallet thick with money and credit cards came the lineup of photos of these beautiful children.

So what was he doing, this successful man, sitting on a bar stool out here, next to his brother, me, the lowly checkout clerk?

"Does anybody have enough friends?" he asked me. "Does anyone have enough *brothers*?" He asked this calmly, but the questions, as questions, were desperate. "Here's what it was," he said. "Two or three times a week I felt like checking in with someone who wasn't a wife and wasn't just a friend. Brothers are a different category, right there in

the middle. It's all about *relatedness,* you know what I mean?"
I must have scowled. "We can't rush this," he said. "Let's go
have dinner somewhere. My treat. And then let's do something."

"Do what?" I asked.

"I've given that a lot of thought," he said. "What do you
do the first time out with your brother? You can't just eat
and drink. You can't shop; women do that." Then he looked
me square in the eye, smiled, and said, "It's summer. Maybe
we could go bowling or play some baseball." There was a
wild look in his eye. He let out a quick laugh.

WE WENT IN HIS Pontiac Firebird to a German restaurant
and loaded up on sauerbraten. I had a vague sense he was
lowering himself to my level but did not say so. He ordered a
chest-sized decorated stein of beer but I stayed on the cola
wagon. I tried to talk about my wife, but it wouldn't come
out: all I could say was that I had a problem with myself as a
family man. That wasn't me. The crying of babies tore me
up. Feeding time gave me inexplicable jitters. I had acted
like Godzilla. When I told him this, he nodded hard, like a
yes man. It was all reasonable to him.

"Of course," he said. "Of course you were upset and confused." He was understanding me the way I wanted to be
understood. I talked some more. Blah blah blah. Outside, it
was getting dark. The bill came, and he paid it: out came the
thick wallet again, and from a major-league collection of
credit cards came the white bank plastic he wanted. I talked
more. He agreed with everything I said. He said, "You're
exactly right." Then I said something else, and he re-
sponded, "Yes, you're exactly right."

That was when I knew I was being conned. In real life
people don't say that to you unless they're trying to earn
your love in a hurry. But here he was, Kurt Sykes, visibly my

brother, telling me I was exactly right. It was hard to resist, but I was holding on, and trying.

"Here's how," he said. He lifted his big stein of beer into the air, and I lifted my glass of Coke. Click. A big blond waitress watched us, her face disciplined into a steel-helmet smile.

AFTER THAT, IT WAS his idea to go outside and play catch. This activity had all sorts of symbolic meanings for him, but what was I going to do? Go home and watch television? I myself have participated in a few softball leagues and the jock way of life is not alien to me, but I think he believed he could open up if we stayed at my level, throwing something back and forth, grunting and sweating. We drove across town to Buhr Park, where he unloaded his newly purchased baseball, his two brand-new gloves, and a shiny new bat. Baseball was on the agenda. We were going to play ball or die. "We don't have to do any hitting." he said. While I fitted the glove to my left hand – a perfect fit, as if he had measured me – he locked the car. I have never had a car worth locking; it was not a goal.

The sun having set, I jogged out across a field of darkening grass. The sky had that blue tablecloth color it gets at dusk just before the stars come out. I had my jeans, sweat shirt, and sneakers on, my usual day-off drag. I had not dressed up for this event. In fact, I was almost feeling comfortable, except for some growing emotional hot spot I couldn't locate that was making me feel like pushing the baseball into my brother's face. Kurt started to toss the ball toward me and then either noticed his inappropriate dress-for-success formality or felt uncomfortable. He went back to the car and changed into his sweat clothes in the half-dark. He could have been seen, but wasn't, except by me. (My brother could change his clothes out in the open, not even bothering to look around to see who would see. What did this mean?)

Now, dressed down, we started to hustle, keeping the rhythms up. He threw grounders, ineptly, his arm stiff and curious. I bent down, made the imaginary play, and pivoted. He picked up the bat and hit a few high flies toward me. Playing baseball with me was his way of claiming friendship. Fine. Stars came out. We moved across the field, closer to a floodlit tennis court, so we had a bit of light. I could see fireflies at the edge of where we were playing. On the court to my right, a high-school couple was working their way through their second set. The girl let out little cries of frustration now and then. They were pleasurable to hear. Meanwhile, Kurt and I played catch in the near-dark, following the script that, I could see, he had written through one long sleepless night after another.

As we threw the ball back and forth, he talked. He continued on in his résumé. He was married but had two girlfriends. His wife knew about them both. She did not panic because she expected imperfection in men. Also, he said, he usually voted Republican. He went to parent-teacher organization meetings.

"I suppose you weren't expecting this," he said.

No, I thought, I was *not* expecting you. I glanced at the tennis court. Clouds of moths and bright bugs swarmed in insect parabolas around the high-voltage lights. The boy had a white Huron High School T-shirt on, and white shorts and tennis shoes, and a blue sweatband around his thick damp hair. The girl was dressed in an odd assortment of pink and pastel blue clothes. She was flying the colors and was the better player. He had the force, but she had the accuracy. Between his heat and her coolness, she piled up the points. I let myself watch her; I allowed myself that. I was having a harder and harder time keeping my eyes on my brother.

"You gonna play or look at them?" Kurt asked.

I glanced at him. I though I'd ignore his question. "You got any hobbies?" I asked.

He seemed surprised. "Hobbies? No. Unless you count women and making money."

"How's your pitch?"

"You mean baseball?"

"No. Music. How's your sense of pitch?"

"Don't have one."

"I do," I said. "F-sharp." And I blew it at him.

He leaned back and grimaced. "How do you know that's F-sharp?"

"My daddy taught me," I said. "He taught me all the notes on the scale. You can live with them. You can become familiar with a note."

"I don't care for music," he said, ending that conversation. We were still both panting a bit from our exertions. The baseball idea was not quite working in the way he had planned. He seemed to be considering the possibility that he might not like me. "What the hell," he said. "Let's go back to that bar."

WHY DID I HIT my brother in that bar? Gentlemen of the bottle, it is you I address now. You will understand when I tell you that when my brother and I entered the bar, cool and smoky and filled with midsummer ballplayers, uniformed men and women, and he thoughtlessly ordered me a Scotch, you will understand that I drank it. Drank it after I saw his wad of money, his credit cards, his wallet-rubbed pictures of the children, my little nephews. He said he would save me from my alcoholism but he did not. Gentlemen, in a state of raw blank irritation I drank down what God and nature have labeled "poison" and fixed with a secret skull and crossbones. He bought me this drink, knowing it was bad for me. My mind withdrew in a snap from my brain. The universe is vast, you cannot predict it. From the great resources of anger I pulled my fund, my honest share. But I do not remember exactly why I said something terrible, and hit my brother in the jaw with my fist. And then again, higher, a punch I had learned in the Navy.

HE STAGGERED BACK, and he looked at me.

HIS NOSE WAS BLEEDING and my knuckles hurt. I was sitting in the passenger side of his car. My soul ached. My soul was lying facedown. He was taking me back to my apartment, and I knew that my brother would not care to see me from now on. He would reassert his right to be a stranger. I had lost my wife, and now I had lost him, too.

WE STUMBLED INTO MY living room. I wobbled out to the kitchen and, booze-sick, filled a dish towel with ice cubes and brought it to him. My right hand felt swollen. We were going to have ugly bruises, but his were facial and would be worse. Holding the ice to his damaged face, he looked around. Above the ice his eyes flickered on with curiosity. "Ships," he said. Then he pointed at the worktable against the wall. "What's all that?"

"It's my hobby," I said. The words came slow and wormlike out of my puzzled mouth.

He squinted above the ice. "Bottles? And glue?"

"I build ships in bottles." I sounded like a balloon emptying itself of air. I pointed at the decorator shelf on the west wall, where my three-masted clipper ship, the *Thermopylae,* was on display.

"How long have you done this?" he asked.

"So long I can't remember."

"How do you do it?"

He gave me a chance. Even a bad drunk is sometimes

forced to seize his life and to speak. So I went over to the worktable. "You need these." I held up the surgical forceps. I could hardly move my fingers for the pain. Alcoholic darkness sat in a corner with its black bag waiting to cover me entirely. I went on talking. "And these. Surgical scissors." Dried specks of glue were stuck to the tips. "Some people cheat and saw off the bottom of the bottle, then glue it back on once the ship is inside. I don't do it that way. It has to grow inside the bottle. You need a challenge. I build the hull inside. I have used prefab hulls. Then you've got to lay the deck down. I like to do it with deck furnishings already in place: you know, the cabin doors and hatch covers and cleats and riding bits already in place on the deck. You put the glue on and then you put the deck in, all in one piece, folded up, through the neck; then you fold it out. With all that glue on, you only have one shot. Then you do the rigging inside the bottle. See these masts? The masts are laid down inside the bottle with the bottom of the mast in a hole."

I pointed to the *Cutty Sark*, which I was working on. I did not care if my hands were broken; I would continue this, the only lecture in my head, even if I sounded like a chattering magpie.

"You see, you pull the mast up inside the bottle with a string attached to the mast, and there's a stop in the hole that'll keep the mast from going too far forward. Then you tie the lines that are already on the mast off on the belaying pins and the bits and the cleats." I stopped. "These are the best things I do. I make ships in bottles better than anything else I do in my life."

"Yes." He had been standing over my worktable, but now he was lying on the sofa again.

"I like ships," I said. "When I was growing up, I had pictures on the wall of yachts. I was the only person in the Harris family who was interested in ships."

"Hmm."

"I like sailboats the most." I was talking to myself. "They're in their own class."

"That's interesting," he said. "That's all very interesting, but I wonder if I could lie down here for a while."

"I think you're already doing it."

"I don't need a pillow or a blanket," Kurt said, covered with sweat. "I can lie here just as is."

"I was going to turn on the air conditioner."

"Good. Put it on low."

I went over to the rattletrap machine and turned it on. The compressor started with a mechanical complaint, a sound like *orrr orrr orrr,* and then faster, *orrorrorr.* By the time I got back into the living room, my brother's eyes were closed.

"You're asleep," I said.

"No," he said, "no, I'm not. My eyes are just closed. I'm bruised and taking a rest here. That's all. Why don't you talk to me for a minute while I lie here with this ice. Say anything."

So I TALKED AGAINST the demons chittering in the corners of the room. I told my brother about being on a carrier in the Navy. I talked about how I watched the blue lifting swells of the Pacific even when I wasn't supposed to and would get my ass kicked for it. I was hypnotized by seawater, the crazy majesty of horizontal lines. I sleepwalked on that ship, I was so happy. I told him about the rolling progress of oceanic storms, and how the cumulonimbus clouds rose up for what looked like three or four miles into the atmosphere. Straightedged curtains of rain followed us; near the Strait of Gibraltar it once rained for thirty minutes on the forward part of the ship, while the sun burned down on the aft.

I talked about the ship's work, the painting and repairing I did, and I told him about the constant metallic rumble vibrating below decks. I told him about the smell, which was thick with sterile grease stink that stayed in your nostrils, and the smell of working men. Men away from women, men who aren't getting any, go bad, and they start to smell like metal and fur and meat.

Then I told him about the ships I built, the models, and the originals for them, about the masts and sails, and how, in the water, they had been beautiful things.

"What if they fell?" my brother said.

I didn't understand the question, but thought I would try to answer it anyway. It was vague, but it showed he was still awake, still listening. I wanted to ask, fell from where? But I didn't. I said if a man stood on the mainmast lookout, on a whaler, for example, he could lose his balance. If he tumbled from that height, he might slap the water like he was hitting cement. He might be internally damaged, but if he did come up, they'd throw him a life buoy, the white ones made out of cork and braided with a square of rope.

I brought one of the ships toward him. "I've got one here," I said, "tiny, the size of your fingernail."

He looked at it, cleated to the ship above the deck. He studied it and then he gazed at me. "Yes," he said. It was the most painful smile I'd ever seen in an adult human being, and it reminded me of me. I thought of the ocean, which I hadn't viewed for years and might not, ever again. "Yes," my brother said from under the icepack. "Now I get it."

LIKE STRANGERS SITTING randomly together in a midnight peeling-gray downtown bus depot smelling of old leather shoes, we talked until four in the morning, and he left, his face bruised dark, carrying one of my ships, the *Lightning*, under his arm. He came back a week later. We sat in the park this time, not saying much. Then I went to see him, and I met his wife. She's a pleasant woman, a tall blonde who comes fully outfitted with jewels I usually see under glass in display cases. My brother and I know each other better now; we've discovered that we have, in fact, no subjects in common. But it's love, so we have to go on talking, throwing this nonsense into the air, using up the clock. He has apologized for trying to play baseball with me; he admits now that it was a mistake.

When I was small, living with Harold and Ethel Harris and the other Harris children, I knew about my other parents, the aching lovers who had brought me into my life, but I did not miss them. They'd done me my favor and gone on to the rest of their lives. No, the only thing I missed was the world: the oceans, their huge distances, their creatures, the tides, the burning water-light I heard you could see at the equator. I kept a globe nearby my boy's bed. Even though I live here, now, no matter where I ever was, I was always homesick for the rest of the world. My brother does not understand that. He thinks home is where he is now. I show him maps; I tell him about Turkey and the Azores; I have told him about the great variety and beauty of human pigmentation. He listens but won't take me seriously.

When my brother talks now, he fingers his nose, probably to remind me where I hit him. It's a delicate gesture, with a touch of self-pity. With this gesture he establishes a bit of history between us. He wants to look up to me. He's twenty-eight years old, hasn't ever seen Asia, and he says this to me seriously. Have you ever heard the sound of a man's voice from a minaret? I ask him, but he just smiles. He's already called my wife; he has a whole series of happy endings planned, scene by scene. He wants to sit in a chair and see me come into the room, perfected, thanking the past for all it has done for me.

KATE BRAVERMAN

Temporary Light

IT IS EARLY IN DECEMBER. Suzanne Cooper drives down
Wilshire Boulevard through Beverly Hills and the city is not
as she knew it. Overnight, wide red ribbons have been entwined around street lamps, there is simulated snow and
frost in shop windows, and legions of slaughtered pines are
everywhere decorated and displayed. It is as if the earth had
suddenly divested itself of the ordinary and revealed its pa-
gan interior. Or perhaps the world had without warning
gone mad, she decides, garish red and green and silver like
a bleeding forest under moonlight. This is a landscape of
dangerous wounds and corrupted vegetation.

At a traffic light she finds herself staring at a Santa Claus
with a sleigh of reindeer strung on wires across the intersection. Everywhere, strands of light bulbs rise into the air.
Even the sky seems delirious and experimental. It is the winter of the wild surprise. The old regime does not apply.
Have a drink, the voice in her head says.

It is Suzanne Cooper's second sober Christmas. She has
learned to recognize the voice of her illness, the demonic
chorus it employs and the genius motivating its attempts to
destroy her. The voice could be articulate, brilliant, and seductive. It is the disaster that never sleeps.

I have a killer disease that wants me dead, she remembers. I have a daily reprieve based on the maintenance of my spiritual life. She repeats the slogans from Alcoholics Anonymous she has memorized, the banalities designed to provide a rudimentary form of counterattack against the onslaught of her alcoholism. It is like a chess game played by two computers to a series of perpetual stalemates. She is always black and on the defensive. Her sickness is aggressive and white, the color of vodka, gin, and wine.

At the next stop sign, she glances into a shop window dense with a red-and-green geometric motif. Mirrors amplify the distortion. Mannequin elves offer demented smiles. They look as if they have taken enormous doses of mescaline.

You're pathetic, the voice says, with your tiny arsenal, your squalid weaponry. And it won't be enough, not nearly. Consider the thin air beneath you. You have no net. You will fall and shatter and your blood run. One small glass of eggnog with a drop of brandy. No one will know.

Suzanne Cooper turns her car into the monumental parking structure beneath the Beverly Center. This year she is shopping early. Last Christmas she was in the hospital. This year will be different. This year she will see her children. Stephanie and Mark will spend Christmas Eve and Christmas Day with her. This has become her imperative, the irrefutable meaning of her present life. Her actions derive from the fact of Christmas. It has become the spine of her world, the anatomy she accepts as necessary.

In a boutique on the sixth level of the mall, yard-square aluminum representations of snowflakes sway above her head. She wonders if each one is in fact different from the others and unique. "Jingle Bells" plays relentlessly, asserting itself from unseen speakers. The voice in her head substitutes the word *martini* for jingle bells. "Mar-ti-ni, mar-ti-ni, mar-ti-ni to-day," the voice intones tirelessly as she lifts scarves and sweaters and cannot focus her eyes. She is conscious of the sharp-edged metallic snowflakes just above her. She is holding clothing between her fingers, bolts of fabric. She feels confused, suddenly hot, as if she has been struck with a virulent flu. Then she walks out of the store.

On a higher level of the mall, Suzanne finds herself standing in a shop excessive with Christmas manifestations. Six tall trees straddle stacks of wrapped and ribboned gifts. A colossal wreath is suspended from the ceiling. The walls glow with strings of gold lights. This is not Christmas as Suzanne Cooper remembers it.

Last year she did not even send Christmas cards. She was only one month sober. She could barely walk the hospital corridors. It seemed that there had been rain, and carolers had come, schoolchildren wearing bells. She had closed the door.

It occurs to her that the other Christmases of her life are partial memories, images in a blackout, something like a village glimpsed in a blizzard. There are the meals she burned, the gifts she forgot to wrap or send. The line in the post office was offensive and boring, she thought as he drank from a bottle stashed in her car. She would return later, when the line was smaller, but of course she didn't, drove to Malibu instead and crashed the car. She is thinking of the Malibu sheriff's station and the ambulance on the Pacific Coast Highway as she stands beneath a gigantic wreath suspended from the ceiling. Then, somehow, she buys her first gifts of the season.

Even as the packages are being wrapped, the dark blue velvet dress with a white lace collar for Stephanie and a red-and-green sweater with a border of reindeer for Mark, a discreet implication of Christmas adorning the area near the shoulders, Suzanne feels dissatisfied. The wrapping paper is red, embossed with green trees, and the red seems to glare challengingly. She is conscious of the voices in her head complaining, mimicking her children. "Oh, another dress," the condemning voice of Stephanie says. In the silence, Stephanie would not have to say, how dull, how could you? It's riding pants I long for.

"There are reindeer on here," Mark says with mock astonishment. "Mother, I can't wear reindeer," the approximation of Mark tells her, his voice soft like his father's, the tone that of a lecture.

In their eyes she is like a slow child who needs to be tutored. She realizes they do not expect much from her, she of the ruined dinners and automobiles and hospitals. She of the diminished capacities. And she recognizes that their image of her is similar to her image of her mother. Somehow she has managed to replicate that which she most loathes.

And somewhere, always near, her mother Candace, her tone sharp and offended, says, "Put that down, dear. You can't afford it. They won't appreciate it. They never do. How could they, with that breeding? I told you, put that back." It occurs to Suzanne that she is trembling. She reaches out her hands for the packages, the red that glares dangerously, and walks out of the extravagantly wreathed store. For a moment, she experiences a sense of triumph.

She has at last purchased something. Suzanne feels as if she has finally drawn blood in the consumer hunting season. She enters a stationery store. A wordless version of "Jingle Bells" descends from the wall- and ceiling-speakers like an invisible flock of tiny, menacing birds. "Mar-ti-ni, mart-tin-i, mar-tin-i today." Then she begins to study the boxes of Christmas cards. She considers her potential selections methodically, working her way first vertically and then horizontally across the rows.

Suzanne Cooper weighs the resonances of the cards, not merely the issue of style and content, typeface and graphics, but the more elusive fundamental essence. There are subtleties. She rules out snow scenes in any guise. This is California and it would, after all, be contrived. Santa Claus in any form is too childish and cute. The elves are unspeakable. Birds of peace are a possibility. And flowers and bells and cards from nonprofit agencies. There is also the matter of recycled paper. She stacks her first round of potential selections in a pile near the counter. The stack rises beside the cash register.

Suzanne Cooper considers the implications of "Merry Christmas" versus "Joy," and the distinctions between "Season's Greetings" and "Happy Holidays." The voice in her head objects to all of her selections. Too religious, it chides her. Too flamboyant, it comments, voice stern. Suzanne feels inadequate. She experiences a sudden sense of rage that takes her breath away.

Of course, "Merry Christmas" is too specific. What if one doesn't celebrate Christmas? What if one isn't merry, has just gone through a divorce, or had a suicide, drug overdose, or cancer in the family? What if one is an alcoholic and has been removed from her family and then banished to a small apartment in Santa Monica? Was there a card appropriate to her circumstances?

She finds herself holding a box offering "Joy" in pastels. The motif is simultaneously intimidating and seductive, avant-garde in a terrifying way. It could mean anything, this "Joy," even things she could not articulate or control. Finally, Suzanne decides to buy three boxes of "Season's Greetings." These permutations seem manageable. Still, she feels little confidence as she departs from the store.

On the top level of the mall, in a kind of enclosure past the movie theaters that remind her of a Greyhound bus station in a depressed city, Suzanne Cooper drinks a café au lait and wishes that she could smoke again. If she had a cigarette, she could make more accurate assessments in her shopping, she would be calmer and more assured. Her brain and hand-eye coordination would be vastly improved. She watches someone smoking near her and it occurs to her that if she smoked, she would look glamorous and capable. Store clerks would not dare defraud her. Smoke a cigarette, just one, the voice in her head says. It's Christmas. You can have one.

Suzanne turns her attention to the Christmas cards she has just selected. She views the cards as if they were the distillation of her personality, the highest tangible achievement of her sensibility. She notices that the card approximates a kind of typewriter script and duplicates the phrase "Season's Greetings" relentlessly, as if struck by a mental illness or a form of repetitive nervous disorder. She feels repelled and somehow betrayed. There is a lack of authenticity about the card that profoundly saddens her. She recognizes that she would not wish to receive such a card.

She walks to a Mrs. Field's Cookies bordering the eating enclosure and purchases four large white chocolate macadamia nut cookies. She eats two of them, quickly, and immediately feels better. This year she will manage the ritual of Christmas, with all its garish atrocities and bizarre paraphernalia. These pathetic rituals are our cumulative definition, she thinks, simultaneously agitated and resigned.

This year she will decorate a Christmas tree and hang a wreath of noble pine on her front door. She will bake cookies shaped like Christmas trees. She will cover them with green sugar that resembles bits of glass. She has practiced the recipe already. She has told Stephanie about their striking stained-glass appearance. Stephanie, with polite silence, has reluctantly agreed to participate. They will wear matching white aprons Suzanne has purchased just for this activity. She has imbued the baking with spiritual qualities that require special garments like vestments. They will bake cookies together and this action will subtly bond them. She will duplicate the winter landscape with a version of her own, green and white, like a form of voodoo.

The stained-glass cookie project has assumed an almost mystical significance for her. She wants her entire life filled with tangible manifestations of the calming and predictable. Her personal evolution has been characterized by what she

now views as fierce years of barbarism. Her own private ice
ages, so to speak, her centuries of retrograde behavior and
perception. Now she is committed to the larger traditional
demarcations. Events such as Christmas have been clarified
and redeemed. She no longer views them as acts of indifferent hypocrisy but rather as collective cultural statements of
faith.

She eats another white chocolate macadamia nut cookie
and reflects on her personal evolution. It occurs to her that
she might be preparing for an oral exam in a subject in
which she is not comfortable and has merely memorized
facts and equations. She glares at the Christmas cards with
their leaden assertion of greetings, and the words seem to
leave the page, to somehow retreat and pale.

"I don't drink anymore," she told Candace. It was the
previous summer. She had taken her mother out for lunch.
It was July. They sat in the Polo Lounge at the Beverly Hills
Hotel. The air seemed yellow and pink, tropical but tamed
and elegant. She had taken Candace out of the institution
on a half-day pass.

"But you can have one glass of wine with your mother. Of
course you can," Candace chided her. Her mother was
dressed entirely in pink, a pink Chanel suit and hat and silk
scarf. Even the diamonds on her brooch and rings seemed
pink in the filtered and restrained midafternoon light. Such
a sweet lady, a passing stranger might think. Candace ordered scotch on the rocks. She drank it quickly and signaled
with a diamond-tiered hand for another.

"Have a drink with your mother," Candace ordered. Her
voice was fueled with rage. Her face was flushed. Even her
eyes looked pink. Her eyes were the pink of certain preda-
tory birds, or perhaps more distinctly reptilian, like chame-
leons. Have a drink with your mother, you must, the voice
within her announced.

"You're contemptible," Candace decided, drinking with exaggerated relish and ordering another. She wore pink lipstick. The scotch in her glass looked pink.

"What kind of celebration is this?" Candace demanded. "You always disappoint me. No"—she paused, then faced her daughter—"you betray me. That is a constant."

Candace pushed her chair away from the table. She stood up, unsteady. She pointed a finger encased with diamonds at her. Her voice was loud now. "You always lie to me," Candace shouted. She was still holding her scotch glass. She studied the glass in her hand as if she was uncertain what the object was. Then she threw it in Suzanne's face.

Suzanne had been startled by the liquor, how cool it was, how familiar the scent. She closed her eyes then, the better to breathe it in.

Later, she had telephoned her former husband. She told Jake that she had been forced to call the hospital. Candace had been taken from the Polo Lounge in an ambulance.

"Naturally," Jake said distantly, as if adjusting something while they spoke, a shoelace, perhaps, or the television, the newspaper, the skirt of a new woman, or jogging shoes. "She's mentally ill."

"I didn't drink," Suzanne told him.

"Why would you?" Jake had answered, surprised, as if the thought had never occurred to him. "You don't drink any-more."

He made it sound as if she had had a minor infection and had received the appropriate medication and now it was over, done with, ancient history, less than a footnote. It was remote to him because she was no longer important. He had filed for divorce while she was still in the hospital. The out-come of her hospitalization did not matter to him. She could drink herself to death or remain abstinent; in either event he was finished with her. He had kept the house in Beverly Hills and the children remained with him. She had gone from the hospital to a one-bedroom apartment in Santa

Monica. She had been banished. It had never occurred to her that this might happen. It had been, literally, unthinkable.

SUZANNE COOPER DRIVES from the Beverly Center shopping mall west toward the ocean. The landscape is manicured and swept clean, a perpetual warm winter of bougainvillea and poinsettia on sunny hillsides above the loitering Pacific. On impulse, she parks her car on the bluffs above Santa Monica Bay. It occurs to her, suddenly, that there are certain moments and angles that are almost bearable. There are white sailboats on the bay. The water seems anemic and dazed. Waves break slowly and without malice. The Pacific is simply a fact for her, a blue beyond judgment, taken for granted. A sense of definition asserts itself at the periphery of her awareness. She realizes that nuances and the blue increments will come later, if at all.

She finds it necessary to reiterate the central facts of her existence, that she is thirty-seven years old, the divorced wife of Jake, the mother of Stephanie and Mark. She is a sober member of Alcoholics Anonymous. She doesn't drink anymore, ever. This year her children will spend Christmas Eve and Christmas Day with her. She will not fall asleep with a lit cigarette burning in an ashtray or pass out in the garden with her nightgown on. She no longer smokes and she no longer has a garden. She is reliable now. Even Jake's attorney has finally agreed to accept, provisionally, this concept. Yes, she is becoming the sort of woman who puts the appropriate change into parking meters and mails her Christmas cards on time. She is becoming the sort of woman one could exile to an apartment in Santa Monica knowing that she would accept it with quiet dignity. She is the sort of woman one could banish with little expense.

Suzanne Cooper walks along the Santa Monica cliffs feeling oddly hollow, as if her bones are merely a grid, a suggestion of an armature not yet developed. She walks into a gift shop bizarre with decorations, its shelves flaunting color and pyramids of oddities she can barely decipher. She holds a plastic ashtray with a picture of the Santa Monica Bay, overly representational – the water is never that shade of ineffable blue anymore. *"Feliz Navidad"* is written in an offensive red script across the exaggerated too-green shoreline. Her hand feels soiled.

You need a drink, her voice reminds her. It is a patient voice. No one will know, it tells her. They don't care anyway. Drunk or sober, they have no use for you. One Bloody Mary. It won't kill you. 'Tis the season. 'Tis the season to be jolly. And you won't be surprising anyone. They expect it. They expect you to slip. They'll forgive you. You can always go back to AA after the holidays, in January, when the world turns dull and normal.

As she walks to her car, the light sea breeze brushes her body and she feels insubstantial, as if she might blow away. Then she drives to her noon AA meeting. She raises her hand and is called on to share. She wants to tell them how she has been exiled to an apartment in Santa Monica but she does not. Instead, she talks about her difficulty selecting the absolutely perfect Christmas card. Everyone laughs sympathetically. The women nod their heads in recognition. But she does not tell them that Stephanie and Mark will be spending Christmas with her. She imagines her children climbing the stairs to her apartment with their sleeping bags, their eyes expertly adjusting to her limited perimeters. Stephanie and Mark exchanging glances that say, Look at her minuscule domain. She is even less than we thought.

Suzanne Cooper spends her alloted three minutes making a humorous anecdote of her inability to choose a Christmas card that will solve all of her problems. She does not mention the fact that Stephanie and Mark will be spending Christmas with her under duress. They have both telephoned, separately, asking to be released from this obligation. Jake is going skiing in Aspen with his current girlfriend, the redhead with the free concert tickets. The one who took them to David Bowie and U2. Jake has suddenly become a skier. He has discovered rock and roll. He can take airplanes now, his fear of plane crashes has disappeared. It is as if her miniaturization has somehow enlarged him. This is what Suzanne is actually thinking while she talks about Christmas shopping. When she finishes, she glances at the women she has successfully deceived. Quite unexpectedly, she realizes that she detests them all.

THAT NIGHT THE WIND becomes agitated and cold. There is a storm and then, almost immediately, another. It rains for the next two weeks. The night wind seems increasingly personal and specific. She prepares her apartment for the arrival of her children, who do not want to be there. She has never before managed the literal details of Christmas by herself. She ties a Christmas tree to the roof of her car and drives with branches splayed across the windshield. She drags the tree up the stairs to her apartment as it rains. She decorates it with new ornaments. The hand-sewn sequined snowflakes her grandmother made remain with Jake and the children. Her tree seems pathetic in comparison, deformed like a kind of dwarf, something small enough for her to carry, and adorned with the standard and ordinary. She tries to erase her sense of humiliation about the tree as she hangs a wreath on her front door. She stockpiles cookie-baking ingredients.

It rains the night of her children's Christmas pageant. It has been decided that she will pick them up after their performance. Jake's attorney has relented and she will be allowed to be with her children in an automobile for the first time in years. Then she will take them to her tiny dominion, which they will translate into something squalid. They will be excessively polite with her. Their eyes will be angry and bored.

She is imagining her children's eyes as she parks her car in the school parking lot. She is struck by the force of the wind as she walks. The sudden cutting press of it seems more than a function of climate. It seems to be a revelation of some brutal interior.

She finds a seat in the school auditorium. A seat for one. There is a moment of darkness and then the lights come on, soft and pink and radiant, as if there has been a kind of clarification. The pageant unfolds gracefully. The program is titled *Fiesta de las Luces*. Children rush across the darkened stage holding flashlights. They are comets. They are comets in the void or perhaps they are meant to represent random pulses of inspiration. Suzanne considers this, breathlessly. A child with a white robe speaks into a microphone, explaining that it is not only Christmas and Hanukkah, but a rare conjunction of planets and calendars makes this also the Islamic celebration of Ramadan and the African festival of Kwanzaa.

Suzanne Cooper is stunned by the implications of this universal recognition of light. Children appear and sing a Christmas carol in Spanish and then a chant in an African dialect. An older boy appears and recites passages from Genesis and the Upanishads. Suzanne is struck by the thought that somewhere, candles are being put into boats and they are gliding across unpronounceable rivers. Stephanie appears and stands in a circle with five other girls, singing a lullaby about stars in winter. The stage fills with children wearing African masks and others dancing like dervishes.

It occurs to her that this is her first Christmas pageant. Last year she was in the hospital. Before that, each year by this time she was drunk. Now she is sober and the spectacle seems to be winding down. There is a song in what seems to be Chinese. Later, she recognizes the music as Bach. Children part the shadows with flashlights, simulating comets and inspiration, desire and intelligence. The simplicity of this resonates through her with an intensity for which she is absolutely unprepared.

She realizes that this essential drama is being enacted, in slight variation, throughout the world. White-gowned children sing of the light in remote nations and languages. It is more than a holy day, one holy day or another, but a recognition of the evolution of life. From the fundamental darkness, there is a random juxtaposition of energy, of thought and light. On this night and this night only, Buddha, Christ, Muhammad, and Moses inform the winter waters with a brilliance that glows. Suzanne Cooper finds herself weeping.

When she meets her children after the performance, Mark with his saxophone case, Stephanie still in a white robe, they seem distant and restrained. She notices that they are not carrying their sleeping bags.

"We've decided to go skiing," Mark informs her, barely looking at her.

"That is, if you agree, Mother," Stephanie adds. Her eyes say, Deny me this and I will hate you forever.

Suzanne recognizes that she needs a cigarette. They will go to Aspen and she will go to a 7-Eleven and buy a package of Marlboros. She sees her former husband on the far side of the almost deserted auditorium. Stephanie and Mark are joining their father. They call good-bye to her over their retreating shoulders and this sentiment, at least, sounds sincere. Then she is alone in the auditorium. She walks to the parking lot in the rain, buys a package of cigarettes at a liquor store, and drives to her apartment.

She lies awake smoking and listening to the rain. She has had insomnia since she stopped drinking. She is used to this forced examination of the night while the voice within her demands that she drink. The voice is male and yet speaks with the cadence of her incarcerated mother, she suddenly realizes.

In the morning Suzanne gets down on her knees and prays to the God she does not believe in to keep her sober one more day. She has been instructed to do this by her sponsor, a woman with eight years of sobriety who has rebuilt her life one painful molecule at a time. Her sponsor did not believe in God in the beginning, either. Suzanne Cooper begins each morning of her sobriety in this fashion, feeling fraudulent and somehow debased. For the first time, the voice of destruction within her is silent when she prays.

Something feels as if it is awakening, inside, where she has lived with her secret glaciers, the fields of ice that surround her, encase her, keep her protected and inaccessible. The ice that seems pink when the sun chances to touch it. On impulse, she telephones her mother in the hospital. She describes Stephanie in her ankle-length white robe singing about stars in an African dialect. There is something transcendent that she wishes to transmit to her mother. She expects nothing in return, not shared recognition, certainly, not even polite indifference.

"I would have wanted to see this," Candace says from the hospital. Suzanne does not reply. She is looking out her living-room window, into the window of an apartment identical to her own. She can see a Christmas tree and Christmas cards opened across the mantel.

Suddenly Suzanne finds herself offering to pick up her mother. She is telling her mother that she can have a Christmas pass. Suzanne had not planned to see her mother. Candace is too disruptive. It is simply too much pain.

"I'll be good," Candace says, and softer, after a pause, "I promise."

"You won't throw a drink in my face?" Suzanne asks, lighting a cigarette. The package is almost finished. She recognizes that she has started to smoke again.

"I would never do such a thing," Candace replies, voice hurt. "I know you don't drink anymore."

"But I'm smoking," Suzanne reveals.

"You'll stop again, I'm certain," Candace assures her. "You don't drink. That's the important thing."

"The children aren't coming," Suzanne says. She reports the fact of it, simply.

"They will appreciate you when they are older," Candace tells her. "You will see. They will surprise you."

Later, Suzanne Cooper will drive to the hospital, pick up her mother, and carry her suitcase into her apartment near the ocean. Candace will behave appropriately or she will not. They will, perhaps, wear matching white aprons and bake cookies in the form of green stained-glass Christmas trees or they will not. Perhaps they will sit on a bluff above the slow lingering white sails of boats on the Santa Monica Bay, sipping hot chocolate and recalling anecdotes from her childhood. Perhaps Stephanie and Mark will telephone from a ski lodge, suddenly missing her. They might say that Jake and his girlfriend keep the door of their room locked and it doesn't seem like Christmas, really, in that distant lodge, without her.

Of course she will always be disappointed by the traditional demarcations. She accepts this dispassionately. The voices she has internalized will always degrade her efforts and pronounce her inadequate and flawed in all circumstances. They will evaluate the stimuli and tell her she is not loved enough.

But it is this particular morning, following the *Fiesta de las Luces,* that occupies her attention. She is hanging up the telephone, staring out the window and taking the morning into her. She is smoking a cigarette in the living room of her apartment in Santa Monica. The storms have stopped. The morning is brilliant with the kind of purified light often seen in high altitudes, a light that implies the revelatory, absolution and forgiveness. It is the light of Christmas and Hanukkah, Ramadan and Kwanza. It is the light of candles on mantels and candles in boats on rivers and moored in harbors in the ports of all the world. It is the light of a billion school children wearing white robes and white gowns rushing across auditoriums to announce the birth of myriad deities. It is the light of children everywhere holding flashlights as they sing into the darkness, and beyond that darkness are great ridges of white mountains covered with white snow and punctuated by uncountable pines, all the massacred trees of Christmas somehow risen and returned. And further, there are green rivers lit by the white of flames in boats. There are ports where rivers empty their caravans of temporary light. And somewhere, in the place above that men perpetually pray to, comets startle the void and inexplicable juxtapositions inspire the darkness into forms of birth.

Suzanne Cooper is smoking a cigarette, racks of cookies are cooling. Her kitchen curtains are wide open. Sunlight is pouring into the room, brushing against the white apron she is wearing. And she is startled by the thought that she is somehow a candle in the window, and she is lit, at this moment, from within.

KAREN BROWN

Destiny

Marianne is named after a song by Frankie Valli and the
Four Seasons. I named her myself – her father doesn't even
know we're alive. He's probably still driving his pearl-white
Chevelle down some turnpike every night, plugging in
eight-track tapes of the Raspberries, who sing out the open
car windows, "Please go all the way," to any teenage girls
within earshot.

I've vowed that I will not let Marianne be fooled like I was.
I've been trying to set an example – staying chaste, unin-
volved – but sometimes I find myself imagining Marianne
years from now, at fifteen: brown hair streaming under violet streetlights, a silver charm bracelet jingling on her wrist,
staring up at someone's face, or at the moon . . . and I ache
with jealousy, with a mysterious excitement that has nothing
to do with my life in the past. I'm fooling myself, of course. I
already know that Marianne is the only thing I can love and
not pay for, ultimately, with my soul.

We have lived in Florida for two years – one with James
Copper, the makeup instructor I met at modeling school in
Massachusetts, and one on our own. I'm still not used to this
damp heat, this thick air, but Marianne doesn't care that her
clothes stick to her skin. I've even taken her with me, job
hunting, in my old Chevy Impala that's got no air condition-

ing. A few months ago, on the way home, the Impala died in the middle of an intersection. Marianne cried, "Go Mommy go," scattering her crayons as she climbed from the backseat to the front to tug on my arm. Other cars screeched and swerved to avoid hitting us, and finally three men in white clothes came from nowhere and pushed the car into a Sears parking lot. It was a hot day and their white shirts were wet. Marianne kissed the top of my arm as we watched the men disappear down the sidewalk, wiping their foreheads with the backs of their hands.

At first we didn't get out of the car. I was thinking about the photographer I'd just seen, who'd examined my proof sheets with a magnifying glass and said, "There's something about the mouth... " — as if it weren't *my* mouth in the picture, as if *I* weren't sitting there on the low couch in front of him, with my knees jutting, pointed and thin, out from under a tight black skirt. I looked at my mouth in the rearview mirror. Then Marianne whispered something in my ear, pointing to a display of bright metal swing sets assembled on the concrete in front of Sears.

We had to walk home. Heat rose off car bumpers and the glare of sidewalks. Cars flew past and blew the heat up my skirt. I am not living, I remember thinking. The living thing inside of me has left, and I am just a shell of a person walking down a street, holding a little girl whose legs dangle to the knobs of my knees, who takes my face in her two small hands and says, "Ask me *Who do you love?*" Her hair was sticking to the side of her face. I pushed her head down on my shoulder and kept walking, past the tire place where the men stopped working to whistle at me. I wanted to scream *These legs hurt,* and *There is something about this mouth,* but I didn't. I was a shell of a person. Yet the bones of the child pressed into my arms, warm and real, unbearably small, achingly beautiful.

Finally, we reached our house — almost hidden in the shade of the neighbor's trees — a tiny building with reddish brown paint peeling off all four walls. The sky hung over our heads, dismal, gray, and weighted with rain. Inside, the smell of old wood and mold was familiar, oddly consoling. Milk stood congealed in a bowl outside the back door. Marianne brought it in and dumped it in the sink. She was very quiet, staring out the door at the bare backyard, the one lean tree, and the railroad track.

"It would fit right there," she said.

I wanted to tell her that those swing sets are cheap, that they have to be cemented into the ground or they come up and tip, that the metal bends and the screws fall out. Instead I said, "I used to have one of those."

"With two swings?" she asked. "With two swings and a slide? Tell me."

So I told her about the swing set in Massachusetts that I got one year for Christmas, all set up in the garage on the gray cement, just like at Sears.

"When are we going there?" she wanted to know. We are always half packed, ready to go somewhere. The living room is lined with cardboard boxes. We just dig things out as we need them: clothes, hairbrushes, electric rollers.

"We've already been there," I began—then stopped, my voice lost under the sudden slap of rain on the roof. I stood at the door and watched it blur weeds and leaves into bright green smears. Behind me, game-show contestants screamed on the television, and Marianne lay curled in a ball on the couch with one finger in her mouth.

For the first two years of Marianne's life we lived with my mother in the house where I grew up. She is a divorced woman possessed by a lingering sadness that makes her mouth droop. The sadness hangs about her body, smelling of Chanel No. 5. In the late afternoons, sitting at the white iron table in the damp shade of the backyard, she drank double old-fashioneds from a large tumbler with a red P.G.A. insignia on it. I always thought this glass belonged to my father, a man I created who played golf and wore sweat-

ers that smelled of tobacco. Now I think it could have belonged to some other woman's husband who left it on the
counter one day. The neighbors always strolled across our
lawn with drinks in their hands. I would hear them below
my window while I changed Marianne: low voices laughing,
and ice cubes banging against the sides of heavy glasses.

The rain didn't last long. Once it stopped, Marianne and I
sat outside in one of the dripping lawn chairs someone had
left here long ago. The woven plastic slats are worn
through, and sometimes lizards slide out from under the
armrests. We just sat and watched the railroad track steam.
Our neighbor's trees were dense and shiny with rain, reminding me of my mother's giant green umbrella and her
hallway tile floor that was like ice under my bare feet, even
in summer.

My mother loved Marianne. When she kissed her good-
night, she would clutch the crib rail and sway down until her
mouth was right by Marianne's tiny ear. Her lipstick
brushed Marianne's face and she would whisper to her,
sometimes calling her my name by mistake. "I love you,
Roxanna," she would say – the only time I have ever heard
her say those words. The memory made me uneasy, waver-
ing in and out like the noise of insects in the trees around
us. When Marianne insisted that the noise is made by spi-
ders, weaving webs with machines, I couldn't help laughing.
She pinched my arm and gritted her teeth. It's all right for
her to hate me, I thought. I'm prepared for it. I have se-
cured a soft wall around me, waiting. It is normal: all daughters hate their mothers.

I told this to Janine, my friend from across the street who
had joined us in the backyard. She stood in front of me,
shaking her head, her hands on her hips.

"Who says?" she wanted to know.

"James Copper," I said.

"Oh," she smiled and rolled her eyes, "the makeup guy.
Why would you believe him?"

"Why not?"

Janine looked at me as if she knew something and didn't want to tell.

"You mean you would believe a guy who fed you all that crap about being a model, who carted you all the way to Florida and left you and a two-year-old alone for months at a time in a dumpy apartment?" Her face was flushed and she was waving her hands in the air. "Think about that!" she shouted.

I did. I thought about being in the Impala that my mother bought for me after Marianne was born, about Marianne asleep in the backseat with her legs buried under a pile of my dresses, about me crying and James Copper smoothing my hair and telling me things that I had to believe then—having already driven six hours on the interstate, with my mother's swing records from the forties stacked on the floor, and all my shoes (twenty pairs in bright-colored boxes) wedged in the trunk. Janine would not understand any of it. I looked at her soft, puffy face and furious eyes. I could never tell her about pulling off at Stuckey's while Marianne slept, how he drove around back and pushed my head down into his lap, stroked my hair and my neck and my back. How I imagined the waitresses in their brown uniforms leaving work, squeaking past the car in their white rubber-soled shoes, wondering: What is that man doing alone in that car with his head thrown back? Is he dead?

Janine glared at me as if she wanted to punish me, but then her eyes softened. She tried to turn away before I could see that she loves me. It was getting dark and she squinted at the empty dirt drive, moved a few steps back so she could see the street.

"Where's your goddamn car?" she asked.

"At Sears," I said. I didn't even look up at her. With Marianne squirming on my lap, I imagined sitting in this spot forever, becoming part of the outdoors with vines in my hair and weeds sprouting from my toes. I was comfortable.

"Even you, Roxanna, have a right to be happy," Janine said quietly.

"I am happy," I said. I closed my eyes and listened for the rustling of stems winding around my ankles. Marianne's legs were making wet marks on my thighs. We wore identical ponytails and I lifted hers, kissed her neck where it was salty, soft. I wanted to cry but decided to hold it in, to wait until it burned in my chest, a sweet pain.

SOON AFTER THE CAR was repaired I took Marianne to the beach.

"Florida is a beautiful place," I told her. "We can be anything we want."

"I want to be a model," she said. She can already put on lipstick expertly, without a mirror.

"Then we need tans," I said. We held hands and smiled, the sand scalding the bottoms of our feet. I had bought Marianne polka-dotted sunglasses and a pair of rubber thongs, but I still couldn't bear to look at her squatting on the bright towel, holding her knees, her tiny bones poking against the white skin of her back.

"Some things," she told me, "aren't very fun, even if they're supposed to be."

NOT LONG AFTER THAT I found a job through a modeling agency. I've had to work nights, but Janine has been willing to come over and watch Marianne for some time now. Her husband doesn't mind. She makes him dinner and leaves him with it in front of the TV. "Like an animal," she tells me, "only I put it on Corelle instead of in a metal bowl."

She had just arrived last night when my mother called and screamed at me over the phone: "I want my records back, do you hear me!"

"I don't have those anymore," I said, as Marianne swished around the room in one of my full slips, moving to the rhythm of "Love Me or Leave Me." Cicadas whined through the screen door, and the wind was pulling the cream curtains out and back.

"You had no right to do that," my mother cried, so close to hysteria that I hung up on her. Usually she'll just call back the next day and ask for Marianne, angry with me without knowing why.

I left Janine and Marianne and drove to my job at a popular nightclub. I dance there, in a square cage made of metal bars enameled black, with a Plexiglas floor. I wear costumes that match the theme of the night — Biker Bash, Wild West, Pajama Party. If someone is sick the manager sometimes asks me to waitress. Either way I make money, but I'd rather be behind the bars where no one can touch me. People my own age come to the club, right out of high school with fake IDs — girls in their mother's designer clothes, guys with long hair tied back and wearing shoes of buttery, expensive leather. I've gotten to know them. I watch them fall in love with each other. I see who two-times, who lies, which ones to trust. They act out their lives in the club while I dance and watch them. Older men throw money onto the square floor of the cage, and I fold the bills into tiny squares, tucking them in the toes of my patent leather pumps.

This job is only temporary. I don't have any other plans, but I know things will change soon. I felt it last night, driving home at two A.M. with the car windows down, in the way the air moved the hair on my arms. Then, I had to stop at a convenience store to buy cigarettes for Janine, and I saw a man in a green army coat sitting on a duffel bag under the pay phone. He looked straight at me, and I was startled by his eyes — and the silence of a face like that of a statue. When I came back out, a police car was parked next to mine and the cop was telling the man to leave, waving his stick in the air while he talked. I opened my car door and the man stood up and looked at me again. I motioned toward him with my hand.

"Let's go," I said. I felt bold and strange. He got in the car, leaving the cop openmouthed, and we drove away.

His name is Jeffrey. He smells of the outside, of fresh open air. "I'm nomadic," he told me, laughing quietly.

When we reached my house I went inside alone, gave Janine her cigarettes, and watched her walk home. Then I sneaked Jeffrey in. I showed him Marianne, sleeping in the bedroom. Her body was nearly invisible under the patterned sheet: a small raised spot, a fold that I could flatten with my hand. Jeffrey and I slept without clothes on the prickly material of the secondhand couch. Before dawn he disappeared, and I crept back into the bed I share with Marianne. Her fingers curled around the pale sheet, revealing small crescents of dirt under her fingernails. As I brushed her thin hair from her face my hand shook.

In the morning a train went by, rattling everything in the house. Open windows banged shut by themselves. I sat on the edge of the bed, awakened by the noise. I'd been dreaming about Marianne's father, a boy I barely knew except for his mouth and the dull weight of his hips. In the dream I see the Chevelle parked in our yard, the white paint shimmering pink and blue in the sun. A ripe orange falls from a neighbor's tree onto the hood, plunk, and rolls to the street. He stands inside the door and, without words, I know what is expected of me. I do not undress, but I am back on the tiled floor again, the blue-gray slate under the dim hall light. My mother's green umbrella leans beside the door, my shoulder blades push against the ice-cold tile. Somewhere up the carpeted steps my mother sleeps, dreamless.

I crouched on the edge of the bed, far from Marianne, my knees pulled up close to my chest. The train and the dream seemed the same, and I tried to hold my breath until it passed, but the rumbling and the clattering didn't stop so I gave up and breathed in the dust and grease sifting under the door. I tasted the memory in my mouth, sharp, unwanted: a boy in a white car, and myself, lifeless, silent, pressed to a gray slate floor. The train moaned in the distance, the iron bulk of it now past our house, the dust settling at the foot of the bed. And I was filled with guilt and shame for the thing, though I do not remember ever wanting to do it, and I do not remember ever saying I would. Suddenly I was sick, hunched retching over a brown plastic wastebasket. I watched Marianne turn and sigh, and sleep on.

This afternoon Jeffrey showed up at the front door, wearing the same green army coat with the brass buttons, but looking younger in the daylight with a blond beard that must have grown overnight. Marianne hid in the bedroom for two hours, until Jeffrey made her a wand out of the TV aerial and some aluminum foil.

"It's magical," he said. She watched him through the crack in the door. "C'mon, Marianne."

She tiptoed across the linoleum floor and slipped between my knees. "I still don't like you," she told him as she grabbed the wand. On her fingers she wore rings with colored plastic stones attached to tarnished metal bands.

"Do you have bells on your toes?" Jeffrey asked.

Marianne showed him her bare feet—rings on each of her big toes. She wiggled them at him and smiled. "How do you like that?" she asked.

"I like that a lot," he said. "You have pretty feet."

Within minutes Marianne is showing him her dress-up clothes, modeling a flowered kimono and my patent pumps, taking him outside to look at the yard. They walk up the white gravel bed, step onto the railroad track, and wave at me where I lean in the frame of the back door with my arms wrapped around my waist. Marianne moves her shoulders up and down and claps her hands. She does a little dance on the track. The phone rings but I decide not to answer it. I am immovable in the doorway, watching them smiling at me, watching Jeffrey take Marianne's hand and help her down the graveled slant. Then they move toward me, fast, running, like people in a home movie.

For dinner we eat tacos from the fast-food place down the street. "Time for bed," I tell Marianne, but she shrieks, pulling away from me and leaping onto Jeffrey's lap.

"We're going to wait for the train tonight, Roxanna," she says. She picks up a crayon and, holding it between two fingers, raises it to her mouth and exhales.

Jeffrey looks at me but I try to avoid his eyes, which are sad and soft like a saint's. We go outside and unfold two of those old lounge chairs. It's almost dark, surprisingly cool.

"This is like spring in Massachusetts," I say.

"This is magic weather," Marianne whispers, clutching the wand. We adjust the chairs until they lean almost all the way back, and we push them close together so there is no gap. Marianne fits beside me, under my arm. Jeffrey drapes his big green coat over us all. Underneath it he holds my hand.

"What are we waiting for?" I ask.

"The magic circus train," Marianne says. She turns toward Jeffrey and he smiles.

I do not want her liking this man, climbing up onto his lap, believing in him, but I've grown tired of holding back. The bare yard dissolves in the dark, yet overhead the stars are blinding. My toes peek out from under the heavy coat, alive, covered with skin instead of moss.

While we wait for the train, I imagine a man tied to the tracks. I make out the shape of him – lying prone on top of the glowing white gravel – but the face of the man changes. It is Marianne's father, it is James Copper, and then it is Jeffrey with his pale blue eyes pleading, with his only possessions crammed in a duffel bag by the door. He will mark me in some way, like the rest, leave the imprints of his arms and fingertips like tattoos under my clothes. I do not care.

Marianne's breathing moves her against me, slow gentle breaths that spill out mist into the green night. She too will learn the cycle of things, the irresistible wheel that draws us into its spokes. Even now, as we sit in these lawn chairs, the three of us together under the dark wide sky and the overbright stars, our lives happen – all around, just then, forever.

DOROTHY BRYANT

Blood Relations

T HEY HAD THEIR USUAL season tickets and, when the first play opened, Frank realized that he wanted to go. David, back in the hospital again, encouraged him. "Take Paul, or Jay." But Frank didn't want to see any of their friends.

There were his sisters, his parents, his cousin. No. He decided he wanted his grandmother, who had never gone to plays and concerts and was now over eighty, with failing sight, hearing, memory. "Come with me, Nonna. It's a musical, *Sunday in the Park with George.*" He knew she would come. The only grandson of a large family, Italian on both sides, he could count on her old unjust preference. For once he was glad of it, shameless.

They drove down Geary Street through gradually thickening traffic. At a long stoplight, he suddenly asked her one of the old questions about his grandfather, whom he knew only through photographs and the stories Nonna told him. It had been years since she'd told this one, his favorite. How he and his grandfather were together all the time in those last months, puttering in the garden until he was too weak. How Frank, barely three years old but talking constantly in either English or Italian (he could not speak a word of Italian now), understood his grandfather perfectly. No one else could, not after seven operations on his cancerous jaw.

Frank's memories began after his grandfather's death, when Nonna became the settled, widowed old lady he knew. He never thought of her as ever having had a husband. He never asked her how she had endured those two years of his grandfather's terrible dying. Frank's mother said that Nonna nursed him day and night, never complained, never cried. Only that by the time he died, she had a slight tremor, an almost imperceptible shaking of her head that still remained after thirty years. It was as if she were constantly whispering inwardly, No, no, no.

FRANK DROPPED HER in front of the theater while he parked the car. Alone, he felt a stab of guilt. These stabs came regularly now when, absorbed at work, he forgot for a few minutes, then suddenly remembered David sitting at home, probably staring out the garden window. Or when he took a deep breath of cool, foggy air, felt a surge of ordinary well-being, and rejoiced in it. And then remembered David with silvery-blue plastic oxygen tubes in his nose. He wondered if Nonna had ever felt guilty for not being able to share each moment of her husband's pain.

HE FOUND HER JUST where he had left her, shivering a bit in the crowd. It took them some minutes to inch their way across the jammed, noisy lobby, to squeeze into the elevator, to find their seats. The theater, filling quickly, was already hot and stuffy, and Nonna looked tired. Usually she was in bed by this time. It had been cruel to bring her. She would not enjoy this kind of musical. Even Frank preferred the old-fashioned kind, with tunes you could hum.

She sat silent beside him, as usual. Living alone all these years, she had no one to talk to. She spent hours working jigsaw puzzles, as she had done with his grandfather during those final months. It had been something they could do without his having to talk. A visitor could join their silence, watching, fitting in a piece or two. When Frank was there, Nonna had told him, his grandfather would hand him a piece and show him how to fit it in, which he did with great concentration and satisfaction. No, he could not remember that either.

Aside from the puzzles, she read an occasional best-seller, watched television, telephoned her grandchildren. Yet even on the phone she said little. There was silence in her eyes, too. They looked, they saw, they expressed nothing. Frank was grateful for that tonight. It would have been a mistake to have brought his mother. Her eyes said everything. Whenever she looked at him, they widened into an abyss of prophecy, full of images of him in David's place. Last week, suddenly infuriated, he had snapped at her, "Don't bury me yet!" It was a strange phrase for him to use, more like something Nonna would say.

A few minutes into the play he was sure they should not have come. He did not want to sit in the dark listening to these tones of abrasive, intellectual sentiment. It would have been better if they had gone to a movie, where he could cry. Like Nonna, he never cried. Except at the movies, where sometimes, at the most banal scenes, tears suddenly spilled down his cheeks. How David laughed at him! But he had not been to a movie these past two months. The flat, simplistic images that usually relaxed and distracted him had become unbearable, torture by stupidity.

Only his job, only work brought him relief. Nonna had had no job during those two years, no break from nursing her husband, using up their savings, then going to work after he died, on night shift for the next twenty years, "not to be alone when the sun goes down." After the first week, Frank realized he was lucky that he had to go to work every day.

Lucky. It was a word he and David used often now. Lucky to have each other, not like some poor bastard all alone. Lucky to have their own house, no panicky roommates or landlord to evict them. Lucky that family, friends, employers, all were behaving well, impeccably, like Nonna who had, as usual in any family crisis, sent jars of soup, ravioli, and her incomparable veal cutlets. David had laughed and said he wondered where on the hierarchy of "luckier than they" he and Frank stood. Surely his former lovers were calling themselves lucky not to be Frank. He and David laughed a lot these days, alone together, or with friends and family. Everyone roared at each other's jokes. They had become the ideal audience for a stand-up comic, all eagerly pitched on the edge of laughter, dreading the silence that followed.

FRANK FOUND HIMSELF drawn into the play in spite of, or because of, the abrasive, repetitive music. Maybe he felt in tune with this music that wasn't trying to be sweet and this story that led nowhere. Ragged and hesitant and fragmented, the story lurched from side to side rather than forward, as George, the impressionist artist, conceived his painting from the bits and pieces of his life, fitting them together into beauty no one else could see.

Frank wondered if Nonna was paying attention or daydreaming. Could she follow the play? Or did she see and hear and then forget a moment later, as she forgot so many things now? How much did she actually understand before she forgot? Did she understand what was happening to David and would possibly – probably – happen to Frank? He stopped that thought, grabbed it, firmly put it aside. Stopping thought was a new process for him, requiring great discipline. Maybe Nonna didn't really forget, but had learned to put aside certain thoughts she must live with.

WHEN THE HOUSELIGHTS came up for intermission, she nodded, yes, she was enjoying the play. No, she did not want to leave her seat. She sat watching people move about. Frank knew she would not speak again unless he asked her a question. "Did you ever get mad at my grandfather, I mean when he was sick?"

She seemed unsurprised by the question, nodding as if always ready with the answer. "At the end, the last months, when he was leaving me."

Frank nodded. It had come sooner to him, the rage, and to David as well. Anger exploded in small ways, in telephoning from work and yelling when he learned that David would not, could not, eat his lunch. In low, petty ways, like his sulking when David called the AIDS Project to ask for a counselor, someone who would "come between us," Frank whined, flinching at the contempt in David's eyes, in his cutting response, and then, worst of all, in his silence. They apologized, forgave, quarreled again, made up, forgave, wondered at the ignoble form their anguish took. They were not prepared for this, they who had prepared so well.

They had been together five years when the blood test became available, and they took it, glad of the chance to escape the cloud hanging over their friends, confident that their fiercely defended monogamy would be vindicated. They could hardly believe the results. Positive. Each had picked up the virus years ago. Or one had carried it to the other.

They made their wills, took vitamins, went to bed early, stopped drinking even wine, talked about death-with-dignity, quoted statistics. Only ten percent of positives got sick. Twenty percent. Thirty-five to forty percent. The statistics changed as the year slowly passed, until David became one.

Now, their suicide seemed like childish romanticism. Their contempt for heroic measures shriveled and, abjectly, they accepted medical assault. Dignity dissolved in the ocean of petty necessities—the unwashed dishes, the disability application, the mortgage payments—the dozens of reminders that, while everyone must die, life lurches on.

THE LIGHTS DIMMED AGAIN. Now the setting was modern, and the great-grandson of George was the artist, still struggling with the same questions, his own life a fragmented puzzle. The baby in the first-act painting was now a grandmother, dozing and drooping in a wheelchair, singing in a weak, piping squeak, "Children and art, children and art." Those were the only things, she sang, that you leave when you die, that are worth anything. "Children and art, children and art."

Frank waited to see if the insistent chant of that simple equation would take him in like a movie and wet his eyes, but it did not touch him. He would never have children, and he didn't make art. Whatever he left would not be so easy to name. What did Nonna think of that song? Not children and art, just children. They were all that mattered to Nonna. That was why she was here with him, why she would sit in the dark through anything with him. So, the force that held them together was, in reality, a huge gap between them. Did she even know him? Did she understand why he needed her tonight, needed to begin to learn what she had known for thirty years?

He reached out to take her hand, gently, respectful of her arthritis. She gave his hand a quick, hard squeeze. Her strength surprised him, hurt him. She had never been so abrupt with him, so rough. He had never felt so grateful. They sat and watched the rest of the play, hand in hand, dry-eyed, two old soldiers in the long war.

KATHLEEN CAMBOR

Concessions

Sᴀᴍ ᴡᴀs ᴀ Cᴏᴜɢᴀʀ that spring, Harry a Shorthorn. Harry had just turned eight and was in the Peewees. Sam was eleven, in the Minors, with a pitching arm he hoped would take him to the Majors after just one season. It was April, Texas, Little League, practices four times a week, then games; the parents had to work two shifts in the Batter's Box—the concession stand—for each boy they had in the league. And since Mike was gone, Lily had to do it all. In her bedroom, she pulled her red hair back in one wide barrette, donned a white cotton skirt and T-shirt, tennis shoes and tennis socks, a blue baseball cap and matching apron— the uniform required for volunteers. In her station wagon, she looked at herself in the rearview mirror and set her face into the necessary smile, then practiced her baseball repartee with the empty seat beside her as she drove to the field. Small talk was required in the Batter's Box. Team spirit. Goodwill. She knew that she should act as if all this were fun for her, as if she *loved* it—serving hot dogs and barbecue and pizza to the players, parents, siblings, nostalgic passersby who heard the springtime baseball sounds and wandered in. But in truth, she'd never loved it, and had come to love it even less since she'd been alone. Her resistance to it took the form of a brain that wouldn't function. She became an awkward, simpleminded version of herself, unable to recall the price of anything. For five years Nerds had been twenty cents, Sweetarts, thirty-five. Nachos were a dollar plain, a dollar and a quarter with jalapeños. Lily's was an ordered, able mind, but on nights in the concession stand it failed her. By seven-thirty she had a crick in her neck from having to turn so many times to check the price list.

And then there was Birgit.

"You're running out of tea, there's no more popcorn. The water in the bun warmer is almost out." Birgit came in the back door as she did four times each three-hour shift to confirm what she already knew—that things in the concession stand fell apart without her. She was in charge, a pretty Dane with a sharp, small-featured face, an accent that she slurred and rounded in an effort to hide it. Her blond hair was long and frizzed; she wore a miniskirt and sleeveless T-shirt, giant dangling silver hoops as earrings. In the bleachers, on the sidelines, with the coaches, she had a breezy, flirty style. But in the concession stand Birgit was all business—there was a plastic, zippered bank envelope tucked under her arm, a beeper in her skirt pocket. Birgit looked at Lily and the three other volunteers and frowned. It was a look that Lily knew. *They* had forgotten to call for more pizza, *someone* was putting too much cheese over the nachos. Birgit folded her arms across her chest and sighed her disappointment, then placed herself in charge. She put more buns in the warmer, filled the popper with more corn, lifted the lid on a vat full of smoked and shredded beef. "You need more sauce here on this barbecue," she said.

"The sauce is in the microwave, heating up." Lily smiled with exaggerated sweetness at this one small thing done right.

The bell on the oven rang. Before Birgit could get to it, Lily opened the door and reached in for the two-quart measuring cup, only to find that the handle was too hot. She began to open drawers and cabinets, looking for pot holders.

"Here, I'll get it," Birgit said impatiently, and she moved as if she were, in this way, too, superior—asbestos hands, impervious to pain. She wrapped the palm of her bare hand around the handle of the Pyrex cup. Birgit's cry came first, then the crash. Lily watched the measure shatter at her feet, then saw the steaming sauce rise as if in slow motion, a miniature, red tidal wave that spread over her shoes and splashed across the shin and calf of her right leg. Tomato sauce and spices, scalding grease. Lily bit her lip to keep from crying out, then grabbed the closest cold thing, an extra-large Coke, full of ice, to pour on her burned leg.

THREE TO ELEVEN. Lily used to like working those hours at the hospital. She liked the slow movement from afternoon to evening, the smell of hot food, dinner served, the clatter of cleared trays, the dimming of the lights, the settling down, the tucking in. She liked it in the days when she was young and new to nursing, when hospital halls were green and tiled, when her crepe-soled shoes squeaked against the antiseptic-smelling, endlessly mopped floors. Now the halls and rooms were carpeted, windows draped. Hospitals were supposed to look like home.

She stopped in the hall at the isolation cart for gloves and mask and gown. She was methodical about procedures; in most things she favored precision over abandon. Even when she'd played piano six, eight hours daily, she loved Bach more than Beethoven, preferring the rigors of études and fugues to the passionate requirements of sonatas. She put on her mask and gown, and knocked twice on Jorge's door before she entered.

He turned slightly in his bed as she walked toward him. In recent days he'd hardly left his bed at all. His old determination to keep up, keep moving, had waned, then disappeared. His slow walks up and down the hall had ceased. He'd hoped bed rest would renew his strength; instead it sapped it. A low-grade fever made him flushed and sleepy, his voice was tremulous and low, his hands shook when he tried to cut his meat. Illness hadn't dulled his senses; instead it made him more alert, more sharply focused.

"What happened?" He gestured at her bandaged leg, barely visible beneath her gown.

"A long and boring story," Lily said through her paper mask. The burns were minor, except for one long, blistered second-degree burn along her shin. She could give the oozing blister air at night at home, but at work it needed the protection of gauze and tape, thick white stockings, and a sterile gown that almost reached her ankles. She placed a bottle of IV fluid on Jorge's bedside table and pulled on sterile latex gloves. "Did your doctor tell you? IV time again."

He had a picture on his bedside table of himself when he was well – dark Latin eyes and hair, wide seductive grin. Since she'd been to work the day before, Jorge had placed the photo face down so he wouldn't have to see it. There were no flowers in his room, no cards, he'd never had a single visitor. One helium balloon that said. Get Well Quick! was tied to Jorge's IV stand. An aide had taken it from another patient's balloon bouquet.

She loosened the sterile wrapping on the needle. "Your choice," she said. "Which arm?"

He reached under his pillow, took a quarter out and flipped it. He'd been in the hospital six times in the last year; he'd come to know her pretty well. His left arm lost, and he offered it to her.

He made small talk while she tried to find a vein that wasn't bruised or broken. How clear the air looked outside his window, how bright the sun. Almost as bright, he said, as it used to be in Acapulco, where his parents had a lovely, sprawling summer house that overlooked the bay. "I used to get brown as an Indian when I was a boy," he said. "Some-

times I speared fish as if I was a barefoot native, not the priv-
ileged city child I was. I imagined diving from those cliffs as
natives do to entertain the tourists." he wished he was at
home, he said. In Mexico. He wished he could go out to the
sun porch he could see from his hospital window. Could she
arrange that with the day shift? A moment in the sun? He
fingered the sleeve of her white uniform where it pro-
truded from her gown, the kind of plucking that the very
old and the dying sometimes do. He closed his eyes as she
probed his arm. "I'll bet a dollar you can't get it on the first
try."

Lily found a vein, the needle went right in. She smiled at
him. Could he tell, she wondered, when she smiled behind
her paper mask? "You've lost a lot of bets, you owe me sixteen dollars now." A little blood oozed out around the
needle. She wiped it with a sterile cotton ball then disposed
of it carefully, into a triple-thickness bag with "CONTAMI-
NATED" printed on its side. "When are you planning to pay
up?" she asked him. He was thirty years old, but his arm was
thin as her eight-year-old son Harry's.

"When my mother comes. When she gets here we'll make
everything... how do you say it?... square."

His doctor said he had to tell his parents, that it was time
for them to come. Every day Jorge promised he'd call Mexico City, every night he made excuses for why he hadn't
done it. "How do you find words for that?" Lily was on her
way into his room with medicine one day, and heard him ask
his doctor. "You tell me, what words would you use with
your mother?"

"So you've called your parents? They're coming?" Lily
hung the IV bottle on the stand beside the bed and squeezed
the bulb below, counting drops, adjusting the flow.

He shrugged and turned his face toward the wall. "The
lines to Mexico are often damaged. It's hard to get
through."

She propped his arm on a small pillow, folded his sheet and blanket down across his chest. "You've really got to call."

He nodded. "Yes."

"You could do it now. I could stay with you while you dial."

"My arm where you just stabbed me hurts too much." He smiled. He wanted to go back to teasing. "This afternoon," he said. "I'll call then, right after dinner." He closed his eyes, inviting her to go.

"Do you swear?"

"I swear."

She paused before she left to push his hair back from his forehead, then caught a tear at the corner of his closed eye with the back of her gloved hand.

LILY MISSED MIKE MOST when she watched the boys play ball. She missed the way he stood beside her at the games, his running commentary on the parent inter-actions – the board and the women's auxiliary, harmless flirtations on the sidelines, the occasional long affair, begun in spring, abandoned for the fall and winter. Mike called it the Ins and Outs of Little League. And Lily laughed each time he said it. As she pulled into a parking place beside the field for an early evening game, she remembered how she laughed.

She'd come straight from work and was still in her white uniform, her hair pulled back and up into a twist. The sky over the Peewee outfield was a wash of pink and orange and smokey blue. Late April, early in the season, but it was muggy, already getting hot.

Shorthorns versus Cubs. Harry was the shortstop. He was tall for eight, light-boned and skinny, with a baby face and long eyelashes, a bounce-on-the-balls-of-his-feet, loping sort of walk. When Lily picked him up at school she could always see him in the crowd, his brown head bobbing up above the others. The baseball field transformed him; there his stance was firm, he was alert and quick and unafraid, even though he'd got a bad black eye when he was hit by a grounder in the first game of the season. Despite his fearlessness, something about him irritated the coaches. It wasn't enough for them that the boys play with determination, they must also look determined, breathe with determination, change their on-the-balls-of-their-feet walk in order to look like competitors. "Get your butt moving!" the head coach shouted at them. "Get that glove down! Be a hitter for me."

The league had four fields, but there were bleachers only on the main field where the Minors and the Majors played. So parents brought their own chairs to the Peewee field — brightly-colored woven plastic on a metal frame, K-mart new each season. Lily bought one once but never used it; she preferred to stand and watch, to curl her fingers through the wire fence, to be where she could see Harry on the field.

"How's that leg?" Red Benson came up behind her. She felt his breath on her hair. He was taller than her by a foot, blue-eyed and curly-haired, a Texas drawl that made each word sound casual and easy. He came to every game, and found a way to drift off from the other parents and to stand beside her. A ray of the setting sun caught the silver buckle on his belt.

"My leg's fine," she said. "A little burn, a blister. Nothing really." The pitcher blocked her view of Harry. She took a step away from Red.

Red took his baseball cap off and ran his hand back through his hair. So often had he stood so close to her that she knew the smell of his shampoo, a sweetly herbal scent.

"You should be more careful in the Batter's Box." His voice was low and smooth. "Pretty legs like yours. Shame to have them covered up with Band-Aids."

He was an oil and gas attorney. Hard times in Texas, but

he didn't let it get him down; he made self-deprecating jokes, wore a T-shirt with an oil rig silk-screened on the back. Lily had heard that Red's wife was pregnant almost constantly for four years running, had three girls, then finally a boy who'd grown to be a tough, aggressive, bulldog kind of kid who played first base and hit like hell.

"Harry's up." Lily clapped, called his name. In the ondeck circle Harry took one final practice swing, licked his sweaty upper lip, then walked to the plate to take his stance – knees bent, back arm up, cleats dug into the dirt. His mouth was a thin, straight line, his lips so tightly pressed together that they were bloodless, white in his tan face. His metal bat quivered.

The first pitch hit the plate, the second was high and inside. The umpire, crouched behind the catcher, called them as he saw them. Ball one. Ball two. Harry stepped back from the plate, kicked the ground, nodded to the shouts of his batting coach. "Take two steps back in the box. Clutch up on that bat now. Concentrate. You hear me, son? I said pay attention." Harry spat into the brown dirt at his feet.

Lily stood on tiptoes, calling to him. "It's all right, Harry, take your time. Relax." The things Mike would have said. But even as she shouted reassurance she knew he couldn't hear it. All he wanted was a hit. One moment of contact, bat to ball, would make the game for him. The smack, the impact trilling up his arms. If he was lucky, he'd get to round first base and head for second. He'd get to throw his feet out, bring his backside down and slide. A rivulet of perspiration coursed down Lily's back between her shoulder blades and made her shiver.

"Fine boy," Red said. "Good eye." He placed his hand over hers where her fingers curled through the wire fence.

A swing. A miss. Strike one.

Lily worked her fingers free of Red's big hand.

"Nice follow-through," said Red, approvingly. But on the second swing and miss, he was less approving, mama close enough to touch or not. "Keep your eyes *open,* son," he shouted.

Lily took another step away from Red, and when she glanced down to get her footing, she missed Harry's third fierce swing, and knew what had happened only when she heard the umpire's call.

"Stee-rike three."

"Goddamn, he should have let that one go." Red punched the heel of one hand with the curled fist of the other. Harry dropped the bat into the dirt, took off his batting helmet, walked flat-footed back to his dugout, shrugging reassurance to his coach and teammates; he's not upset, these things just happen, don't anybody think that he's about to cry. He plopped down on the dugout bench. Lily worked her way through a row of lawn chairs to come up behind him. Then she reached through the wire fence where he was sitting and slipped a bag of M&M's into his pocket, hoping it was full of green ones, the ones the boys said always brought them luck.

"Russian roulette."

"I can't hear you."

Wayne, Mike's father, looked down over the edge of the roof at her and took the cigar out of his mouth. He cupped his hands and shouted.

"I said, Russian roulette. That's what that job is." He motioned to her to move aside, threw a half-dozen worn-out shingles to the ground, then backed down the ladder.

Lily, in her yard, wearing blue jeans and a sweaty T-shirt, picked up the shingles and threw them onto the pile already in the wheelbarrow. She hoped Wayne knew what he was doing. "I work in a hospital. People get sick, they come in, you take care of them. I don't pick and choose."

He took a handkerchief out of his work-shirt pocket, mopped his face. He was almost bald, but parted his hair low on one side, bringing a few thin strands across the shiny surface of his head. His scalp blazed red with sunburn. His belly bulged over his belt. He was too out-of-shape for hard work, too old for Texas sun and heat.

"Well, change jobs. . . teach or something. Couldn't you teach nursing? You'd be good at that. I mean, I know these people aren't dangerous to folks like me. But you're handling their blood, it spills on you, you have a cut, and before you know it. . . " He used his index finger to make a quick slice across his throat.

Wayne came to visit from Terre Haute once a year. He said he came to see the boys, to help.

Lily handed him a glass of iced tea.

He took a sip, then kept on talking. "You've got those boys to consider."

"Look," she said. "I do consider the boys. I'm careful."

What she couldn't admit to him or to anyone was that she, too, was worried. About herself and blood and body fluids. About the boys and their bad dreams. She had applied to computer-repair school last summer – "Your Bright Future in Electronics" – thinking that she should get out of nursing, of the Texas heat, thinking she should try to make more money. Through her second year in college she had thought she'd be a concert pianist. She studied music theory, history, excelled in composition. She practiced hours every day, perfecting her keyboard technique as well as her low, sweeping bow. Nursing had been for her a backup, a way to make a living in case music failed. And when it did (her talent was not great, her instruction had been uninspired), it only made sense to stay in nursing, and to make herself good at it, so good that when she stood on the verge of choice last summer, she finally realized that any other job would be impossible for her.

"Come on," she said to Wayne. "Don't push me. And don't you say anything to worry the boys."

She heard their voices in the house, home from school,

calling for her. She and Wayne went around the back, through the torn screen door into the kitchen. Wayne had just arrived that morning; this was the first the boys had seen him. Sam, too old for kisses, shook his hand and grinned. Harry hugged Wayne's waist. Lily got milk from the refrigerator, then went to the pantry to fetch cookies for them all.

"UNIVERSAL BLOOD AND body-fluid precautions" were recommended for all health-care workers. When a patient came into ER with a bleed, before you knew it everyone was soaked. It was too late for precautions after the blood tests came back. So, as prevention, ER staff were often gloved and gowned.

Lily's unit was Medicine, but these days as many as one-third of her patients were HIV positive. Depending on what care they needed, sometimes she had to suit up, too. She often wondered how it felt to be tended to by someone so armored, so protected, safe in a way you would never be again.

May Day was a Friday. Windy, cool, a spring surprise. Alan was going to be discharged over the weekend. As Lily was leaving for the day, she stopped in to say good-bye.

Fred, sitting on a chair next to the window, rose to greet her and handed her an index card on which he'd typed his recipe for pesto. He was a weight trainer by trade, a connoisseur by avocation. "No ordinary pesto," he explained. "Goat cheese, walnuts, and fresh cilantro. Very Southwest." He kissed the gathered fingertips of one hand in a gourmet salute. "Eat your heart out, Italy."

Alan, in bed with a mirror propped on his over-the-bed table, was applying pancake makeup to a lesion on his chin.

He looked up at Lily. "Well?"

She looked closely, then stepped to one side to see him in different light.

"You want the truth?"

He straightened his back, gave her an I-can-take-it look. "The truth," he said.

"It looks like a giant zit."

He laughed. "So long as it doesn't look like what it is."

When Alan first got sick Fred had wanted to get out, to run. Lily saw it in his eyes the day they made the diagnosis. But some sense of duty stopped him; he required himself by an enormous act of will to stay. When Alan was too weak to eat, Fred fed him. He fought with the nurses, insisted that Alan get his medicine for pain on time. The chair from which he rose when Lily entered had been home to him for seven weeks. He slept in it, he read aloud from it—*Little Dorrit*—in a droning, soft, hypnotic voice when nothing else could soothe Alan. From his chair he watched while Alan slept, he memorized him—the rhythm of his breaths, the angles of his limbs, the long perfection of his fingers. He stayed and did the necessary things, until feeling followed the course that action set.

Fred urged Alan to keep on working with the pancake makeup. He was settled back into his chair, taking notes on a legal pad. He'd just endured a discharge-planning meeting with the social worker. Weekly visits to the clinic, expensive medicines, a support group for both the patient and his lover in a downtown Y. They both knew that down the road there would be hospital beds and special nurses, maybe a short stay in a hospice. Alan wanted to work as long as he could, save some money, keep his insurance, but the purplish lesions on his face and neck and arms threatened to give him away. His employer was a wary man and was suspicious.

"What are you planning for Alan's homecoming dinner?" Lily asked. Fred's blue sport shirt was open at the neck. The muscles there were sinewy and strong. Fred pondered Lily's question, pursed his lips. "French," he said, after a moment's consideration. "Veal, maybe. Or quail. What about quail?" A nod to Alan. It would be his choice.

Alan smiled and leaned back on his pillow, pleased to be the reason for a party.

DURING ONE OF THE two weeks of Wayne's visit, Lily worked the evening shift. It gave the boys a chance to be alone with their grandfather, and made it possible for her to avoid his well-intentioned help and questioning. It also gave her a chance to end the day with these, her patient charges. She could be the one to set the tone for nighttime, the one to dim the lights, to walk the shadowed halls, and say the final words before sleep came. At 10:30 precisely, Lily started the rounds of all her patients one last time.

Jorge, growing steadily more fearful, almost always wanted her to stay.

"Tell me about your boys," he'd say. Or, "Tell me about Little League. One of your funny stories. Make me laugh."

But on this night in early May, Jorge was even more insistent. "Sit," he said. His voice was flat, his eyes were bright with fever. "I've told you everything about my life. Tell me about yours."

He wanted her story. She sat down beside him and gave him the abbreviated version, a fairy tale.

"MONOCOT OR DICOT?"

"Excuse me?"

"All flowering plants are either monocots or dicots. Lilies have petals in groups of three, a single cotyledon. A lily is a monocot."

"Thanks very much," she'd said.

Lily was working overtime in the emergency room when Mike came in with his broken ankle. He was a high-school biology teacher, a soccer coach, but a scientist at heart. The monocot or dicot question was one of hundreds he would pose, first to her, then later to the boys.

What is the life span of a star? In what position does a sea otter sleep? Who first taught that the heart was a muscle?

Some volume of their encyclopedia was always open, their library cards dog-eared and stained. For the boys it was a great, impossible game, Who could find the answer first? Who would win the prize? A goldfish from the five-and-dime, eight slabs of bubble gum and fifteen baseball cards, a poster of the periodic table.

What was the name of the first U.S. baseball club? What color were Marie Curie's eyes?

Lily was twenty-eight when she met Mike; she'd waited a long time. He said he wanted to be a doctor, he was going to school at night to make up two math courses he needed to get into medical school. He coached his soccer team, taught his students frog anatomy, he was advisor to the science club; she helped him chaperone their springtime camping trip. He kissed her fingertips, sweet praise, each time she serenaded him on the piano. And through it all his questioning continued. It was as if he believed that he could know everything, that together, nothing would be impossible for them. They married, bought the tiny bungalow in which she still lived with the boys. She got pregnant right away, not part of their plan, but they could do anything, they fit it in. After Sam was born she worked nights and weekends when Mike, the student, could be home with the baby.

What was Albert Einstein's favorite plaything given to him by his uncle when he was twelve years old? What is a neutrino?

She took six weeks off when Harry was born, then went back to work again, became a nighttime fixture at the hospital, a sleepy daytime mother. Did she mind? Mike wondered. Was it too hard for her? It was the day he got his first stethoscope. He listened to her heart with it.

What was the major accomplishment of Alessandro Volta? In what hospital were rubber gloves first worn for surgery?

"*Did* you mind?" This from Jorge. He sounded sleepy, far away. Her voice was like a balm to him, and to herself as well, she realized, opening eyes she'd closed to memory.

Two sons, father-raised and so much like him that the first words each one spoke came out formed into a question.

"Moon?" asked Sam as the clouds parted on a summer night.

Four years in a medical school, three years a resident in medicine, a pulmonary fellowship. Then there would be money, there'd be time.

How wide is the wall of a cell? What is a manometer?

"But nine years is a long time. *Didn't* you mind?" Jorge wondered again.

Mind?

Mike loved baseball, and taught the boys to love it too. The thud of a ball caught in the well-worn pocket of a glove became the most familiar backyard sound – Mike and the boys, then, when Harry got big enough, the boys alone together. Lily was the relief pitcher on the evenings when Mike had to be on call.

At the beginning, both boys lived for Little League, but after a while Sam especially began to feel the disadvantage of a kid whose father was too busy to coach. He sat on the bench too much, played outfield even though he was a better catcher than the coach's son. Pitching was a way for him to end that. Good pitchers were rare, control and concentration come hard to the young. He threw the ball in every extra moment he could find, against a Pitchback, against an old mattress Mike had propped up beside the garage, even, reluctantly, into Lily's glove. He went running with his dad to stay in shape. Mike called it cardiovascular fitness, Sam called it training; they hit the streets, ran the neighborhood. "Be careful," Lily said each time they left. She bought each of them a dog tag with his name and address on it. They humored her and wore the tags, and looked just like one another, bare backs, long legs, arms pumping in unison. She liked to stand on her sagging front porch and watch them disappear under the canopy of live-oak branches that arched over the street.

Jorge wanted to hear the end of her story, but it was time for change of shift, her boys were waiting. As she was about to leave him, he reached out for her hand. "More tomorrow?" He wanted her to promise – that she'd be back, and that he would still be there to listen.

Lily made Fred's pesto, spooned it over boiled new potatoes, and took it to the Shorthorns' team picnic. Parents gathered around a picnic table and a rough stone barbecue pit where Red was roasting hot dogs, while the boys played ball close by. Sam, the big boy, made himself the umpire.

It was only the end of May, but the coaches were already talking next season. They'd spent the last two weeks going to every Tadpole game, scouting the boys who would move up to their Peewee league. Lily, sipping lemonade, overheard two of the coaches talking about getting a winter team together. Red's voice rose above the others. "I like the winter-league idea," he said. "Damned good for the boys and would give us all more time for the work we have to do." He looked at Lily. She looked away.

"I'd stake my life on it." Red's wife, Suzanne, was at the far end of the picnic table where Lily sat. She was talking to the catcher's mother. Lily didn't know Suzanne well, nor did she know any of the other mothers; she did not invite their overtures, and they, in turn, regarded her with something like suspicion. She was alone, she stood apart. When they saw bloodstains on her white uniform, they feared her, she seemed tainted. The catcher's mother leaned toward Suzanne and stroked her arm, and Lily felt a momentary yearning for all the things that that touch seemed to promise – safety, closeness, trust.

"I always thought it was just flirting," Suzanne whispered. "That was how Red caught my eye at Texas, after all. But now I think there may be someone else." A picture of Suzanne's son in his baseball uniform dangled in a Plexiglas square at the end of her key ring. The catcher's mother nodded. Go on. Lily had the urge to warn Suzanne, to call out, "Don't, it's best to keep some things a secret." But Suzanne seemed driven to continue. She touched the picture of her son's face with her finger. "I think it's Ginger Marshall." Her voice caught. She looked straight at the catcher's mother. "You know Ginger," she said. "Her son's a Colt."

Red was talking with the other coaches, giving thumbnail sketches of the boys he thought he wanted for next year's team. Who hit well and who was fast. Jokes about which ones had good-looking mothers.

AND SO SPRING PASSED. Wayne went back to Terre Haute. Alan held his own at home in his and Fred's apartment. Jorge's diagnosis was pneumonia. *Pneumocystis carinii.* Azaleas bloomed, then faded. June and summer came. Sam's last game was just a week away. Rumor had it that he would get to pitch, and that scouts from the Majors would be there. Lily, in her bedroom, examined her leg in the circle of light cast by her bedside lamp. It was healing well, the bandage was no longer a necessity, but she still could not be certain whether she'd have a scar. Sam found her sitting on the edge of her bed, running her finger along her healing wound. He asked her if she'd practice with him.

The backyard was long and narrow. Lily and the boys took turns and kept it mowed and tended. But the beds that edged it were wild with sage and verbena, plants that bloomed and flourished on their own. Old roses climbed the backyard fence, hundreds of them, volunteers that had spread from a single plant Mike bought for her when Sam was born. Lily got the catcher's mitt from the shelf above the dryer, walked to a worn spot in the grass, hunkered down and called to Sam that she was ready. There was thunder in the distance. For a long time the only sound was that and the rhythmic thwack-thwack as the ball passed through the air from glove to mitt.

"Do you think I have a chance of making pitcher in the Majors?" It was getting dark, Harry was sleeping over at a friend's, there was no one around to hear them.

"Sure I do." Thwack.

"I do too. But I'm not sure I'll get it. And I'm afraid if I don't make it, I'll be really disappointed. I mean *really*." Sam stood sideways, with one shoulder toward her, preparing for his windup. He shot a quick hard glance over his shoulder at an imaginary runner on an imaginary base. His face was expressionless. He'd learned to make himself unreadable, as all good pitchers must. "So I wonder if I should try to prepare myself somehow. In case things don't work out. Like, make a tape to put under my pillow to play when I'm asleep." He stopped suddenly, brought his glove up to his face and laughed into it, an uncharacteristic boyish gesture. "You remember, like the mouse in *Dumbo* who whispers at night in Dumbo's ear, 'You can fly. You can fly.'" His smile disappeared. He let his hands drop to his side. "Do you remember?"

She looked at him standing alone in the middle of the lawn. "Yes," she said. "I remember."

"Except my tape would say, 'Don't get your hopes up, don't count on it too much.'"

She brought her mitt back up. "Do you really think that would help?" she asked.

"Yeah. Maybe." The windup, the pitch. The ball was high and way outside, but Lily made a dive for it and caught it.

Sam stepped forward on his right foot for his follow-through, then turned his back to her and stepped onto the pile of leaves and dirt and grass he called "the mound."

"Sometimes I wish Dad had been sick awhile so that we could have gotten ready. I wish that I'd been ready."

A clap of thunder, close at hand. A flash of lightning ripped across the sky. Two raindrops, fat and cold, fell on Lily's hand, and then the downpour came. The blinding rain made Sam, at the far end of the yard, invisible to her. She tucked her head down, started running. He beat her to the porch, then reached out to hold the door for her. "I heard Grandpa talking," he said. "About your job. Is it dangerous? Do you have to be brave to be doing the work you do?"

She shook her head. "No," she said. "You don't have to be brave."

LATER, AT THE KITCHEN table, sharing pizza, Lily had a sudden urge to tell Sam all of it. She wished he was the man he so much wanted to be so she could confess that she was not brave or generous or kind, not even very good. For four months after Mike died she'd kept everything the same. She kept his ashes in a wood box on her dresser, his shoes lined up across the closet floor. She thought she'd be faithful to him always; she thought she was true, loyal, so much in love. Then, just like that, she took a lover, a first-year resident, a twenty-six-year-old kid. He was married with a pregnant wife—that ought to have stopped her but she didn't care. She helped him with medication orders, summary notes, then helped herself. And it wasn't just a fling for her—she was serious as hell, she would have stayed with him, asked him to leave his wife; she even thought of leaving her own boys, of running away from her collapsing house, her empty bed – a coward in the truest sense when it came down to it. She slept with him in the on-call room, in a nearby motel; she took enormous, foolish risks and would have kept it going if he had not begun to hesitate. She broke it off only when she saw that he'd lost heart, and then reluctantly. Perhaps that's why Red pressed her so. Maybe, Lily thought, he sensed and saw what no one else could – that she, like he, understood lost hope and a failure of resolve. That she, too, had broken faith.

It was almost two years ago, and still, to Lily, it seemed like yesterday. Her lover and his wife and newborn baby left Texas at the end of the affair. Spring came again, and Lily oiled both boys' baseball gloves. Wayne arrived for the first of his yearly visits. In her bedroom she had listened to the sound of Wayne whistling and working as she cleared Mike's closet and packed his things away. As she worked, her hands began to shake, her knees threatened to give way beneath her. In order to go on she had to lean against the door frame, breathe in deeply, and require herself to focus on Mike's blue running shorts bedecked with silver stars, his otoscope with its cracked handle, the scissors that he used to cut his own shaggy hair. The details of a life without him.

ON LILY'S UNIT THE nurses took turns working with the sickest patients; it seemed the only fair way to divide that labor. But Jorge had asked for her specifically – his fever made him ache; an aide could bathe him, but he longed for familiar hands. When she turned him to change his bed, she moved him very carefully and pulled hard on the sheets, so that they would be cool and smooth. Then, on her way home, she bought a Spanish/English dictionary, and the next day, while he slept, she broke the rules of patient confidence and ethics and made the call herself.

Static, Spanish-speaking operators on the line. Then a sudden clearing. A woman's voice.

"Bueno."

The introduction, explanation. "Su hijo está muy enfermo. Your son is very ill."

A ONE-ARMED MILK-TRUCK driver had brought Mike home. The driver rang the doorbell, stood on her doorstep in his white slacks and shirt. He held his visored cap in the hook that was his artificial hand.

Five-thirty in the morning. A full moon and the porch light made it possible for Lily to see him. He said his headlight beam found Mike, sprawled face down at the roadside. "I was a medic in Vietnam; I checked his pulse, I gave him CPR, but I knew he was already dead. I should have called the police, I know, but when I saw his dog tag, it seemed right to just go ahead and bring him home. I couldn't drive away and leave him."

A heart attack. He'd had a physical the week before, a treadmill test. "Too bad we can't afford more insurance," he'd said, kidding. "This body is worth millions." Forty years old and perfect. He was perfect. Iron Man, he called himself. "My dad, the jock," Sam laughed. In another year, when he wasn't quite so busy, he would train for a triathlon. The boys, he said, could help him.

Lily stood at her front door in her silk nightgown, with Mike's old soccer letter sweater wrapped around her like a robe, and listened to the milk-truck driver. A norther had blown in, the wind drew strands of hair across her face. As she listened, she saw everything about that moment in exquisite, stark detail: the bowl of dark sky filled with stars, the droning motor of the milk truck, the vapored clouds of the milkman's breath, the way the muscles of his shoulder tightened when he worked his artificial arm.

JORGE ASKED TO BE shaved. The hospital barber came to his room to wash and trim his hair.

Jorge's mother held her husband's hand as they stepped from the elevator. Her dark hair was pulled back severely to reveal an aristocratic chin and cheek, a widow's peak, delicately shaped ears, the lobes strained by the weight of her gold earrings. Her smile was hesitant, disarming. They had come quickly, on the first plane. Lily could see that she was exhausted, and that she couldn't have felt at all like smiling, but good breeding and grace prevailed. She smiled, then wept when Lily took her to Jorge's room. Without the benefit of mask and gloves and gown, she kissed him, she showered him with kisses. His hands, his hot, hot head. She wondered, begged, How had he gotten so sick so suddenly – he was fine when he'd come to the States to study. How had it come to this?

Jorge had prepared himself. "SIDA," he said. AIDS. Just that, he told Lily later. Never once in their long hour's visit saying "homosexual." Lily thought he could have trusted them with that, but he chose not to, and in so doing, missed the chance to tell them all that he'd told her. That he had been in love. That what he'd finally found was love. And that even after he had lost it, the memory, the sweet surprise of ever having it at all, was what sustained him.

"MOVE YOUR BUTT... Get that glove down... Elbow up, now, watch those feet!" Instructions from the coaches never stopped. It was as if they believed that there was some correct instruction, some right way to play that would assure that there would be no errors, no accidents, that nothing would go wrong. Like magic, every pitch would be a strike, each swing, a hit, each outreached glove would pick a ball out of the air. Everything would be fine because they did it right. "Be careful," she'd said to Mike that last morning when he went running. And he was, he was. He wore his dog tag, he watched for speeding cars and trucks, he used designated paths. But hearts, she knew, were deaf and arbitrary things, incapable of heeding warning.

It was ninety degrees and humid, but a light breeze blessed the air for Sam's final evening game. Lily came straight from Jorge's bedside to the field and climbed the bleachers slowly, wanting to find a place where she could sit and be alone. The floodlights flashed on as she reached the topmost tier, filling the field with a harsh, white light. Lily saw Sam standing near the dugout, shielding his eyes, searching the bleachers for her. She turned and waved.

Sam pitched the first three innings, as he'd hoped to, and gave up just one run—a competent, controlled performance, Lily thought. She'd kept herself tense, she'd willed success for Sam through every windup, every pitch, and she didn't relax until Sam walked off the field into the waiting arms of his congratulating teammates, slaphappy kids who greeted him with boyish thumps and whoops and accolades. Only when Lily saw Sam's flush of pleasure did she rub her neck and put her feet up, let her mind drift from the boys, the game, the score. The noise of the fans three innings later was what brought her back. While she'd drifted the Cougars had fallen two runs behind. Now, in the sixth and last inning, two Cougar singles had gotten one man to first and one to third. A hit would even the score. A home run would mean a Cougar win. They'd moved so often through the batting order that Lily had lost track. It was when the fans began to chant his name that Lily realized Sam was batting next, that good pitching hadn't been enough—he'd have to be an expert batter, too. Everyone would look to him to save the day. Lily wished she'd sat down closer, where she could see him better, where she could send good thoughts to him, through air, through flesh. She stood, about to go down and grip the chain-link fence. But Sam was too fast for her, too eager. He was at the plate in moments, pumped up, ready, waving off the shouts and gestures of his coaches. He fixed his batting helmet on his head, then bent his legs, and even from so far away, Lily saw the quiver of his ready bat, his easy grip around the handle. His tense, yearning face. Lily gripped the railing that edged the bleachers. She thought she'd grown so hardened that winning didn't matter anymore. Now it seemed it did, in spite of all the odds against it. She crossed her fingers, prayed for grace to shower down.

The pitcher brought his leg up, pulled his right arm back, and threw. The well-aimed ball sliced cleanly through the air toward Sam, and Lily saw Sam pull back fast and hard. But when she heard the slam as his bat hit the ball, she closed her eyes instead of watching. She didn't want to see. If it was caught, or missed, a long drive into center field, or an over-the-wall homer. She wanted to be blind, to let hope rule her.

ELLEN HUNNICUTT

Energy

On the day he learned his son was planning to quit high school, Grafmiller ran out of gas on the expressway. Rolf, seventeen and his only child, lived with Grafmiller's former wife. For a moment her phone call had surprised him, then it seemed the next inevitable step in a pattern of decline.

Nothing was going well for Grafmiller. His office had installed a computer that worked erratically; when the main trunk from the home office in St. Louis broke down, his work had to wait, sometimes for hours. His car had serious transmission trouble. He no longer knew what his dreams meant. He'd become interested in his dreams in college while reading Carl Jung's autobiography, and had kept a journal of them from time to time since. He had taken keen satisfaction in watching his own inner narrative unfold and fancied he was good at spotting tendencies in himself, keeping his life on an even keel. Now everything seemed gibberish. He had dreamed, for example, that workmen were enclosing the shopping mall near his home. In the center of the mall was a building that resembled a small Greek temple, but also looked a bit like an animal cage. He had never seen such a building in real life. In the dream, the foreman was explaining to him that this building would not be torn down as originally planned. Rather, a new structure would be bolted onto its roof. The bolts the workmen were using resembled the headbolts on his automobile engine. Grafmiller suspected the dream had something to do with his most primitive instincts, and that one way or another he was being buried, but it really made no sense to him.

He had been seeing a woman from his office, Rochelle, and found he no longer took pleasure in the association. At thirty-eight she was not really young, but still four years younger than Grafmiller, and pretty enough, with a short, rather buxom figure, neat brown hair that was surprisingly soft to his touch, and large, quite beautiful hands. He had found her sensitive and intelligent. Only a short time ago their liaison had seemed perfectly pleasant and he'd thought of asking her to marry him, but now their walks and little suppers had become desultory, their couplings mechanical, even stifling. Once, lying in her arms, his face nuzzled against her neck, Grafmiller had felt he could not get his breath, and had pulled away suddenly, leaving Rochelle, nude and disheveled, lying across the bed looking ridiculous, like an old woman who had slipped and fallen.

Into this malaise had come the phone call from his former wife (one more thing, always one more thing).

"You'll have to talk to Rolf."

"Of course. Give me a few days to organize my thoughts."

"You can't put it off." Her tone laid blame squarely on the father.

He accepted it without argument. "Of course."

In fact, what he had sought to organize these four days were thoughts about himself, the order and magnitude of his failures. He saw a pattern beginning, growing, culminating in the trouble with his son. (*Failing,* an archaic term from childhood. When the elderly — Grafmiller pictured a man — began their measured march toward death, drying, shrinking, slipping into confusion, people of his parents' generation had said, "He is failing.")

"Certainly," said Grafmiller, welcoming this joy although he had no idea what it involved.

His former wife sighed lightly and smiled a little. She continued to look tired.

Rolf found a denim jacket with the sleeves torn out. Grafmiller supposed it matched his faded jeans. He put the jacket on over a T-shirt that was decorated with splashes of iridescent paint. His limp hair, dark like Grafmiller's own, hung nearly to his shoulders, and he wore a headband of sorts that made him look a little like a farmer. Grafmiller thought the boy needed a warmer coat for the chilly night, but said nothing, not wishing to begin the evening on a critical note.

Rolf directed him to drive to a nightclub in a seedy section of the city. "It's pretty early but we can stay awhile. We've got all evening, right, Dad?"

"Right," Grafmiller said guardedly. He had expected they would be having a talk about the value of completing Rolf's education, but the boy's joy was contagious. Grafmiller felt good for the first time in days. He decided there would be time enough later to talk.

The club was in an old automobile showroom. The large front windows had been painted green. They were meant to suggest a forest of palm trees. The bar near the entrance was nearly deserted at this early hour. The few patrons and the bartender greeted Rolf with friendly nods. Rolf led Grafmiller to a small, round table near the empty bandstand—all of the other tables were empty—and a waitress in a leather skirt and vest immediately brought them two glasses of wine. "This is my father!" Rolf said to her.

"Wow!" said the young woman. "Oh wow, your father!" She grinned and rolled her eyes upward as if Grafmiller's presence was too much to be believed. Grafmiller looked at the wine—Rolf was not legally old enough to be served—and decided to say nothing.

"Dad, I've got all these things to ask you." Rolf leaned

Now, driving through the bleak March night towar
apartment Rolf shared with his mother, Grafmiller fo
himself doubting all of his certainties, inverting everyt
and giving it its opposite meaning. Although he had
divorced for years and had never managed to establish
ally close relationship with Rolf, he felt a strong cor
ment to the boy. He had invested much of his own em
in his hopes for his son. Hadn't he tried to do his best,
by event, across the years? Then it seemed to him tha
was precisely what was wrong, that his association wi
son had been a series of disconnected incidents that
up to nothing. As he pulled into the driveway he won
(of all things) if he truly loved the boy, and he thoug
one giddy moment that everything in his head was go
spin like a slot machine, then stop suddenly and revea
terrible truth. This thought was somehow connected
drawing suddenly away from Rochelle, and again, sit
his car, he experienced a brief sensation of suffocati

"Come in," said his former wife. Pale, blondish, s
been thin and angular for many years. He could not
call ever having felt passion for her. He felt no anim
ward her either. She worked in an office, as he did
seemed to Grafmiller that they now had more in c
than when they had been married. They both ros
morning and went to work, budgeted their money, s
on the way home, felt alarm over the cost of thing
concerned for Rolf. She was a little like a sister to hi
ther had remarried. Now, silhouetted in the doorw
looked old to Grafmiller, older than Rochelle, an
from her day's work.

Rolf appeared behind her. He was already an in
than his father but thin, like his mother, and more d
constructed. To Grafmiller's surprise, the boy seer
mated. He came forward with an eager smile, bot
outstretched. "Dad! Can we go out? I want to take y
place."

forward, tense now and excited. "There were musicians in your family, right? And artists? A dancer? I asked Mom, over and over; there's no one in her family. Nothing. Nobody."

Grafmiller's reaction to this, even before he took time to sort it out, was that his former wife had been having a hard time of it; Rolf had his mother under some sort of concerted siege. This sort of thing probably happened often. The mother was the boy's most convenient target. He, Grafmiller, had probably not been sufficiently sympathetic to her position. "Hmm," he said now to his son, "artists, musicians." He wondered if mother and son were both coming at him, but from slightly different angles, *triangulation*. The word made him think of strangulation and he wondered for a moment if he might have another attack of breathlessness.

"You know, Dad, you told me about an uncle who played the guitar and had these special talents." Rolf's manner was urgent; he was growing irritated.

"Oh yes, my Uncle David. His special talents were with bees. He raised bees and could take honey off without being stung."

"No!" Rolf cried. "On the guitar! You told me that!"

People were drifting in now. Grafmiller noted they were all young, many as young as Rolf. No one seemed to be over twenty-five. Musicians were setting up equipment on the jerry-built stage.

"He wrote songs!" Rolf persisted. "Don't you remember that?"

"Yes, he did." Grafmiller was going on instinct, reluctant to lose the earlier camaraderie with his son. He vaguely remembered that his Uncle David had made up songs, played a guitar. He had probably told Rolf that.

"I mean," said Rolf, "it probably didn't seem like much to you before. That's why you forgot."

"I'm sure that's it," said Grafmiller, grateful for the boy's conciliatory tone.

"And somebody danced. You said when you played in the attic as a child there was a ballerina costume, and shoes."

"That was my sister," Grafmiller said cautiously. His sister had taken dancing lessons, perhaps for a year.

One of the musicians, carrying a guitar, approached the table. From a distance and in the dim light of the club he looked dissipated, in outlandish clothes and with his face heavily rouged. Closer, Grafmiller saw he was actually a boy only a little older than Rolf. His costume was vaguely Middle Eastern, loose wine-colored bloomers, a lime green shirt, bands of metal on his arms.

"Hey!" Rolf cried out. "Meet my dad!"

A smile broke from behind the makeup. "God, your dad!" Grafmiller shook hands with the boy. "God, that's really great! I can't imagine bringing my dad here. But you're from a musical family, Mr. Grafmiller. Rolf told us all about you. That would figure."

The room was filling with customers. Other young people approached and Grafmiller realized he had become the center of attention. He felt like an overweight, middle-aged Buddha being adored. Rolf beamed.

"Look, Mr. Grafmiller," said the guitarist, "you gotta hear this now. After all, that's what you came for."

"Yeah, yeah," said someone in the group.

"We'll do 'Eyes' first," said the guitarist. "That's the block-buster."

Rolf reddened. "Whatever you guys think."

The guitarist and three other musicians in similar gaudy attire assembled on the bandstand. They were two guitarists, a drummer, and a young man in a leather tunic who now appeared to be the vocalist. A blast of sound, painfully loud, erupted and Grafmiller strained to understand the words. Rolf quickly drew a songsheet from his pocket and thrust it at his father. Grafmiller read at the top, "'Eyes,' Words and music by Rolf Grafmiller," and then could decipher that the vocalist was shouting:

Eyes . . . eyes
The eyes of crowds
Look back at me
From midnight mirrors.
In each falling tear I see
Reflections of ecstasy
Lost in tears
Forever lost in tears.

Then it was all repeated with slight variations, in a mono-
tone and at intense volume. Young people squirmed all
about them, dancing and moaning as if in religious fervor.
Grafmiller felt cast adrift and pretended careful concentration on the printed lyric to give himself time to get his bear-
ings. "Eyes" was followed by "Alone," to which it bore a
marked resemblance. Rolf's images of melancholy and
alienation pounded against Grafmiller's ears, assaulted his
mind. The variations on "Alone" continued for a very long
time.

When the musicians ended the set, they gathered once
again around Grafmiller's table. He knew they were waiting
for him to speak and chose his words carefully. "The songs
have . . . tremendous energy," he said, "real vigor. I don't
think I've ever heard anything quite like them." He wondered if Rolf would detect his guarded tone.

But the boy was too excited to notice. "I knew you'd like
them, Dad! I knew it!"

"Yeah," said the first guitarist, "Rolf said that. He really
did!"

Grafmiller felt his breath catch, his throat close momen-
tarily, and held the table firmly to avoid panic. "I have to admit I don't understand the music very well."

"Jesus!" said the young vocalist. "That's nothing! We
hardly understand it ourselves. Rolf's way ahead of his time.
This son of yours is so damned creative! When the rest of us
look ahead, we just see shadows, but Rolf sees it all. He turns

this stuff out so fast, over and over!"

Rolf was embarrassed. He tried to look earnest. "But you get it, Dad. With your instincts, I knew you'd *get* the music."

Grafmiller nodded slowly. He wondered if they were going to ask him for money.

"You know, Dad," Rolf continued, "it's about the individual in society, about all the pain."

"That's it," said the drummer. "That's all there is today, pain. That's what Rolf sees so clearly."

"The music has energy," Grafmiller said again, and wished he had not, but they really did not seem to be listening to him. "What are your plans?" he asked Rolf. "You don't even play an instrument."

"I'm learning guitar."

"Is he ever!" the guitarist offered. "You never saw anybody learn so fast in your life! Another month, we'll put him up on stage. That's where he belongs."

A sudden perversity swept over Grafmiller. "I suppose you need money," he said. He had none to give them, and the sooner they knew it the better.

But they shook their heads. "We've got club dates, Dad," said Rolf, "some really good bookings. They're getting better all the time. That'll finance demo tapes."

The guitarist nodded vigorously. "And if we don't have an album out in six months... " He shrugged, too overcome to finish the sentence.

Grafmiller began to chuckle, and then to laugh uncontrollably, until his shoulders shook and tears appeared in his eyes. Rolf had brought him to this place seeking his approval, nothing more. The thought was incredibly clean, pure, beautiful, ridiculous, hilarious. He began to tremble and could not stop.

"It's emotion," said the young waitress, who had started patting his back as if he were choking. "Jesus, that music does the same thing to me, every time."

"My father is a very sensitive person," Rolf said gravely.

Someone gave him a tissue and Grafmiller wiped his eyes, blew his nose. He wondered why his former wife had given him no warning. Had she said to Rolf, "We will just let your father see this spectacle for himself"? He felt certain she had. He could imagine it, see her standing with her hands on her scrawny hips, suffering with her pained, martyr's face, a face he now brought back to mind perfectly across the years.

He could not be certain if the powerful, exhilarating feelings rising in him came out of spite for her or from participation in his son's joy. It occurred to him they might even have been roused by the music. He took in breath slowly, fully, and felt it course through his lungs, felt the beating of his heart. "I'm speechless," he said, and sat back in his chair.

The young people were satisfied. They turned their faces on him as one person and smiled . . . at Rolf's latest success, his father. Grafmiller smiled too.

MAURICE KENNY

And Leave the Driving to Us

"WILL YOU LET ME KNOW when we get to San Jose, California?"

The boy's request astonished his older seat companion.

"Will you let me know?"

The man grumbled a strange "OK." He turned to his newspaper, straining his blue eyes under an overhead light.

Denver slowly careened away, vanishing below heavy clouds of pollution. In the distance, dark mountains hunched like animals, quiet and dangerous. As the Greyhound zipped through the land, the older man looked across the youth into the night. Neon signs flashed: Stop – Eat – Gas – Vacancy. The boy turned the pages of a comic book.

"Is San Jose, California, a long way off?"

Against the glow of the highway lamps, under the emergency exit light, his dark flesh turned orange. His black hair shimmered, and his eyes, though essentially uncommunicative, held a touch of expectation, a flicker of excitement like the scared thrill of a first roller-coaster ride.

His seat companion was daydreaming.

"Is San Jose, California, a long way?"

The man bolted, remarking to himself, "Of course it's a long way. Too damn long of a way. Half around the world from here." But to the boy he softly answered: "Yes."

Go west, young man, go west! He thought as road signs passed.

A long chain of lights begins at Trinidad, near the New Mexico border, and ends just before the approach to Cheyenne, Wyoming. It links town to village, hamburger joint to gas station like the cold blue signs of a mortuary.

"Yes, son, San Jose is a hell of a long way. That's where you're heading?"

"Yes."

"You'll be riding this bus for the next couple of days."

"Oh!"

Silence moved between them. Then on across the plains, plains no longer considered empty and vast, but eternal.

THE TRAVELERS STOPPED at Cheyenne for a short coffee break. They crawled like ants through the late night hour to the bathrooms and cafeteria. The man spied the boy heading for the Coke machine. He went for the coffee machine.

The driver gathered his passengers like sheep, and soon had them boarded.

"Is it still a long way to San Jose, California?"

"Yes, son."

"I am going there. To San Jose!"

"San Jose is a mighty long ride. Gotta be a thousand miles, more maybe."

"Oh!"

THE GREYHOUND BYPASSED Laramie, Rawlins and Rock Springs. It careened up mountains and crossed wide valleys. Night hung close.

Dawn broke. A bone-dry day rose slowly above rocks and

arid land. Antelope stared at the roaring bus, then charged into the hills.

The bus pulled into Fort Bridger.

Awakening, the boy sat up and peered out the window.

"Is this San Jose?"

His companion, still half asleep, shook his head "no" before looking around. "No son, this is Fort Bridger."

"Fort Bridger? Is that in California?"

"Heavens no! We gotta get out of Wyoming yet. Gotta cross Utah... that's a pretty stretch of country. Gotta cross Nevada. And we gotta cross the whole width of California... mountain to sea."

"I guess it must be far." Disappointment etched his words.

"So you're going to San Jose?"

"Yes."

The boy slumped into his cushioned seat and pulled out the comic book he had been sitting on.

"Fort Bridger's where the Donner party bought provisions. Ol' Jim Bridger warned them of the dangerous route they planned to take. The Donner people wouldn't be put off, an' paid him no mind."

Perplexed, the boy asked, "Were the Donners going to San Jose?"

"No, son. Not exactly. Don't you know who the Donners were?"

"Were they from Denver?"

"They were ol' time emigrants, boy. Set out from the Midwest for California way back in the 1860s, I guess it was. Set out to make their fortune. They took some bad advice from a man they didn't know and on that advice they took the wrong trail. Well, they got lost, and almost all of 'em died of hunger and cold when winter caught them on the Sierras. They were held up in heavy blizzards."

The boy's composure reflected a total lack of interest.

"Some of them turned cannibal. They ate each other. Mean as wild cats. Poor miserable things. Poor lot they were. Poor ticks. This is the beginning of their country... here at Fort Bridger."

"But it's still a long way to San Jose?"

The man nodded "yes."

THE WARM MORNING sun flooded through the green tinted windows. By then most passengers were alert and eager to have breakfast. The driver announced the next rest stop would be Evanston, Wyoming, in half an hour. Ladies combed hair; men felt growing whiskers.

The boy continued staring out onto the flat plains with the purple mountains in the far distance. It looked hot out there, dusty, sterile, frightening. He glanced toward his companion. For the first time he noticed the older man's attire: his flowered shirt and gray slacks, his shiny leather shoes bright to a high polish. Thick graying hair lay combed in great slabs to either side of the head, parted in the center. Pomade gave it a greasy steel look. His tired face was not quite as old as the boy first suspected. Maybe he was thirty-five, forty at the most. It didn't matter, he was old.

"I'm kinda hungry," declared the older passenger who had been thinking about his last time through Evanston. The Post House Café had employed a waitress who seemed to take special interest in him.

The boy held back a response. The man looked questioningly at the youth.

Though physically small he was not as young as he had first supposed. The kid must have been thirteen-fourteen. Short, thin though actually not frail, but lithe. A chest was in the process of development. No doubt the kid was Indian. Funny he had not noticed it before. Strangers coming upon each other usually sense these things immediately. You could tell a whore, a college kid, a sailor out of uniform, a divorcée. Sometimes you didn't want to know. For an Indian kid he wasn't bad looking. Clean as a pin in his new Levi's and checkered shirt... even the T-shirt circling his neck like the white feathers that rim a buzzard's throat looked clean. "Well," he thought, "some Indians are clean, I guess." His jet black hair hung below his ears... thick and heavy, but groomed. He half-looked for a feather tied in the raven strands.

"What are you going to San Jose for?"

The boy brightened.

"I'm going to see my father there."

The silver coach stopped.

The man went to the lunch counter to order ham and eggs, but his 'admirer' was not there.

The layover burnt rapidly.

Once his passengers reboarded, the driver announced the next stop. Salt Lake City. Short squeals followed his announcement then changed to grunts and groans from the passengers. "There will be a two-hour layover."

The ride across the desert was uneventful for the companions. A baby who had whimpered in the night cried the distance of the desert, unnerving everyone aboard. Finally the Mormon Tabernacle was sighted and the dip into the valley aroused curiosity. The Rockies jutted against the blue sky. Snow held on the highest peaks as June wildflowers blossomed along Interstate 80. The city stood straight, clean and crystal, icy. The Greyhound growled up street and down, at last pulling into the station dock.

Passengers trekked off, some naturally disgruntled about the long stop; others took an opportunist outlook. The boy disappeared immediately into the crowded terminal; the man headed for the plastic cafeteria.

Time waddled like an old duck with ducklings. Despite its surroundings, cool mountaintops checkered with snow, Salt Lake City was blistering hot. The sun's glare caught unpolarized eyes, casting a blinding, sickening dizziness to the pit of the stomach. The polished sidewalks were poker hot. Few travelers ventured from the air-conditioned depot.

The boy's companion had remained in the cafeteria the entire break. Now he rose and lumbered to the men's room. He sighted the Indian boy standing at a urinal. Down the aisle a man in a white suit stared at the youth.

The boy turned. His face was screwed into a scowl. The companion realized the Indian kid was neither as short as he had originally believed, nor as thin, nor as young. He must have been at least sixteen.

THE BUS SPED ACROSS the Utah flats along the salty shores of the lake and through the area of the vast copper mines. Haze obliterated most of the view. Mountains hung in vague clusters on the horizon. The boy stared out the window for fifty miles. His companion doubted he saw anything.

"How much farther to San Jose?" the Indian blurted out at last.

"At least another day."

A ten-pound weight of silence fell between them before the man spoke. He sought one crack, the opening of the figurative curtain between them.

"So you are going to see your father?"

"Yes." Another long pause. "I've never been out of Denver before."

"Oh, no! You live there... Denver... huh?"

"I've never been any place. I've never been on a bus before."

"Oh, no? I've traveled quite a bit myself... mainly between Denver and California. Always by bus. I leave the driving to them." He chuckled.

The joke was lost on the youth.

They crossed into Nevada. Ten miles farther up the road

the bus lurched to a halt before a restaurant on the edge of nowhere. There was a casino crammed with one-arm bandits and game tables. Sweaty, nervous middle-aged people jammed the chandeliered interior, their eyes smeared with greed, their open mouths licked by hungry tongues chasing down house drinks.

The boy ignored the machines, but bought a Coke. His companion moved quickly through the crowd and found an unoccupied stool before a nickel machine. He dropped a fistful of coins into the slot one at a time and pulled the crank; one cherry, one plum, one lemon! Losing combinations spun into place.

The ten-minute rest stop dragged into forty minutes. The driver rounded up his gamblers. Two old ladies laughed. They had hit a small dime jackpot. The driver kidded them about buying his dinner in Reno.

Down the highway, the boy turned to his companion, who was reading a racing form.

"I have never seen my father. That's why I'm going to San Jose."

"Never seen your father!" He answered with surprise.

"No."

The man was embarrassed and flushed, his gaze wandering down over the heads of fellow passengers. What could he say? Small talk? The youth clipped the conversation by turning to the window.

"Say! My name's Dan. We never introduced ourselves!"

No response.

"My name is Dan."

"Nice to meet you, Dan," ignoring an extended hand.

"Dan Spires, I'm a car agent. I drive cars to Denver and then ride the bus back to the coast. Some life, huh! Dull as dishwater. If it wasn't for pretty waitresses in the restaurants I'd give up."

The boy managed a thin smile.

"Dan Spires."

He had not yet hit the responsive note.

"What's ahh... ahh, what's your name, son?"

The boy stared him down.

"Mike Hightower."

"Hi! Mike. I mean, hello."

Again he extended his hand. It was ignored.

"We've been riding together almost a full twenty-four-hour day and we didn't even know each other's names. Kinda silly, isn't it?"

The boy gave a frail grin.

"We'll be climbing soon. Get off this insufferable desert. You can see the range from here. Looks pretty black off there. That's Ponderosa country, I guess. TV land. That's where they filmed that TV show."

"The cowboy movie?"

"Yeah! Ever watch it? Pretty good one, I think."

"No. My mother doesn't have a television set. She doesn't much like cowboys anyway."

"Maybe your father will have one."

"Maybe."

He noticed the lack of spirit in the boy's remark. "Well," he thought, "all kids aren't alike. Then he is Indian. Maybe Indians don't like cowboy movies. They always get the bullet."

THE BUS CLIMBED THROUGH rock and gorge, ravine and conifers. Slowly dusk fell on the desolate land. Light failed. Hills rose dark and threatening. The passengers roared into the west.

Relaxed, the boy squiggled in his seat close to the window.

"Where are you going, sir... Dan?"

"Me? Richmond."

"California?"

"Yep! Richmond, California. Right side of Oakland."

"Is that near San Jose?"

"Well, not exactly... though it isn't too far away."

"Will you let me know when we get to San Jose?"

"Sure! Sure I will. If we go that way."

THE INTERCOM ANNOUNCED they were approaching Reno, Nevada. All passengers would change. San Francisco and the east bay passengers would change to one bus, San Jose and the south bay passengers to a different bus.

At the Reno depot Dan turned to Mike, who stood before the Coke machine.

"You sure drink a lotta Coke, Mike."

"I like Coke. It's better than Seven-Up."

"I mean... well, I mean... I prefer Seven-Up myself."

"I don't."

"Guess this is as far as we go together, son. We both have to change to separate buses. I guess I won't be able to tell you when you've reached San Jose after all. But your father'll be waiting there for you. So it's OK."

"No, he won't."

"He won't?"

"I'm going to telephone him. I don't know what he looks like. I've never seen him. I think he knows what I look like though he's never seen me."

Again Dan was embarrassed.

"It's a good thing you've got his phone number. Well, good luck, Mike."

He watched the kid move off. For a moment his black-haired head was lost in the crowd and then again reared up from the mass of bobbing heads.

Dan smiled. "Cute kid."

He said this aloud to anyone within earshot. He climbed aboard his bus for Richmond. In the darkness along the Sierra highway he tried to sleep, but his thoughts dwelled on Mike. In the rear of the Greyhound two hippies played guitars. One of the boys sang:

> "I'm a wanderin' cowboy with no place to go.
> I'm a wanderin' cowpunch with no family.
> So I spend my days drinkin' rough whiskey
> And lookin' for women who won't say no.
>
> I'm a wanderin' loner with no place in sight.
> I'm a wanderin', wanderin', wanderin' all night. . . . "

NANCI KINCAID

Spittin' Image of a Baptist Boy

I DO NOT LOOK one thing like Mother. Maybe just have some of her face. How her cheeks sit out there like little round biscuits of flesh that got put on last, as an after-thought, after the rest of the face was finished. My cheeks did like that too. Sat out there all by themselves, looking added on. And my hands and feet were like Mother's. Very square and neat. No fat-looking fingers or toes. Trim and square. We could pick up most anything as good with our toes as with our fingers. A marble. A thumbtack. Mother could be holding two arms full of grocery sacks and pick up the car keys off the ground with her toes, bend up her knee and hand them to Roy. It was a natural thing. Walter said it was amazing and that Mother must have some monkey in her. But I could do it too.

I had some of Mother's ways, but not much of her looks. It was Roy that had those. Brown Roy with his black, shiny, almost wavy hair. Roy, who could have dirt all over his hands and face and it wouldn't even be noticeable hardly. Not on his brown self.

It was funny how we were. Roy brown like Mother. Me

golden like our real daddy, which is not what somebody said, but I just saw that. How he had this straight yellow hair like me. And we had those blue eyes and those white eyebrows that go away, invisible, all summer long and come back some in the fall and winter. And then Benny looks like Walter. Kind of, he really does. He's like me and our real daddy about his white hair and skin and all. But like Walter in his build, which is big. Thick. Husky. And like Walter in his quietish ways. And it was not unusual at all for folks to say, "Lord, that boy takes after his daddy." Meaning Walter. People that didn't know would say that. "You sure can't be denying that child, Walter Sheppard!" People could see it. Even Mother could.

When folks got to telling Walter how Benny was exactly like him, just him made over, Walter would smile and say, "That's one lucky boy there. Damn lucky." And he'd wink at Mother. And it was just generally recognized how Benny was Walter's spittin' image.

WALTER'S PEOPLE LIVED in Valdosta. That's in Georgia, not too far off. There's a bunch of Sheppards there, a slew of them. Walter said he has more cousins than you could shake a stick at. Walter said every other person you'd meet on the street in Valdosta was a Sheppard, or married to one, or lived next door to one. He said there is such a thing as too much of a good thing. He said that's why he came down to Tallahassee. That, and because he had a chance at a right good job with the highway department.

None of us ever laid eyes on any of Walter's people. Not a one. He never did say that much about any of them. Just his brother Hugh. Hugh Henry Sheppard. He was Walter's little brother, grown and all now. Walter liked the heck out of ole Hugh. But that was about all.

Mrs. Sheppard, Walter's mother, was very disappointed that Walter didn't make a better marriage. She called

Mother "the divorcée." When Walter was fixing to marry Mother and he called Mrs. Sheppard to tell her about the wedding to see if she could come or not, she could not. Mrs. Sheppard couldn't come because it plumb broke her heart, Walter marrying a divorcée. And one with kids. She said Walter deserved his own flesh-and-blood kids. And here he was going to be bringing his hard-earned paycheck home to somebody else's leftover wife and another man's kids. And it plumb broke her heart. And there wasn't any need in her coming clear down to Tallahassee to cry her eyes out at a terrible mistake of a wedding like that. She wasn't up to it. Walter was just gon have to understand that. So Mrs. Sheppard had never even seen Mother, or any of us. We didn't think she ever wanted to. Walter said we were not missing one thing. He said he'd seen enough of the woman for all of us.

And then one day out of the blue she calls up Walter and says she is coming to visit. She's taking a Trailways bus down to Tallahassee and can he pick her up down there at the bus station. She says her conscience cannot rest until she sees Walter, meets his divorcée wife and all. She just has to come because she can't rest until she does. Walter was married to Mother almost a year by then – and his poor mother can't rest.

Mother went into a frenzy over the idea. Not mad exactly, just a nervous wreck, worrying about what to fix for dinner. Does your mama like this or that? Does she like biscuits better than cornbread? Does she like sweet pickles in her potato salad? And then Mother wished we could go on and paint my bedroom. It had been needing it so she wished we could paint it. She wanted Walter to mow the grass, and wash the car and his highway truck, and fix the tear in the screen door. She wanted Roy and Benny to get them a haircut. She wanted to clip our fingernails – and our toenails. She did speeches on us acting nice, stuff about not just yes ma'am, no ma'am, please and thank-you. But also about chew with your mouth closed, put your napkin in your lap. Do not pick your nose. Keep quiet. Don't scratch. Say excuse me. Be polite. No fighting and yelling. No slamming the screen door. No grabbing food. Smile. Say nice-to-meet-you. Walter's mother coming was not one thing like when our granddaddy came.

We kind of had the feeling we were in a contest to see if we could be nice enough to win Mrs. Sheppard so she might want to be like our grandmother or something. Like she was the Grand Prize if we won the niceness contest. If we could be good enough.

Walter tried to calm Mother down because she was about to wear herself out, and us too. And Walter said it wasn't the queen of England coming, just his mother, Emma Jean Sheppard. And there wasn't no sense in trying so hard to please her. No sense at all. But you couldn't tell Mother that. On the day Mrs. Sheppard was coming, Mother changed clothes a half a dozen times. Brushed the curl right out of her hair. Got all the rest of us nervous too. She burned the first batch of homemade dinner rolls she put in the oven. Walter told me to go on up to Melvina's and get her. Mother did not know one thing about dinner rolls. He said to get Melvina in the kitchen before it was too late. So Mother went on in the bathroom and brushed her hair some more. Melvina got in the kitchen mumbling all kinds of this and that.

When Mrs. Sheppard finally came walking in the house with Walter one step behind her carrying her suitcase, she was not exactly what we were expecting because we didn't know what we were expecting. Walter standing there behind his Grand Prize Mother. Everybody, including Melvina, gathered up around her and stared like she was some outer-space creature or something. Mrs. Sheppard in her little pillbox hat with the flowers on it, with her silver-blue curled hair and her seashell earbobs. She was a pretty regular grandmother type we thought. She didn't look so bad.

Walter said, "Mama, I want you to meet Sarah here. My wife, Sarah."

Mother reached out her hand and said, "Mighty glad to meet you, Mrs. Sheppard. Walter has told me an awful lot about you."

Mrs. Sheppard did not go to shake hands with Mother, but just looked her over some. Just stood there with her hands folded across her stomach and let her eyes fix on Mother. "You are a pretty thing. I'll say so. Walter, she is a pretty thing. How is it a pretty girl like you come to be a divorcée?"

"Mrs. Sheppard, meet the children," Mother said, putting her arms around us. "This here is Lucy . . . and Roy . . . and little Benny. . . . " She didn't add that at that moment we were the three squeakiest clean children in Tallahassee. But she could have. She did not say, "Look here, Mrs. Sheppard, look behind these kids' ears, clean as a whistle. See that?" She did not make us show our teeth, how toothpaste-white they were, or make us hold out our hands for Mrs. Sheppard to check how our fingernails were clipped so nice and all. She didn't do it, but she could have.

We said, "Glad to meet you." Then Mrs. Sheppard told Walter she sure was tired and thought she would like to lie down and rest some. No howdy-do or nothing. And that was how the visit started. And it never got better.

Mrs. Sheppard was a right peculiar woman. She went and laid down on the bed in my room – with her flower hat still on her head and all. She laid on her back with her hands still folded over her stomach, her shoes still on her feet. She looked like somebody waiting to get buried in a grave.

Mother went and put on a Tennessee Ernie Ford religious record on the record player. She thought some music would help Mrs. Sheppard rest better, and it would drown out any noise me and Roy and Benny made, which wasn't much. Mother told Melvina she could go on home, since

supper was under control and everything. But Melvina
didn't want to. She said she ain't come clear down here for
nothing and she's gon wait till after we eat supper. That was
because if there was something good left over from this
company dinner she was gon take it home with her. She always did like that. Fix her a big plate and take it up to her
house. Meanwhile she was gon sit in the kitchen with a fly-
swatter in her hand and wait.

Most of the afternoon passed with Mrs. Sheppard lying
up in my bed. Finally Walter went in there and woke her up
to come eat supper. Mother made him do it because she
didn't know how much longer the three of us could keep up
with being so good. It was like she was afraid our good behavior was going to run out just about the time Mrs. Sheppard woke up and we sat down to eat, and Roy and me
would go to chewing with our mouths open and grabbing
food. And Benny would start crying and rub Jello in his
hair. She wanted to get supper over with before our good-
ness ran completely out.

When we were all seated at the table, Benny in his high-
chair by Mother and all, then we bowed our heads and
Mother asked the blessing, like she always did. Sometimes
she would let me or Roy ask the blessing, but on an occasion
like this with Mrs. Sheppard eating with us, then Mother
said it herself. And she meant every word of it, you could
tell.

We started up passing the food around in a quiet way, and
Mrs. Sheppard looked at Mother and said, "What church do
you go to?"

Walter made this noise in his throat.

"Well," Mother said, "I was raised Methodist, and I'm
raising the children Methodist."

"What is the name of your Methodist church?"

"It's right in downtown Tallahassee," she said. "A big ole
church. Trinity Methodist. It's a very nice church."

"Walter was raised a Baptist," Mrs. Sheppard said. "Been

a Baptist all his life. My boys were raised Baptist. I saw to
that."

Walter kept on eating.

"Walter never missed a day of Sunday school or church
growing up. Did you, Walter? If the doors were open the
Sheppard family was there. Walter's daddy was a deacon,
rest his soul. Walter's been a Baptist all his life."

"There's not too much difference between Methodist and
Baptist," Mother said. "They're pretty close."

"World of difference," Mrs. Sheppard said, putting
spoonsful of sugar in her already sweetened tea. "World of
difference. I know because I've been a Baptist my whole life
and raised my boys Baptist. If it was good enough for John
the Baptist, then it is good enough for me. Baptizing is. Real
baptizing, like the Bible says. Dunking yourself clean underwater, head and all, washing away those sins, being reborn right on the spot. Wet as a newborn baby. Baptized
and reborn."

"Mama," Walter said, in his please-don't-get-started-
with-this voice. The same one he used on Mother sometimes.

"It's so," she said. "It is so. Methodists might think sprinkling a little dab of water on their heads is baptizing. But
they're wrong. The Bible says that. Sprinkling is not baptizing. It is sprinkling. God does not care one thing about a few
drops of water on your head – not even enough to mess up
your hair. He wants wet. He wants hold-your-breath, underwater, soaking wet. That's baptizing. Nobody ever got
born again over a little sprinkle of water on their heads.
There's a world of difference."

Mother acted like she needed to be cutting up Benny's
pork chop for him and wiping off his mouth with a napkin
and all. We could just tell she was biting her tongue.

"Walter is baptized proper. Aren't you, Walter? Didn't I
take you and Hugh Henry and get y'all baptized? I certainly
did. Because if the Bible says it, then I believe it."

Mother was looking at Walter eat. Her eyes were beating on him. If her legs could have reached him, she would have kicked the daylights out of him as a signal for him to say something. It looked like she was chewing her food, but really she was biting her tongue. And beating on Walter with her eyes.

We all ate quietly for a few minutes. Me and Roy had not said one word. And we had not spilled our milk or dropped food in our laps. Since we did not know much about grand-mothers, we just sat there watching Mrs. Sheppard. She was our first close-up look at a real grandmother.

"So," she said to Mother, "where is your first husband?" Mrs. Sheppard was mashing her Jello square with the back of her fork. That Jello was shaking like crazy. "Your first husband. Where is he?"

Mother darted her eyes at Walter, and then said, "Mrs. Sheppard, we ought not to talk about this at the dinner table with the children and all." Mother looked at Walter again.

"Sarah don't have a first husband and a second husband, Mama. All she's got is one husband, and that's me."

"I am just asking a harmless question, Walter. It is normal for a mother to have some curiosity about her boy's wife. It's perfectly normal."

"We're not gon talk about this now, Mama."

It was quiet a long time, us sitting at the table eating. Us using nice manners. Sometimes somebody said pass this or that and somebody would do it. Sometimes Walter cleared his throat. All there was was knives scraping across plates and forks tapping, and ice cubes melting some and clanking in the glass. And sometimes somebody said pass the butter please. Then Mother started saying did anybody want some dessert? Me and Roy did. Everybody did. So Mother starts fussing around the table, moving the plates and all.

Mrs. Sheppard put her hand on Walter's arm. "Son, it's normal for a mother to have some curiosity about her boy's wife. It's normal."

"Don't the Bible say something about curiosity, Mama? It's bound to say something on the subject."

Mrs. Sheppard looked at Walter in a mean way. "Well, I'll tell you one thing, Walter Sheppard, the Bible says plenty about a divorced woman. It says submit unto your husband, which means your one and only husband. It doesn't say one thing about trade this one in for that one."

Mother went carrying the dinner plates into the kitchen, they were all piled up with forks poking out between them and they rattled when she walked, like skeleton bones banging together. She closed the door with her foot.

Walter pushed back his chair from the table, and it made this loud scraping noise. Walter made some loud scraping noises of his own saying, "Let me tell you what!" He was about to speak to his mother, but then looked at me and Roy with our wide-open eyes and Benny, with Jello in his hair, and he stopped. "Lucy, you and Roy take Benny on out in the yard a while. You'll get your dessert later on."

We didn't like the idea.

"Right now I said!" And we could tell Walter meant it. So we got Benny out of his high chair and went on outside. We got up under the dining-room window as quiet as we could be – like we did when Melvina came to see Mother 'cause old Alfonso beat her up. We got up there by the window because we wanted to hear.

"Let me tell you something, Mama," Walter started. "This here is my house. You're in my house. And Sarah is my wife. This can be any kind of house I want it to be and I want it to be a Methodist house. You hear me? And if you and John the Baptist don't like it, it's plain too bad!"

We could hear Mrs. Sheppard sniffling. We wanted to look in the window so bad and see if Walter was making her cry. "And another thing, Mama. You cannot come in my house acting like it is your house. You cannot be talking that divorced woman trash to Sarah. Do you hear me?"

"Walter" – Mrs. Sheppard was crying her words – "you

never used to talk to me like this... not before you married her."

"For Lord's sake, Mama!" It was Walter's maddest voice.

Mrs. Sheppard kept up the crying. "I just want what's best for you, Walter. That's all. That's all I ever wanted. For you a Christian home with a wife of your own and kids of your own. You can't blame a mother for that. I just want you to have a good wife that appreciates you."

"Mama," Walter said in a calm way, "I'm gon be picking out my wife, not you. And I picked Sarah. And she ain't making me into a Methodist any more than you made a Baptist out of me."

Mrs. Sheppard blew her nose.

"You don't know one thing about Sarah, Mama. Not one thing she's been through. And you ain't never gon know because it ain't your damn business."

"Walter... " she cried, "you never used to talk like that."

Then it got quiet. Just Walter sitting there and his mama crying into her paper napkin. Minutes passed with her sniffling and sobbing. "Do you think I'm blind? Do you, Walter?" Mrs. Sheppard said. "Do you think I was born yesterday?"

"Mama, what are you talking about?"

"When I got here this afternoon and your wife said meet the children – and I saw that baby. Walter, I cannot tell you. I can't tell you what it did to me."

"What the... "

"It was like you standing there, Walter. Why, he couldn't be any more yours if you named him Walter Sheppard Junior. Did you think I wasn't gon notice that? That little baby looking like your spitting image."

Walter sort of chuckled.

"Don't Mama me. I'm no fool, Walter. I wasn't born yesterday. It just come to me this afternoon, standing there seeing that little baby – you made over. It come to me."

"What did?"

"Why you married that divorcée."

"Mama..."

"Don't deny it. I know you, Walter. I know you like a book. You're an honorable man about a thing like that. And then I just laid in yonder on that bed there, thinking how it was me that raised you that way. Honorable and all. You from a good Baptist home. Some men would be long gone when a divorcée comes up expecting a baby. But not you, Walter. Not one of my honorable boys."

Me and Roy were in the flower bed up under the window. We did not know what to think about crazy Mrs. Sheppard.

"You're dead wrong, Mama. Do you hear me? Dead wrong. This is my house and I'm saying you're dead wrong."

Mother opened up the kitchen door. Her and Melvina had been listening to every word said. They were listening in the kitchen same as we were listening in the flower bed. And so here comes Mother carrying Walter and Mrs. Sheppard plates of pound cake and ice cream. She set Walter's down in front of him, and when she went to set Mrs. Sheppard's down, Mrs. Sheppard said, "I'm sorry but, I do not believe I can eat this. I have just lost my appetite. I think I'll just go back in yonder and lay down awhile. Excuse me." And she got up with her balled-up paper napkin pressed against her nose and went in my room and laid on the bed. Again.

Mother sat down at the table with Walter, who was eating his dessert like on any ordinary day. Putting a spoonful of ice cream in his mouth and letting it sit there and slowly melt. "Is she all right?" Mother asked.

"She's okay."

"Should we do something?"

"Nope."

"It seems like we should do something, Walter."

"Like what?"

"I don't know, go in there and talk to her or something.
Get this thing straight."

Walter was eating his pound cake and ice cream slow, like
he was enjoying the heck out of it. Like it was one million
times more important than his mother lying like a corpse,
crying like she had come down with some fatal truth.

"Well, we can't have her go around thinking Benny is
yours, and I tricked you. Walter, I don't want her to think
that. I'm no tramp. And it bothers me, Walter. It does."

"Look on the good side," Walter said. "It's not you being a
tramp so much as it is her Baptist boy being one hell of a
lover."

"Walter..." Mother smiled at him like she did when he
would not take a serious thing serious. Like it could be the
end of the world and Walter would sit and eat a plate of cake
and ice cream, slow and relaxed. Like bombs were going off
and Walter would sit still and feel good about himself.

In a minute he got up from the table and walked by
Mother, patting her shoulder. "Good supper," he said.
"Good supper for a Methodist divorcée." He walked on into
the living room and sat in his regular chair over by the picture window.

When me and Roy and Benny came back in for our dessert we saw that Mother was crying, with her hands over her
face, and Melvina patting her like Mother was a child. She
turned her face from us when we came into the room and
then hurried down the hall to her bedroom. Mother back in
her room crying and crying, and Mrs. Sheppard lying in my
bed doing the same. Some people would probably say that
Walter didn't have much of a way with women.

Nothing can take away a child's appetite like a mother crying her eyes out. Me and Roy sat at the table sort of jabbing
at our cake, but not eating any of it. Melvina came in and
stood by us, saying very quietly, "Y'all allow your mama to

be sad, now, you hear? Don't she allow you to be sad when you need to?"

We looked at Melvina, and she reached out both hands and took our serious faces in them. Her hands were soft and warm and wrapped most nearly from ear to ear under our chins. "God wouldn't have give folks no teardrops if he hadn't of meant for them to cry some. Now would he?"

We nodded our heads no.

"And Melvina wouldn't of give y'all no dessert if she didn't expect y'all to eat it." We half smiled at her. She smiled too, and gave our faces a squeeze. "See can you eat your ice cream fore it melts all over the table."

The next day Walter took his mother back to the Trailways bus so she could get on home to Valdosta. We said good-bye and nice to meet you like Mother told us to say. We felt disappointed for Mother because she wanted us a grandmother so bad and could not get us one no matter what. Me and Roy tried to tell Mother we did not need a grandmother. Not some blue-haired woman who just sleeps all the time with her shoes on. It was sort of like when you enter into a contest and try your absolute hardest to win, and then find out that the prize is something you never have wanted in your life. Just some contraption that's gon stay broken and tore up, and don't work good when it's fixed. We told Mother never mind about Mrs. Sheppard, but seems like that made her sadder than ever.

Later on when Walter saw how funeralish we were acting, he said his mother would not know a good kid if one bit her. In fact, he said, if she ever came back that's what me and Roy should do. Bite her. Bite her right on the leg. Me and Roy laughed our heads off. Walter is so funny.

MAXINE KUMIN

✖

Beginning with Gussie

IN A WAY, Tweedie's out-of-wedlock pregnancy – did people still call it that? – was mostly her grandmother's fault. Augusta James, born in the opening year of the twentieth century, an internationally respected botanist in the forties, was always exhorting her, "Follow your star, Tweedie. 'Extra vagance! It depends how you are yarded.'"

There was something in Gussie's past, hinted at. Darkly alluded to. Tweedie could never tell if it was real or imagined. There were so many sides to Grammy James. She was earthy, iconoclastic, politically naïve, with an underpinning of good family, old money, and the lingering traces of a private-school accent.

Forcibly retired from the faculty of Smith College at the age of seventy, Gussie had not yet given up field trips to alpine meadows. The year she became *emerita ejecta,* as she called it, she had made a modest find. A species of Arctic rhododendron had been named after her.

Gussie and Tweedie had bonded early. Sometimes Rebecca felt that her mother had pounced on the baby like some fierce, infertile tabby determined to acquire a kitten of her own. She had carried the child off with her every summer to her unrestored farmhouse in the Berkshires, in spite of Rebecca's protests.

"It's good for a baby to grow up in nature. And besides, it's important for children to have a sense of the generations. Would you deny me my rights as a grandparent?"

"What about my rights as a mother?"

"Sweetydarl, you have her ten months of the year."

"But all summer... "

"You will have her the rest of your life," Gussie pronounced.

Grandmother and grandchild shared the dusty, cluttered space in Becket with an array of creatures. One year it was a bummer lamb, the last-born of triplets, being raised on a bottle, and an orphaned raccoon in his own playpen. A nest of baby rabbits saved from the sickle bar, kittens from an adjoining farm slated to be drowned, were commonplace. Succeeding summers produced comparable rescues.

Tweedie at four, the only child of an only child, explained to her parents' dinner guests, "It isn't fair to a mother cat to let her have so many kittens. Grammy James says she should be spaded."

"The word is spayed, darling," Rebecca said. "Do you know what it means?"

"Spaded means to have her kitten room taken out. And the daddy cats should be neutraled, they just snip off their pepsicles."

Gussie had been a bluestocking graduate of Barnard in 1922 and took a Ph.D. from Columbia six years later. She taught for several years before marrying an astronomer, who died of pneumonia not long after. Although she never married again, her daughter Rebecca, who would only dimly remember her father's beard and his pervasive aroma of peppermint, noted the ease with which Gussie attracted younger men.

Rebecca James Gruber, a Ph.D. in history, heading into college administration, was fond of calling her mother "a lovable eccentric."

But Tweedie protested. "Ec-centric, out of center, that

just means out of the ordinary. If people would behave in ordinary, decent ways, there wouldn't *be* any animals to rescue."

Tweedie was ten the year of that pronouncement. Her father had recently decamped, gone to California to write film scripts. They had always called her Tweedie, a child's pronunciation of Sweetie, something Joseph had called Rebecca in those first good years. Her real name was Elizabeth.

Tweedie-Elizabeth was born in 1950. Rebecca married Joseph Gruber, the wildly successful novelist, three months earlier, in the middle of both her sophomore year and his survey of twentieth-century fiction, in which she took an incomplete. It would not have been ethical to compete for an A, she reasoned, even though she deserved one, while carrying his child. Rebecca heard that he now wore an earring. She hoped it was true.

"You didn't have to have me!" Tweedie, age twelve or thirteen, had cried with terrible prescience.

But Rebecca refused the bait. How could she, the woman in the middle, daughter and mother, possibly justify her choice to this furious adolescent? She had been determined to fasten Joseph to her, pin him down, make him serve as father and husband all in one.

What could she have said to Tweedie? *I wasn't pretty. I was almost fat.* Bryn Mawr was a cloister for bright girls like me, all of us fell in love with our professors, made them over into our images of Zeus, Apollo, whatever. I don't know how it happened, I'll never know . . . but he stood there facing the class with that way he had—has—of ramming his hands deep into his pockets, then rocking back and forth on the balls of his feet. He always wore clean tennis sneakers. His lectures were extemporaneous, brilliant, he never spoke from notes. The hour was over almost before it began. He was famous, a giant in that landscape. Of course I didn't know then he was mildly afflicted with satyriasis, I only knew I had been chosen! I was the luckiest girl in the world.

And I didn't tell him I was pregnant until it was too late, really, to do anything about it.

"Your father," she called him to Tweedie, who screamed back, eyes screwed tight as if in pain, "Stop saying that! His name is Joseph Gruber."

Now, when Rebecca remembered him, she had to take little tucks and darts in the picture. Once he had been seamless, shining, perfect. Now he toed out like a duck as he walked. Under his lovely cleft chin another chin had formed. He was of only middling height, of only average athletic ability with his slight paunch, his sloping, almost-womanly shoulders. For ten years he had been the center of the universe around which she and Tweedie gladly spun, a parent to both of them, a friend, a conspirator.

Mama hadn't. Couldn't. Was walled off from Rebecca in mysterious ways. Clear, outspoken, competent Gussie, so full of fun and distances.

"I brought you up to be all the things women were not supposed to be," Gussie told her the night before her high-school graduation. "To be strong and bold and full of adventure. To be forceful and innovative."

Rebecca, who was neither valedictorian nor class president, cheerleader nor Most Likely To Succeed, wanted the earth to open and receive her. She was nothing more than Honor Society, she was a signal failure, an experiment that never jelled.

Not even two years later, Rebecca and Joseph drove to the farm for Easter recess. Their marriage certificate, three days old, reposed in a file folder marked Personal.

Joseph went fishing. Rebecca faced Gussie across the big trestle table that had served for dining, mushroom identification, mail-sorting, and elbows-on discussions for as far back as she could remember.

"You must have been very angry with me not to have told me at Christmas," Gussie said, gesturing at the mound of

Rebecca's belly, which Joseph's white shirttails did nothing to diminish. "Were you afraid I would try to talk you out of it?"

"No. I don't know, maybe. It's just what I wanted. Oh Mom, we're *married!* He's so wonderful! We're so happy!" And to her total surprise, Rebecca put her head down on the table and sobbed.

"I suppose I wasn't around enough," Gussie suggested. "I wasn't... tender enough... long enough."

"It's not in your nature to be tender," Rebecca said, blowing her nose. "With people, that is."

"You're right. I don't know what gets in the way. I wish I had held you more, cuddled you."

"Even though I was half an orphan."

"I'm sorry. I thought about your moral education and your intellect. It was all John Dewey and progressive education. I was too sorry for myself, Sweetydarl, long after your father died."

They stumbled awkwardly into each other's arms. Rebecca could still feel that harsh and salty embrace. It was as close as they could ever come to saying *I love you.*

IF GUSSIE HAD WEATHERED the shock of Rebecca's pregnancy a bit grimly at first, she was weathering this one quite cheerfully. Her letters crossing the ocean to Tweedie contained dissertations on calcium and iron, emollients for the skin, and the magical properties of vitamin E oil.

To Rebecca and Milton, the once-young virologist who lived with her, she said only once or twice, "I *do* wish this baby could have a father. It makes it so hard. I *do* wish, Rebecca, that our Tweedie were a little less... headstrong."

Milton made little murmurs of assent.

The ensuing silence acknowledged the way Tweedie was.

In mid-adolescence, Tweedie had made the leap from animal to human rights. In the ferment of the sixties, she collated and stapled, joined hands and sang, marched and sat in, and was arrested twice. Both times, because she was a juvenile, her case was continued with no finding. Once, she sat in at the Boston Navy Yard with Rebecca and twice she marched in Washington with Gussie. *Grandmother and Granddaughter Arrested at Pentagon* made headlines in the Springfield *Republican* and merited a feature article in the *Washington Post.*

Ten years later, armed with an advanced degree in international law from Georgetown, Tweedie landed a job with Horn Relief, a worldwide agency based in the Sudan. From headquarters in Khartoum, she lobbied desperately for volunteer doctors and nurses and drug supplies. In Juba, she structured food distribution and storage techniques. The Japanese and Australians have been bulwarks in the acquisition and husbanding of water resources. Tweedie has attended conferences in Sydney and Nagoya dedicated to adapting modern technology for use in desert encampments.

Now she has friends in a dozen different embassies, and a few enemies as well. After several months of witnessing the hunger-bloated bellies of children, Tweedie no longer saw the starved and overloaded beasts of burden in the countryside. She hardly noticed the pariah dogs whipped away from cooking fires, or the gaunt mother cats scavenging in every settlement.

Two years ago she took a post with an inter-governmental agency called Migration Assistance Organization, pronounced Mayo, as if it were a binder for tuna or chicken salad. Headquartered in the heart of Europe, Mayo is dedicated to resettling refugees and stateless persons, especially the so-called hopeless cases. Tweedie has shucked the past and been reborn in her humanitarian zeal. She is a gifted administrator in a line of work that requires skillful dealing.

Rebecca remembers Tweedie describing a cocktail party

in Islamabad attended by a well-known Ugandan, who in an earlier time supervised the torture of revolutionaries.

"He's a chameleon, he hangs on through every change of government. Now he's a bureaucrat again, he blocked the embarkation of one of our planeloads of refugees from their airport to a transfer point last week. There were 342 people on board, people who had just given up their hous-ing—such as it was—their cooking pots—God! He kept them sitting on the tarmac for eighteen hours in the blazing heat, not knowing whether they would fly out of there or just get stuffed back into the cesspool of the tent city again. Only this time without identities."

"You know each other? I mean, you're personally ac-quainted?"

"Oh yes. He's very suave. Would you believe, he has a de-gree from the Sorbonne. Anyway, he handled me three or four times... "

"Brushed against you? How?"

"Stroking my arm, my neck. Then managed to corner me between the hall and the stairway."

"What did you do?"

"Stepped on his instep very hard, with my high heel. Then said, *'O, je m'excuse, j'ai perdu mon équilibre.'* Walked away."

This was last Christmas on home leave. Tweedie is ex-tremely loyal to family. Two weeks with Rebecca, two weeks with Gussie, a week in California with her father and his lat-est new family (Joseph has remarried three times), then she's off to Rome or Athens or Dakar to "visit a colleague." Of course there are lovers. Names are dropped and anec-dotes told, but there is something brittle in the telling.

"How would you like to be my birth partner?" Tweedie had asked Rebecca in one of their weekly transatlantic phone conversations. Her voice always faded in and out, as though snippets of syllables had been detached from it along the underwater cable. "We could write a whole new chapter in the history of mother-daughter relations."

Rebecca, president of a small liberal arts college in northern Michigan, her head spinning from the request, riffled the pages of her calendar to cover her momentary vertigo. "When will this be, exactly? Or inexactly."

"January something. Around the tenth."

The scratch of a pen X-ing out a cluster of days. "Good academic timing! I'd love to. I'm flattered that you asked me."

At the other end she could imagine Tweedie drawing a line through this item on her list. It was probably followed by Request Maternity Leave. Order Bassinet.

To be fair, that wasn't the first word of the impending baby. Tweedie had chosen to convey that news in a letter that contained all the appropriate clichés: "Something I've always wanted... very excited about... biological clock [she was thirty-six]... on the basis of good genes... has no wish to be acknowledged as father... promised not to divulge."

She had written Gussie at the same time, but far more frankly.

"You know how I feel about betraying confidences," Gussie said during Rebecca's weekend visit to the farmhouse. Milton had brought them both Bloody Marys and then gone tactfully off for a jog with the dogs. "But really, Rebecca, I don't like this... selectivity of Tweedie's. I think you need all the facts we can muster before you go off midwifing."

She unfolded the letter and passed it over.

"I don't know what you'll think of this piece of *extra vagance*, but I've decided it is now or never. I don't see why I should be cheated out of motherhood for want of a marriageable partner. The man I've chosen is an Indian diplomat, Oxford educated, gifted in languages. He speaks seven fluently and plays the sitar and the saxophone. Since I was but an impolitic dalliance, he is furious at my refusal to have an abortion. I am hoping for a little girl – I have no idea at all how to bring up a little boy – but whichever it is, I plan to bring it home during my four-month maternity leave for you to admire."

"Poor Tweedie," Rebecca said. "She must have had such high hopes."

"So you see why she couldn't bring herself to tell you."

Rebecca nodded, aware that tears were swimming in her eyes. She hoped they would get reabsorbed, she couldn't bear it if they fell, spattering her drink.

"Don't be hurt, Sweetydarl."

"Hard not to."

"I shouldn't have taken her from you every summer. It was wrong of me. Selfish. But I was lonely."

Rebecca wanted to cry out, But what about me? I was lonely too.

"Sweetydarl. I'm getting close to the end, you know. You're still in the middle."

"Meaning you're handing her back to me?"

"As if I could. As if anybody hands Tweedie."

They both reflected on this. Rebecca waited; was her mother about to say something more? There was something more, she was sure of it.

But Gussie, her conscience clear, had gotten up briskly. "Time to pick peas for supper."

AFTER THE PLANE lifted off from Kennedy, Rebecca ordered two vodka martinis. She had already been in transit most of the day, but the fund-raising, morale-building concerns of her job were not easily dispelled. How to keep up enrollments with a broadly based program aimed at married women in the area – ecology, Eastern philosophies, behavioral psychology, and poetry workshops – still ghosted her thoughts. The second cocktail went so quickly to her head that she gave in to the pleasant, mizzly sensation, cradled her head between the seat back and the cool window glass and let herself drift.

Of course what came up was Tweedie. Tweedie and Gussie, on either end of a seesaw. Rebecca as the fulcrum. Thirty-six years of this.

One of the ongoing mysteries of this triad was why the pensioned horses, the old foundered donkey, the fledgling birds, saved alive with eyedropper and worm of hamburger, had never quite seized her conscience in the death grip that tightened on Tweedie. They had, after all, been subjected to almost identical proselytizing.

In a kitchen littered with fungi, wild grasses, and bits of birdshell, the child Rebecca had mastered the identification of a hundred specimens. The family cats slept on her bed. She fed the dogs, rode and cared for a retired police horse named King. But she was restless, anxious to break away. There was never a time – after the age of, say, ten – that she did not feel embarrassed by her mother's huge enthusiasms, her excesses. Do children ever understand how fame overtakes their parents? Just last year, during a month-long expedition in Denali, Augusta turned up a new moss of the tundra not yet classified, but sure to be one of her major finds. And crowed unduly.

This woman is eighty-five years old! Rebecca admonished herself. She is a living legend! Why can't you stop... blaming her? For loving Tweedie more than me? For taking Tweedie away from me?

Dinner arrived on its little plastic tray, a welcome diversion. She ordered a split of white wine and focused on hoping that Tweedie's baby would appear on schedule. She dreaded the prospect of waiting around for a week – God forbid, for two weeks – in attitudes of forced equanimity. They would cheer each other on, mother and daughter, while every neuron had already begun to jitter and twinge. She would aspire to an orderly calm for Tweedie's sake. Tweedie, fighting off the impulse to retreat into the solipsism of late pregnancy, would exhaust them both with little expeditions, projects and bravados that both of them detested. Deferring to each other across the invisible wire that connected them for life.

Mr. Assounyub, the Afghan with impeccable manners, in detention in Papua, New Guinea, has written again. *My dear Madame.* Tweedie reads his jagged script on pale blue paper so thin that the whorls of her own fingertips shine through as she holds the page under the lamp. *Permit me once again to bring to the attention of your esteemed self my wretched circumstance.* But the page unfurls like a scroll in her lap; Mr. Assounyub's complaint grows longer and longer. It will take all morning to decipher this latest saga, and meanwhile his plane! His plane is being posted! She holds his expensive travel documents, his doctored passport in her hands, but they become a sparrow. She can feel its quick heart beating in her palm. Before she can open her fingers to release the bird, she wakes in the chill of January in her own bed.

Each time a jet takes off from the country's major airport, less than a kilometer away, the walls of her floor-through apartment in this converted farmhouse tremble. The wine glasses sing in the cupboard. Planes depart every minute and a half, streaking off to Bucharest and Bombay, Dakar, Damascus, New York. Although daylight only creeps onto the rime-coated pastures at eight A.M., the planes begin to rise from the valley floor between two mountain ranges at six. By the time Tweedie leaves for the office, hundreds of people are halfway to Helsinki or Athens.

In this life Tweedie is called Elizabeth. She is a Protection Officer; she knows how to wheedle and bargain and even, from time to time, extort. Mr. Assounyub's hearing will take place today. If not the Dutch, then perhaps the Danes can be persuaded to take in this former student leader, whose

English is eloquent and Victorian, and whose chief sin, ten years ago, was to lead a strike against the university administration. In Berkeley he would have been acclaimed a hero.

Fully awake now, getting up awkwardly, she hopes again that the baby will be early. Her mother is arriving this afternoon. If it turns out to be a long wait there will not be enough ways to fill the available time. Subjects are bound to come up, to be flung up heedlessly. Questions will be raised, problems for which there are no solutions. Tweedie remembers something the Deputy says: "There are no lasting solutions. Everything is *pro tem.*"

She and her mother are intimate without being confidential. They have lived together so long in their tandem singularity that they have learned, like yoked oxen, not to pull against each other. In fact, they make a conscious effort not to intrude on each other's private domains. This leaves long corridors of untenanted spaces between them, something they are both uneasy about. Even though their mutual sympathies, present if not vigorously articulated, bind them together as surely as the braids of a rope, Tweedie feels a little phobic flutter at the prospect of Rebecca's presence.

She stands barefoot in the kitchen, vaguely aware that something is out of plumb. Once again it rained during the night. Because her only windows at this end of the house are skylights, she cannot open them without incurring leaks. Now, as she empties the buckets and stacks them in the closet against the next rainy night, bending to put them in the corner, she feels the first squeeze of contraction rise across her belly, harden, then slip away.

Magically, she is already in labor as the plane bearing her mother across the ocean passes Gander and heads out over the water. It is a walking-around labor, possibly a false labor, possibly it is nothing at all. She nibbles on a banana and some *petits buerres* and does a load of laundry, balancing the basket on her hip as she crosses the courtyard to the communal laundry room.

The zeal to start out clean, she thinks. She showers, washes her hair, has two cups of tea. More contractions, mild enough to walk through. She is too restless to write letters, but puts Vivaldi on the record player and tries to plan a strategy for the four Sikhs stranded in a luxury hotel at the Tripoli airport, who arrived there via a hijacking in which they were taken hostage. But now it is hard to think clearly; this iron hand across the abdomen is the real thing. By prearrangement she calls her closest friend, a colleague at the office. Indeed, after Jenny arrives with her Jamaican backcountry wild talk, the contractions subside to mere twinges. There is much forced hilarity. Tweedie is surprised to discover that she is on the verge of tears.

Meanwhile, Rebecca's plane is approaching. Rebecca is bringing with her the little hooded towels, the vitamin E oil for the nipples of nursing mothers, and a convertible cradle from Sears Roebuck designed to hang from its own tripod, which has a crank attached to it. A few turns of the handle and the cradle will rock unattended for an hour. It has been an albatross for Rebecca to transport.

Jenny is waiting at the airport when Rebecca gruels through customs and is permitted to enter the public space. Her English is crisply British, though her inflection lends it an exotic quality. The words appear to break open as she enunciates them. Later, reporting the rendezvous to Tweedie, Jenny says, "Indeed, we recognized one another at once."

By the time Rebecca enters the apartment, Tweedie's contractions are five minutes apart. She can still walk, talk through them. The doctor is called. He promises to come by within the hour, but that hour and most of the next pass before they hear him, audible a hundred meters away on his Mobecane. He balances his helmet upright on the kitchen table and, still in his leather jacket, pulls on a rubber glove to examine Tweedie casually on the living-room sofa. She is already two centimeters dilated. Perhaps they should go. He must pay one more call, he will meet them shortly in hospital. His manner is distant, diffident, reminding Rebecca of an uneasy schoolboy.

A last look around. Rebecca takes a banana and a few cookies for sustenance, drops them in her shoulder bag, picks up Tweedie's overnight case, and they set off.

"Left here, then right at that church," Tweedie directs. "You go three cross streets and take another left, by that little *épicerie*, see?"

It is dusk. Peering down the unfamiliar streets, Rebecca tries to assemble landmarks to come home by. The little Volkswagen jiggles and spurts each time she shifts, she has not mastered the distances between gears yet. "Sorry, darlie," she murmurs. Receiving no answer, she reaches over to take Tweedie's hand and is surprised – no, unsurprised – by the fierceness of the grip. "You can do it. Tweedie, you're all right," she says, words older than time.

"You all right, though, Mom?" Tweedie manages. "Not such good timing, you must be... exhausted."

"Terrific timing! We'll have a whole two weeks on the other side of the birth, much the best way," and then mercifully they are there.

Although English is her mother tongue, Tweedie will have this baby in her second or third language. She has gone conscientiously to all the meetings of the childbirth class in her sector, even the final practice ones when each of the other women had a husband for a partner and she had to make do with the instructor, a German-speaking midwife of truly imposing dimensions. Frau Lansdorf's thighs when she squatted to demonstrate an alternate pushing position loomed inside their leotard coverings as massive as old tree trunks. She looked as though she could deliver a baby with the direct dispatch of a hen laying an egg.

Tweedie had taken a stand early on about single parenting. She comported herself as if it were an ordinary happenstance, as if marriage were a quaint custom shortly to fall into disuse, like calling cards or the wearing of white gloves in the evening. And she played this part so faithfully and with such granitic determination that she could no longer (she told herself) feel the bitter envy, the savage, corrosive longing to belong, the harsh inveighings of loneliness or the slow clots of unsatisfied lust she had fought her way past six months ago. She would have this baby. She would have it in the prescribed manner and it would be hers in the way nothing else before had ever been wholly and singly hers. "A son is a son till he takes him a wife but a daughter's a daughter the rest of your life"; that was something Grammy James used to say approvingly of Rebecca, and of Rebecca and Tweedie, and by extension of women in general. The baby would be a girl.

Now the contractions are three minutes apart, they are serious contractions going somewhere, and she breathes as she has learned to breathe, riding the big wave up to the top on a series of puppylike pants, then exhaling as it subsides, to coast for a blessed minute in the beautiful blue sky of painlessness.

Chiding herself, I must not think of these as pains! even as the first harsh moan bubbles out of her mouth. O God it is hard, what liars they all were with their bright talk of lollipops and tea, and cries out, O God! meanwhile clutching Rebecca's hand, mashing it into her own as she rises to the top and then ever so gradually slips down the other side.

When Tweedie is in labor, Rebecca becomes her. She too is feeling the balloon of contraction, how it hardens with a crust like a loaf of round bread, growing and growing. "*Inspirez, inspirez,*" the *sage-femme* urges, her practiced hands measuring the rise and fall. Four centimeters, six... Now Rebecca is lulling her daughter, using the yoga-drift, hypnotically soothing her to rest between rich, gripping seizures. "Go with it, go with it, lie back, drift as if you are lying on the sand in the sun." And indeed Tweedie closes her eyes, the frown lines ease, vanish, she seems almost to doze, then stiffens with the next big one.

Now she *is* Tweedie, but alone, terrified, taken, racked, and praying God O God, just let me get through this, I swear I'll never again, no never. . . and then the murdering oblivion of the scopolamine, followed by huge, wet cobwebs pressed over her face as she fought screaming to get free, *bastards, you bastards* and came to, afterwards, bruises on her shoulders and the insides of her upper arms from where they had held her down on the table, and two spidery hematomas inside her thighs from where they had forced them apart (she supposed; she was not there) at the moment when the head crowned.

And here in this room with white curtains and wallpaper flecked with bright dots, this room with its ordinary bed and pillows, a teapot on the table, a chair, a squatting stool, and behind a screen, discreetly, a delivery table, the backache takes hold of Tweedie, pressing, aching, pounding across the vulnerable small of the back, the lifting and holding arc of her body. Rebecca takes out her aloe cream and rubs, pressing down hard where Tweedie, in a passionate groan, directs. The other midwife, the one who speaks English with a rich New York accent (she worked for six years at Columbia Presbyterian), takes turns with her pressing, and the contractions still come and go. The mother enters the daughter and rises and falls with her as she has all her life, but before this, always in secret, at a remove. Now they are one woman in labor, passing the distended belly between them, puffing up the terrible mountain of rock, slipping half-conscious down the other side of it, filling their lungs at the bottom, making ready. *Ready.* Ready to push. *Now.*

"Mahvelous, mahvelous, dahling," croons the midwife. "I think we have this baby in five minutes now. And push! Push to the count of ten! Push not with the face, not with the neck, push from the chest. Push like the *caca.*"

"Much! easier!" Tweedie calls out, reenergized. But at the last, with all the bearing down, all the *poussez, poussez!* encouragements, the fetal heart wobbles and slows and the indifferent, silent, long-haired doctor, who arrived thirty minutes ago and has been standing at the window peering out as if awaiting a message, now squats to his work. He inserts the *ventouse* and sucks the baby's head to the mouth of the cave.

At that moment Rebecca reenters her own body. She sees a creature come out. A large rat is backing out of the birth canal, the wet, matted hair rat-color and sparse. It is all a terrible mistake. Then the whole head emerges and she sees it has indeed a human face, still cowled in a marblelike material, something at once silken but mottled, like stone. The umbilicus, as thick as a grapevine and braided like the cord of a monk's robe, is wrapped tightly around the baby's neck. The baby holds it in one fist. The midwife quickly inserts a finger between the cord and the neck in order to loosen the noose, and the membrane breaks and the baby's face comes alive, gasping. One shoulder slips free, then the other, then the whole length of him—for it is a boy—slips free and howls in discomfort into the world. The doctor lifts him, floppy and bloody, to his mother's chest and he lies there, almost comforted, while the cord still pulses. Someone dims the lights, just as, with a snip, he is set free on his own support system. The other *sage-femme* takes him now, to suction his mouth and nose as he roars protests.

"Would you like to bathe him?" she asks Rebecca, who nods yes, and then he is in her hands, submerged in a warm bath, and he falls silent. This skill comes back unbidden. In minutes he is swaddled and dressed and put to his mother's breast. New as they both are, he manages to take hold and she to accept. He suckles a few minutes at each breast, a midwife on either side of Tweedie, like devout acolytes, and then lies calm and alert under his *duvet* on the lap of the grandmother who has also delivered him.

The midwives bring a feast of custard and tea and champagne and zwieback and they relive the birthing, like a sporting event, phase by phase, each fiercely proud of the other, and proudest of all of the little pale brown boy (they had both wanted a girl) who is neither exceptionally large nor exceptionally small, neither long nor short, who resembles all the other neonates and is their prize, their conspiracy.

FOUR DAYS LATER, Tweedie and Rebecca sit on the floor of the living room with a bottle of Beaujolais and a full page of diagrams and instructions. They are assembling the Sears Roebuck cradle, which comes with pointed screws, end nuts, acorn push nuts, carriage bolts, knob, hanger wire, washers, and four rubber leg tips.

Tweedie reads: "'A. Slide end cover into motor unit by straddling the inside end plate, as shown. B. Insert two top leg sections into motor unit as shown, and then line up the holes in the upper leg section with the holes in the end cover and inside end plate. Secure with two pointed screws.'"

An hour later they get to E. Rebecca is now reading: "'Insert seat push rod into rear key hole of motor unit by alining push rod ear with keyhole slot.' Shouldn't that be aligning? And why key hole first, then keyhole, one word?"

Finally, a yellow slip in the bottom of the box. Rebecca again: "'Once in a while we are less than perfect and one of our products reaches a customer with a problem or our instructions are not clear. Please use our toll-free number 800-' etc., etc." and they rock with laughter.

THE BABY IS EIGHT days old, vigorous, alert, and a poor sleeper. The mechanical cradle is something of a godsend, when all else fails. In the night Rebecca retrieves him once he is truly awake and squeaking. Sometimes she can fore-stall a feeding and spell Tweedie a little longer by walking the floor with him, a well-wrapped package, high on her shoulder. This too she has not forgotten. She and Tweedie are trying to discover the baby's natural schedule, but he is wildly erratic, sleeping only two hours between some feedings, then going more than six. Occasionally he is happy, a wide-awake little sailor rocking from side to side in the windup contraption.

Tweedie and Rebecca talk to Gussie every day, luxuriously long phone conversations. Gussie is failing, having little blackout episodes that she of course does not admit to, but Milton, her faithful companion, has called to report these ministrokes. The vision in one eye has been affected, but her mind is perfectly clear.

"I meant to tell you this yesterday, Tweedie. The duckbill platypus has no nipples. Milk oozes through the pores of the skin of its abdomen, and the young ones simply suck up the droplets as they appear."

"That's fascinating," Tweedie says.

"Of course it's just garbage-pail information, but I thought you'd appreciate it. How is the vitamin E oil doing?"

"Just fine, Grammy. No problems nursing. The only problem is getting him to sleep."

"Swaddling. Tuck him up tight, he will feel more secure. In a litter the young always lie touching, you remember that? We poor humans are singular. No one should have to sleep alone."

Day ten. Rebecca and Tweedie are reading, on opposite sides of the living room, texts on nursing and child care. On opposite sides of the globe these last several months they had read texts on childbirth; they are staunch believers in book knowledge. How to make a solar heater, how to build a purple-martin birdhouse, six steps to a slimmer you, it's all

there. The British books are best, they agree; breezy, infor-
mational, and noncondescending. The La Leche League is
too evangelical.

The majestic baby, whose dark scrotum betrays the fact
that he is of mixed blood (so the head nurse, a starchy nun,
had announced), for the skin tone darkens only gradually,
is sleeping fitfully, sucking the cuff of his sleeve. Sometimes
he puts his whole fist in his mouth. He has not been circum-
cised, although Rebecca had promised Joseph that she
would urge their daughter to arrange this little amenity. In
this country, circumcision is thought to be a barbarism, me-
dieval. Rebecca and Tweedie will conspire to convince Joseph that it was impossible to achieve, the baby's condition
was not stable enough to permit it. It is dubious that this
child will grow up to be the chief rabbi of Rome or Vienna,
Rebecca reasons.

Tweedie is reading about wet-nursing in the eighteenth
century. It was common practice for poor unwed mothers
to put their babies out to baby farms, where they frequently
sickened and died, and then to hire out as wet nurses to the
wealthy. Often such a woman would substitute her own
baby for the wealthy woman's. The heir would die at the
baby farm and the wet nurse would bring up her own child
in comfort. A great many plots in literature revolve around
this switch – Gilbert and Sullivan's *Pinafore,* for one.
Twain's *Pudd'nhead Wilson* for another.

It is the kind of subject Gussie would love to discuss. Gussie would know that wet-nursing never became deeply established in the United States. She would say, "American
women were always too independent to take on *that* job for
somebody else," and then add, "except maybe in the South.
My own uncles," Gussie would say, "change-of-life babies,
were suckled by the descendant of a wet-nurse slave."

But Gussie's life ends this same evening, which is mid-
morning on the Continent. Milton the virologist calls to say
that Augusta James died peacefully in her sleep. She left a

will, she left notes and messages to them both. He sounds very composed, but sad.

"I want you to know, Milt, that Tweedie and I are deeply grateful to you," Rebecca tells him, but there is more. Gussie left her animals with explicit instruction as to their disposal. The old horses are to be euthanized, as is the donkey. Milton himself will take the dogs; he has grown quite fond of them and they know him.

Should Rebecca return immediately? It hardly seems necessary. They spend some time commiserating. They agree to hold a public memorial service for Gussie at a later date, when Tweedie comes to the States for her maternity leave. Perhaps they could establish a scholarship fund in her name.

The baby is not so fretful this day. He seems finally to be able to lie awake without making those grating, fussy noises that neither the mother nor the grandmother can bear. The fussiness, say the books, indicates an immature nervous system, a condition he will outgrow.

"I HAVE TO TELL YOU something about Grammy James," Tweedie says. "It's something she wrote me a couple of months ago."

"After you told her you were pregnant?"

Tweedie nods. "It's the most astonishing thing, a confession, a document, actually. Wait, let me get it for you."

Rebecca sees it is indeed a document, several single-spaced pages typed on her mother's Smith-Corona with the tail-letters – q's and y's – that always printed a little below the line they belonged on.

"When Grammy was seventeen," says Tweedie, shuffling the pages, "she had a mad, wonderful love affair with the guy who was the chief trainer for the thoroughbred farm across from their property."

"The old Stoddard estate?"

"I guess so. It was 1917, the year of the first flu epidemic. She had just graduated from high school, a private day school, really." Now Tweedie is reading. "'There was no question of an abortion, of course. In addition to the disgrace attendant on one, the illegal procedure, usually performed by a failed doctor or a veterinarian, was extremely dangerous. My parents were besides themselves with fury and terror. I had to be removed from the scene at once! So I was sent off to Indiana to live with some distant impecunious cousins, two dry sticks, staunch Methodists, who ran the local hardware emporium. I was alone in the house all day with two cats whom I observed very closely, keeping records of their sleep and awake times, and so on. Also, I studied Greek. After supper, as soon as it was too dark for my condition to be taken note of, I went for my daily long walk.'"

"God," Rebecca says.

"The day the baby was born he was put up for adoption and she never saw him again. Then she got the flu and she hoped she would die of it, romantically. 'Having lost my lover and give my child away,' she said, 'I was ready to lose my life.' She was so sick that all her hair fell out, 'ignominiously.'"

"I think I always knew about this," Rebecca says slowly. "I mean, not the whole story, but I think I always knew there had been a great love when she was quite young, and that it ended badly. In my mind it had something to do with World War I, the influence of all those stories, I suppose."

"You mean about fiancés being killed at the Marne and the women vowing never to marry?"

"Something like that. They all became high-school English teachers."

"But the way she described it," Tweedie says. "Listen to this: 'I must tell you, Tweedie, this grand passion was the sweetest interlude of my life. Even after almost seventy years, I have perfect recall of our feelings, our gaiety, indeed even our conversations. It was wonderful how he used to lift me up, his hands around my waist – I had a tiny waist, then – and twirl me around in the box stall. "Augusta Wadsworth Kensington," he'd say, "second cousin twice removed of the poet! Watch her fly through the air.""'

Rebecca is crying.

"Don't cry, Mom. Think how happy he made her. 'He taught me how to shake straw on a pitchfork – it's a fine art, to distribute it evenly – and we used to ride out together, galloping the jump course. Even though I was terrified of the drop jumps, I followed him over every one with perfect confidence.'"

"Can't you just see it, though," Rebecca says. "Packed off to cousins in the Middle West, undoubtedly paid to keep it quiet. Abandoned by those bitchy, upper-class parents with their expensive reputation. The groom was probably bought off, too. Banished to Virginia."

"Trainer," Tweedie corrects. "Actually, he went to Kentucky." They are both silent a minute. Rebecca blows her nose.

"They gave her chloroform," Tweedie says. "She described how they put a few drops on a handkerchief tied around her wrist and told her to sniff it when the pains got too bad. So she would sort of pass out and her arm would drop and then she'd come to and sniff again and pass out. Primitive but effective. The thing was, it's very bad for the baby."

"She never found out who adopted it?"

"She said she tried to trace him through the minister of the Methodist church in Leedsville. But I guess back then a natural mother had no rights. They could keep the records from you."

"Strange," says Rebecca. "Mom was so . . . indomitable. It seems to me that if she wanted to know badly enough, she'd have found out."

"Want to hear what she wrote at the end?" Tweedie asks.

She has not known until just now that she would share this with Rebecca.

"'And thus, Tweedie, while I cannot applaud your reliving my history, I am deeply happy to think that my genes are being handed on. Modified, broadened, no doubt improved upon. I know you will hold fast to your baby and that he will be a credit to us all.'"

The baby starts to squeak then and soon works up to full scale. Rebecca diapering him, Tweedie nursing him, separately and silently think how it all comes down to this moment. That the baby begins with Gussie.

COLLEEN McELROY

✖

How I Came to Dance with Queen Esther and the Dardanelles

It MIGHT NEVER HAVE HAPPENED except that one day in the autumn of my senior year in high school, my Aunt Stacia sent my cousin Lulu Mae to the corner store for a loaf of bread. That heifer came home two years later with a baby, and no bread. Lulu Mae had never been known to keep time too well. In fact, she was known for bad timing, and her sudden appearance at our front door, a baby in her arms and a suitcase by her feet, was no more than we could expect from a person who, two years before, had announced that she had every intention of changing her name to Queen Esther so she could go on the stage with the Dardanelles. Those boys just took that name because they'd read about that place, and got it fixed in their heads the place had something to do with Hannibal getting all those elephants out of Africa. They thought using the name could be the hook that would get them out of the Projects. What they knew about Africa you could lose inside a croker sack,

but that didn't matter because those Dardanelles were dancing fools, and next to my Uncle Percy, who was from the Islands, there wasn't anyone for miles who could outdance
Jock and Ferro Maitland. The three of us – my cousins Pepper, Lulu Mae, and I – didn't care what they called themselves. The minute we saw the Dardanelles, we wanted to
dance with them so bad, we were willing to maim each other
for unspecified lengths of time just to get a clear shot at the
chance. We might have been cousins, but blood was never
thicker than a good cha-cha partner. And Lulu Mae standing in the doorway, that baby in her arms, on what otherwise
might have been a dull Saturday morning in autumn,
proved at least one of us had chosen the cha-cha over cousins.

"Lord today," Aunt Stacia said when she saw Lulu on the
porch with that baby. "Lord, Lord, look at you."

At first, nobody moved to open the screen door. Lulu
Mae was on one side of the screen, grinning and jiggling
that baby up and down like she had herself a bottle of Dairy
Fresh and was trying to mix the milk at the bottom with the
cream on the top. Aunt Stacia stood on the other side of the
screen with me and Pepper. There we were, three females
who were known to have more mouth than they had sense,
struck dumb by a woman-child and her baby. I just kept
blinking my eyes, thinking somehow the wire mesh was
playing a trick on me. But Lulu Mae and that squirming
mess of fat fingers and drooling mouth did not go away.

"C'mon in here," Aunt Stacia said. "Open that door,
Maresa, and let that chile in here. Don't leave her standing
out there. Folks be talking bout us if they see her standing
out there like that."

I opened the door, not because of what folks might be saying, but because it just didn't seem right for us to be standing there gawking at each other. Maybe Aunt Stacia had
forgotten how many times folks had gossiped about us al-

ready. What with Grandma Vernida, who used to get the sanctified holiness and scare all the neighbors, and Aunt Stacia with a houseful of girls who were not her daughters, we had given folks more than enough gossip, even if they didn't count my two uncles, Eddie and Percy—especially Uncle Percy, who was handsome and came from the Island and could speak French, which folks around here thought was really strange for a black person to do. By their notion, all black folks were supposed to have been pulled out of the same colored bag. It's like Grandma Vernida once told my mother, "There's more colored folks in this world than them what's slaving down in Dixie. They got some of us everywhere." And since we seemed to have family just about everywhere, I figured we'd given folks plenty to gossip about already, so Lulu's sudden appearance at the door wouldn't change their habits. But I opened the screen door anyway, and while Aunt Stacia snatched her into the house, I got her suitcase. Once inside, that baby took one look at my aunt and held out its arms.

"Lord, how come they all gotta come home to me?" Aunt Stacia said, but we could see how happy she was holding that baby. I leaned over to take myself a good look at the baby. I wanted to know right away whether or not I could figure out just which one of those Dardanelles might be its daddy, and what kind of baby it was. Aunt Stacia cleared up the mystery for me.

"Lulu, is it a boy or a girl?" she asked.

Lulu Mae grinned. "He's a boy. My little man. Me and Ferro calls him D.P. I bet you can't guess what them initials mean."

Aunt Stacia frowned. "What you saying, chile?"

"You know," Lulu answered. "Like his daddy's name stands for the T. in Booker T. Washington. D.P. stands for something, too."

"Oh, now we got to play a game," Pepper butted in.

She had been standing off to the side, watching Aunt Stacia and me make baby noises. Her tone of voice told us Lulu's return hadn't exactly thrilled her. It was as if all the old arguments were right back in place. At any age, a grudge could be a lifetime cause, except at eighteen, time was a relative thing and grudges could be dropped as fast as they were adopted. I saw I had underestimated Pepper's staying power. Her eyes were full of accusations against Lulu for running off with Ferro Maitland, a boy Pepper had picked for herself.

Pepper grunted. "Miz Lulu's back and we gone play let-me-guess. OK, I'll do it. Don't tell me . . . " She closed her eyes and put one hand on her forehead like she was trying to conjure up something.

Aunt Stacia said, "You behave yourself," but Pepper waved away that caution.

"Don't stop me, Aunt Stacia. I see it." Pepper opened her eyes wide. "Yeah. I know what them initials mean. Lulu Mae named that baby . . . " She paused and hummed the "Dragnet" tune: "Dumb-de-dumb-dumb." Then she grinned and said, "She named him DAR-DA-NELLE! Wonder how I knew that. I oughta go on 'The $64,000 Question,'" she laughed.

Aunt Stacia said, "Portia June, that is not funny."

But come to think of it, it was kind of funny — funny in the way some people can look so pleased with themselves when nobody's laughing at their joke but them. Lulu wasn't laughing one little bit. She gave Pepper a tight-mouthed look like she smelled something bad but couldn't quite figure out the direction of the odor. I knew it wasn't that baby. I couldn't smell any diaper smells even though I was standing close enough for the child to grab my nose, my ears, whatever its chubby little fingers could clutch.

"Lulu, what does the D. really stand for?" I asked.

Pepper started to say, "Maresa, ain't nobody asked you nothing," but Lulu interrupted. "Pepper's right. It's Dardanelle," she said.

"See," Pepper sneered. "And it ain't even a real name. It's the name of some old island in the middle of the ocean."

"It's my baby's name now," Lulu told her, and plucked the baby from Aunt Stacia's arms. "Everybody knows the Dardanelles. We the best dancers on the whole circuit, and the onliest reason we come back to this town is cause we're booked at the Club. Everybody's gone come to see the Dardanelles. Ain't that right, D.P.?" She cooed to the baby, then she shoved her glasses up on her nose with her middle finger, and strutted into the kitchen as if to say to Pepper, "Eat that, Miz Thang."

I said, "Oh-oh... Ohhh," signifying without putting words to it.

Aunt Stacia shook her head. The problem wasn't what the Dardanelles called themselves. The problem was my family didn't want any of us falling under some white folks' notion that all black folks could do was sing and dance, or if we had been boys, no matter how great Sugar Ray Robinson was, become boxers. We didn't have to worry about the boxing part. By the time I was born, the only family children near my age were my cousins Pepper and Lulu. It was as if male children had looked at our family and said, "No way, man," then moved on down the street to the Nelsons, who already had three boys, or to the Pritchards, or over to the Projects with the Maitlands, who had give us Talià ferro and Joaquim – otherwise known as the Dardanelles. Lulu Mae ran off with both of those Dardanelles, and when she returned with the first boy-child the family had produced in two generations, part of the family was torn between wanting to exact punishment for her disappearance, and at the same time, wanting to kidnap that fat brown angel-cherub of a baby to see who could spoil it first. For the rest of us – that is, for me and Pepper – the flak over Lulu Mae's return only meant we had to deal with just how the fallout would affect us, because somehow, the family was sure to connect the consequences of Lulu's behavior with us. And it was the family's brand of rules and retribution that had driven us away from our own mothers and into Aunt Stacia's house in the first place.

Aunt Stacia had inherited all of us when we were about fifteen. We had descended on her after our own mothers, Aunt Stacia's sisters, had thrown up their hands–or as in the case of my mother, when I'd moved out before Mama could throw me out. In less than a year, my aunt had gone from being childless to being a mother of three teenage girls, all born within a year of each other. The spring Lulu Mae came home, Pepper had had her eighteenth birthday a couple of months earlier, while I was looking forward to mine right after the school year began. And Lulu Mae? Well, a week after her eighteenth, Lulu Mae was standing in our doorway, wide-eyed behind her horn-rimmed glasses as if she'd simply returned from a two-year walk and had to ring the doorbell because she'd forgotten her key. We sort of figured that after her trip to the store, she'd bypassed that nonsense about celebrating birthdays. It wasn't that we weren't ready to wish her a happy birthday, but after show-ing up with a baby, following two years and no word from her or the Dardanelles, it didn't seem fitting to say, "Oh, by the way–happy birthday, Lulu Mae." Pepper and I would have let the whole thing slide, but later that week, after we had all gotten used to Lulu's return, Aunt Stacia made us wish her a happy eighteenth. Unfortunately, Pepper was in charge of dessert that day, and while she'd come to terms with the notion of Lulu actually running off with Taliàferro Maitland, she just didn't think Lulu should get away with it scot-free. So Pepper made tapioca pudding, stuck a big old church candle right in the middle of Lulu Mae's tapioca, then handed her the matches so she could light it herself.

It's a good thing Pepper hadn't done that on the first day of Lulu's return. On the first day, it was clear that everyone needed a period of readjusting to Lulu Mae again. There were too many things to remember and too many things to forget. Most certainly, we had to forget that Lulu had simply left town two years before, presumably with that loaf of bread still tucked under her arm, and not bothered to look back. At the time, Aunt Stacia had merely made a few phone calls to satisfy herself regarding Lulu Mae's whereabouts without notifying the police. But for me and Pepper, Cousin Lulu's disappearance was like having some part of us ripped away, and the wound had never quite healed over. Now that she was back, we set about the task of recovering from her departure, but I don't think Pepper or I quite understood how Lulu could have just turned us off and gone on about her business the way somebody turns off a leaky faucet and leaves the house, the door unlocked and wide open.

"Bernice done taught that chile to act like she don't see nothing she don't like," Aunt Stacia used to say. "Lulu ain't just wearing them glasses cause she half-blind. After living with her mama, that chile need some help just to see some of what the rest of us been looking at."

When Lulu first came to live with us, I thought Aunt Stacia was exaggerating because she and her sister Bernice used to fight so much when they were young—"Went at each other like cats," my mother used to tell me—but after Lulu Mae had lived there for a while, I understood what Aunt Stacia meant. Lulu had a habit of borrowing things without bothering to tell the owner. One day, something that had been lost would just turn up near her: a favorite pair of somebody else's blue jeans hugging Lulu Mae's narrow ass, a book stuck up under her pillow—the pages all bent—a hair clip lost until it was spotted on Lulu's head, or in the case of Pepper, a boyfriend whisked away as quietly as Lulu used to swish the dustmop across the parquet tiles in Aunt Stacia's living room. In fact, the last time Pepper had confronted Lulu about taking something that didn't belong to her was the last time all three of us had cleaned Aunt Stacia's house. It had happened a few days after Pepper's birthday, the year we were sixteen, the year Lulu had run away.

I had been on my way to the garbage can with the trash from the upstairs bathroom when I'd spotted Pepper standing in the living room doorway watching Lulu, who was doing her usual hit-miss-and-a-promise dusting of the two front rooms downstairs. Pepper had that look of "I'm gonna get this heifer" in her eyes, and I knew she was still seething from the way Lulu had flounced onto the dance floor with Taliàferro Maitland the weekend before. To make matters worse, on that night Lulu had been wearing something of mine: a sweater with mother-of-pearl flowers all down the front of it that my father, who was in the Merchant Marines, had bought in Hong Kong. I didn't care one way or another about that sweater, actually. If the truth be known, all those gifts had been the reason I'd moved to Aunt Stacia's in the first place. Mama had started accusing me of being ungrateful because I was always complaining about Daddy not being at home. So I'd moved out. Living with Aunt Stacia meant I didn't have to care what my father bought for me, when he was going to be at home, or how long he stayed. Mama said it was like cutting off my nose to spite my face, but at least I didn't have to hear all that crap about not being grateful. Like Pepper, I just plain didn't want to listen to my mother's yapping about "Maresa Hayes, you do this." And "Maresa Hayes, you do that." Still, a gift was a gift, and if Pepper couldn't complain about Lulu stealing Ferro from her, she certainly could complain about her lifting my daddy's gift. So on my way back from emptying the trash, I took a detour to the living room to watch the fight I figured was brewing. What I found was Lulu backed into a corner, the telephone in her hand, and Pepper standing in front of her, her hands on her hips.

"So call her. I dare you," Pepper said.

"What's happening?" I asked.

Pepper answered me without once taking her eyes off

Lulu. "This heifer claims her mama gave her one of them pearl sweaters last year. I told her she better prove it. Go on," she said to Lulu. "Call your mama and ask her when she give you that sweater."

Lulu was shaking, but she dialed the number anyway. I couldn't figure out why Lulu would even try to call her mother. Aunt Bernice had made it clear that she didn't expect to hear from her daughter. But Lulu could be as dense about what folks told her to do as my Aunt Bernice could be about telling folks what to do. According to Aunt Bernice, Lulu had fallen from grace when she'd stopped going to church. Moving in with Aunt Stacia only showed how far she'd fallen. Lulu had as much chance of talking to her mother on the telephone as her mother did in trying to make Lulu go back to the Holiness Temple. Sure enough, Lulu Mae no sooner had her mother on the phone when Aunt Bernice hung up on her. Two days later, Lulu was gone. For weeks after that, Pepper had moped around feeling guilty about making Lulu call her mother.

More than once, we'd heard the women discussing Aunt Bernice's behavior – how Aunt Stacia had been the one left to tend Grandma Vernida after she got sick and took to shouting even when she wasn't in church, but Aunt Bernice had been the one who had had the religion rub off on her. The holiness religion had left Lulu Mae's mother unforgiving and stubborn. My mother would say, "She'll come outta it," and Aunt Stacia would add, "Yeah, we all did and look at us." My cousins and I would look and shake our heads. To us, they didn't seem to have come very far at all, and more than that, they weren't about to let us get very far. While we were living in Aunt Stacia's house, our mothers checked up on us to see how we were doing every Saturday. Moving was supposed to have helped us get away from our mothers, but come Saturday, we could count on Aunt Stacia dragging our mothers to the house. And when they came in, it was inspection time.

I remembered what had happened the time Pepper had jumped so bad behind those boys at the dances, she'd started walking and talking like she was from Spanish Harlem, saying "ting" and "mahn" like she was some kind of Island girl. Imitating the way Uncle Percy talked was one thing, but when she started wearing a crucifix in front of the family instead of slipping it on just before we left for the dance, we all got into trouble. Of course, when Lulu came home with that baby hanging around her neck same as that crucifix stuck up under her blouse, it was different, but back then, wearing a cross could get us all into deep trouble. You have to understand, there were two surefire ways of upsetting the women in my family: one was to make fun of Grandma Vernida's Holiness Sanctified Temple, and the other was to tell those women they didn't know what they were talking about. It didn't matter that they themselves talked bad about the H.S., as Aunt Stacia called Grandma's church, and it didn't matter that half the time, they were running their mouths just to hear themselves think—rules were rules, and if we broke too many, we had to find some place else to live. Or as my mama would say, "If you gonna stay here, you gotta walk the chalk line, sister." Living with Aunt Stacia hadn't removed the line, just its location. So when Pepper had jumped bad at sixteen, and started flaunting a bright gold crucifix on a chain around her neck, we figured she was ready to step off the line.

On Saturdays, our mothers breezed into the house on clouds of talcum powder and kitchen odors, their faces full of "Hello, chile" and "Girl, let me look at you," and their arms filled with packages of this and that meant to sustain us during our unlimited stay at Aunt Stacia's. As usual, Lulu's mother was conspicuously absent, but on Saturdays, Lulu helped the rest of us get ready. On Saturdays, the house would smell like cinnamon toast and mango-flavored tea, and the Motorola would be set with a stack of records that ranged from Sister Rosetta Tharpe's gospel songs to Ray

Charles' honky-tonk. "Can't never tell what them women gone want," Aunt Stacia would say, "but I'm gone give them a little bit of Grandma Vernida's music just so's they feel at home." Then she'd throw back her head and laugh in what we called her "holy-roller laugh" – the one that made Uncle Percy get real jumpy and claim he didn't know what Aunt Stacia had on her mind. The only thing on Aunt Stacia's mind come Saturday was her bossy sisters. And they certainly were on the minds of my cousins and me. With our mothers present, we had to make sure we did everything Aunt Stacia asked of us, even those things we'd avoided during the week. Of course, the threat of being asked to return home made discipline easier for Aunt Stacia, but that threat made it harder for us to understand why Pepper took it upon herself to wear a crucifix when she knew our mothers were coming to visit.

Listening to my mother and her sisters talk and eat was like watching hungry folks trying to dance and all the while, grab food from the buffet table. They didn't miss a step. Uncle Percy told a dance story about where folks had been and where they were going. Sometimes the women in my family told the same story, splitting hairs six ways from the part, taking two steps forward and three steps backward. Sometimes they took far too many steps, and other times, none at all.

We had no sooner sat down to lunch when my Aunt Lil'June spotted Pepper's crucifix. With one breath, she stared at it, and in the next, asked, "Eustacia, just where in the world would any of these childrun be getting some kinda Catholic-type neckpiece?"

Aunt Lil'June searched our faces for an answer, but nobody spoke up for the longest time. Finally, she got to Lulu, and Lulu, with her blabbermouth, came across like a champ. "From them Island boys," she said.

Pepper reached behind Lulu's chair and gave her a big pinch. I said, "Shee-it." But I don't know why we were so bent out of shape. We had always made it a habit never to tell Lulu anything we wanted to keep secret. Lulu could keep a secret about as well as Pepper's mama, Aunt Lil'June — which was not at all. Uncle Percy called Aunt Lil'June's mouth "the black dispatch." He'd say, "You got someting you want put on the grapevine, then you go tell Lil'June. Mahn, she send out the news better than Paul Harvey on the radio."

Now Aunt Lil'June said, "Well, Eustacia, I see Percy Portugal done made you go Island all the way, huh? My husband might be Island same as Percy, but I made sure Eddie wasn't gone give that chile no Catholic upbringing in my house. Big Mama would roll over in her grave if she knew you was raising my chile to be Catholic."

Aunt Stacia grunted. "Why don't you go out to the cemetery and tell her about it, Miz Motor-Mouth? I'm sure your big mouth can reach past the grave."

"Stacia, ain't no needa getting mad with Lil'June," my mother said. "You gone get mad at somebody, get mad at me cause I want to know what that chile's doing with that cross, too. Seems to me like you and Lil'June both done turned Island with your husbands. I ain't saying it's wrong, mind you. When you get yourself hooked up with a strange man, you gotta make some adjustments to what's foreign. And even Big Mama musta knowed something bout foreign stuff. That's why she named me Zenobia. You know, like in the ancient times? It means Bathsheba." My mother sniffed. "It's a pretty name, if I must say so myself."

"Can we stop you from saying it?" Aunt Lil'June asked. "If you don't say it, nobody else will."

Aunt Stacia interrupted before Mama could argue with Aunt Lil'June. "Zenobia, stop it. And Lil'June, you listen too. Ain't no childrun round here gone Catholic."

Aunt Lil'June said, "Bet not. Big Mama didn't take kindly to them Catholic folks and all that missionary stuff they did in Africa."

And my mother waved her fork to get Aunt Stacia's attention. "It don't matter what Big Mama thought, honey. She
dead now. But if Bernice finds out you letting these girls
turn Catholic, she gone have a shit-fit and little babies. You
know she think Lulu's leading a sinful life as it is. Lulu, I
hope you ain't thinking bout turning Catholic. Lord help us
if you are. I sho wish Bernice was here to see bout this."

The women nodded their "Amen" to that, but Lulu just
sat there looking down at her plate with her glasses hanging
on the end of her nose, looking all sweet like butter wouldn't
melt in her mouth. That was the way she usually acted when
our mothers came calling, speaking up at the wrong time
and silent the rest of the time, and everybody thinking she
was so good, being mistreated by her churchified mama and
all while Pepper and I took the flak, so busy watching Lulu
that when Aunt Lil'June slammed her hand on the table, we
jumped.

"How come we can't never stay on the subject? How come
y'all can't stop this jawing and tell me why mah chile done
took it upon herself to put that thing round her neck?"

"What thing you talking bout?" Pepper asked her
mother. "It's the same cross what's on the altar at the H.S.
with the same white man hanging on it."

Aunt Lil'June said, "Ohh, Lord today," and my mother
added, "Have mercy, Jesus! Lil'June, you let Pepper talk to
you like that? You hear what that chile's saying? I wouldn't
let Maresa say them things to me," my mother laughed.
"That chile's gone have her grandmama's spirit eating up
this house. Um-um. Calling that church *H.S.!*"

"That's what you call it," I told her.

"Don't you be sassing me, Maresa Hayes. Don't you be
mouthing off. You best watch yourself, Maresa Hayes," my
mama said.

"Zenobia, you hush," Aunt Stacia said. "You talk about
somebody mouthing off and when you was growing up, you
was sassing Big Mama all the time. And everybody else, too.

So just hush, both of you. Long as you sitting round my mama's dining room table, you can just stop your fussing. Don't matter whether you talking Catholic or H.S. The only difference is which slave master give it to us. Now, pass me some of that buffalo fish. And Lulu, you go change them records on the phonograph. Put on something by Reverend Staples' choir."

The sound of Lulu's chair scraping across the floor almost drowned Aunt Lil'June's complaints. "Humph! She talking bout *my* mama stuff. Just cause Big Mama left everything to you don't mean she wasn't my mama too."

"Just pass the fish, Lil'June. We ain't here to be talking bout who inherited what."

Aunt Lil'June handed Aunt Stacia the platter, but she gave her a look that said she clearly wanted to discuss why Aunt Stacia had been the one to inherit all of Grandma Vernida's belongings.

"Eustacia, you still ain't told us what Pepper's doing round some Island boys," my mother said. "I thought the only Island boy was in this house."

Aunt Stacia stabbed a piece of fish. "Ain't no boys in this house, Zenobia. And you know it."

"So where they be?" my mother asked, all sweet-like.

For a minute, there was only the sound of chewing. Then Lulu looked up. Everyone was staring at her.

"What you looking at me for? Always think I'm gone be snitching on somebody. You see me with some cross? I ain't got no cross. Don't nobody in them Projects be asking me to dance."

Pepper rolled her eyes to the ceiling, and I giggled. Lulu had come through again. I caught Pepper's eye, and mouthed the word BINGO!, while the women started having little hissy-fits.

"The Projects!" they yelled in a chorus of soprano voices that would have gained Reverend Staples' attention, if he'd been in the room instead of leading his choir on the gospel record that was just beginning to play. "What y'all doing at them Projects?"

Aunt Lil'June looked sideways at Aunt Stacia and smirked. "If I remember correctly, somebody told me there wasn't gonna be no more doings in them Projects after all the business with they husband going there."

Aunt Stacia shrugged. "That's old news, Lil'June."

My mother interrupted. "I don't care if it's old nor new, nor whose husband been there, I bet not catch Maresa in them Projects."

And Aunt Lil'June chimed in with, "Pepper, I know you ain't gone tell me you been fooling round in them Projects, girl. I told you before not to go there. Ain't you got no better sense than that? No telling what kinda people be in them Projects. Um-um. That's the last straw. I can't have that. I ain't gone have you taking your butt down to them Projects. No, sir." With each word, she got herself more and more worked up, until finally, she had to wipe her mouth with a napkin.

"Hold it!" Aunt Stacia yelled. "Just make up your mind. You more upset about them Projects or about this chile turning Catholic?"

"You know how we all feel bout them Projects, Eustacia."

"Lil'June, all I know is them Projects is here to stay, and don't matter what folks be saying, they give them people some place to live. And I don't know why anybody in this room is so down on the Projects. This house woulda been IN the Projects if the city hadn'ta run outta money fore they got this far. If Papa had bought a house on the other side of Cottage Grove, we'd be Projects sure as I'm sitting here."

"Well, we ain't," my mother said. "And the Projects ain't sitting here. And ain't no chile of mine gone be in them Projects either, not long as she be a chile. Since I ain't heard different bout no childrun sitting in this room turned grown-up all of a sudden, if somebody tell me Maresa's been in them Projects, she ain't gone be sitting here no longer."

Aunt Lil'June nodded her agreement, and my cousins and I saw Aunt Stacia's eyes fill with disappointment over our behavior.

So we'd tried to straighten up. We'd heard the verdict implicit in my mother's threat: no Project dances or home to Mama until we were old enough to find homes of our own. But like Uncle Percy said, we had smarts. We'd changed to Plan B: the Club Rivieria and the Dardanelles, music by a real-live steel band straight from the Islands. If my mother had known that her ultimatum wouldn've caused us to abandon the Project dances for the supper clubs and throw us, headlong, into the path of Jock and Ferro Maitland, she might have relented. On the other hand, if she'd known that meeting the Dardanelles would've caused Lulu Mae to run away from home, she might have called for a stiffer punishment. And I suppose if anyone had predicted which one of us seemed likely to run off with one of those boys we met at the dances, the choice would have been Pepper, not Lulu Mae. But like old lady Holmes next door said when the weather messed with her garden, "Well, that's water under the bridge." A lot of water had passed under the bridge by the time Lulu returned, but most of it had passed a little slower for us than it had for Lulu.

The morning she came home, I watched her waltz into the house and sit down at the kitchen table, comfortable like no time at all had been spent since she'd last sat there. Aunt Stacia and I followed her, but Pepper stayed where she was in the hallway. Still, as soon as she heard us playing with the baby and asking all kinds of questions about the pictures Lulu had brought with her, Pepper came to the kitchen door, looking all down in the mouth and close to tears. And Lulu, as usual, let her forgetfulness cancel out what had just passed between them.

"Pepper, looka here. Here's a picture we took on the

beach before we got on the ship for the Islands. I'm wearing that blouse you give me."

I giggled. I knew full well Portia June Mason had never in her life willingly given Lulu Mae Roper anything. For a minute, Pepper looked like she was going to jump salty all over again, but she shook it off and came to the table to take a look at the picture. As she sat down next to Lulu, the baby grabbed a hank of hair and sort of swung himself from his mother's arms to Pepper's lap, spraying her face with a raspberry of spit as he made baby noises on his way to his destination. Pepper had no choice but to hold him. We all tried to help her, but if there was one thing little Dardanelle could do, it was hold onto something once it was in his grasp. From the way Pepper was looking at that picture, I figured she wished the same could be said for the baby's father.

"See, Pepper. The boys got on them straw hats you always liked. Y'all member them hats?" Lulu asked me and Pepper.

And we said we remembered, pretending we were looking at Lulu's face in the photo, pretending we were only glancing at the boys dressed as the Dardanelles in midriff shirts, the fronts tied in knots just above their navels, the sleeves layered in ruffles like accordions, and their chests as smooth as if skin color had been painted on silk. We pretended not to be interested in Lulu, who was dressed as Queen Esther, Carmen Miranda style, a big flower in her hair, a fluted skirt hanging on the dangerous end of her hip bones and exposing miles of pale brown thigh. It was too close to the memory of us sitting at the back table in the Club Riviera—Sister Vernida June Garrison's granddaughters as far away from the holiness religion as they could possibly get: their legs brazenly crossed at the knees, cardigans opened two buttons too low past the cleavage they hoped for, and red candlelight painting their lips even redder than the slick coats of Coty they'd layered on. At the Club, King Midas used to sing: *"On the Island you find a man. The sun give him such a permanent tan. All the women they think he is grand. So they follow this Island man."* Too bad King Midas hadn't told me and Pepper that Lulu would be the one to follow this Island man, and we'd be the ones left with souvenir photos.

"Ferro looks like he scared of the camera," Pepper said, still trying to untangle the baby's hands from her hair.

Lulu reached over to help her. "Naw, Ferro was tired, that's all. We just finished three shows at the Palm Tree, and all of us was sick off some bad food we'd had the night before. You remember how Ferro useta like Chinese food? We was always stopping by Wu Fong's. Y'all member?" she asked us.

And we nodded "yes," and tried to signal that we also remembered Aunt Stacia didn't want us eating at Wu Fong's. Every time we'd brought her an ice cream box full of roast duck and soft noodles, the soy sauce leaking through the cardboard like blood, Aunt Stacia would scrape the stuff into a bowl and pick through it to make sure it was just duck and noodles. And we always had to eat a little bit with her, although we were stuffed full after helping Ferro and Jock eat about five boxes of the stuff before we got home. Ferro always ate more than Jock, even though he was skinnier, and we always knew he'd had enough when his eyes started to swell up and turn glassy. That's how he looked on that picture Lulu brought back from Atlantic City: a bug-eyed dark-skin boy grinning on one side of Lulu, his brother, on the other side, laughing straight into the camera's eye.

They were both long-legged and bony, their shirts open to expose gold crucifixes, like the one clearly outlined under Lulu's blouse. It didn't matter that the pictures were in that funny shade of brown like the old-timey ones Aunt Stacia had of Grandma Vernida, I knew those crucifixes were gold as surely as I knew those boys smelled of wintergreen cologne and skin turned hot with the sweat of muscles moving like oil. I have to say, I'd always thought Jock was the handsome one. Jock had a sweet look about him, a teacup full of laughter always playing at the corners of his mouth, and his face was rounder than Ferro's. Ferro looked like his name, kind of weasel-like with too many teeth and a pointy chin. And he could be moody, like Lulu. But both of the boys had the most beautiful eyes anyone could imagine, eyes that would make you move one step closer to the water or climb a rung higher on the ladder, even when you knew you couldn't swim and were afraid of heights. Their eyes were full of devilment, like Uncle Percy's, except Uncle Percy's eyes were beige—"des yeux gouères," he called them—while the boys' eyes were brown and full of dark lines that circled in a pattern, the way the straw did in those reed baskets old lady Holmes used when she was gathering vegetables out of her garden next door. That straw was so dark and those vegetables so bright, it was as if someone had taken a photograph called: "Basket with Flowers," or if it had been music, the sound you'd hear when you listened to a flute on a hot sunny day. Those boys' eyes were full of that music. When I danced with Ferro or Jock, I couldn't look in their eyes. That would make me forget to tell my feet what to do, and if I wasn't careful, I'd look right into that pretty brown laughter and find it pulling me back from a wild spin at the last minute, as if the earth had taken over the spin and gravity had snatched me home.

I was lucky Uncle Percy had taught us how to do Island dances, like the rhumba, mambo, merengue, and cha-cha-cha. I could do them all with my eyes closed. Still, the sweet whisper in the eyes of some Island boy could make me lose track of the steps. Even now, with the pictures, we were losing track of where we were.

"You can just put them pictures away," Aunt Stacia said. "We might as well get this table cleaned off so's we can eat something and you can feed that baby."

She was talking normal enough, but I noticed her hands were fidgeting with the photos. So I said, "Aunt Stacia, don't you think them boys kinda look like Uncle Percy when he gets dressed up to go to his lodge meeting with Uncle Eddie?" I figured a question about Uncle Percy and Uncle Eddie, who were cousins, would help Pepper cool down about Lulu and Ferro. What I didn't know was that I was playing into Lulu Mae's hand.

She laughed. "Y'all forgot to ask me what the other part of the baby's name was. He do have two names, you know," she said.

"What you mean?" I said. "We already know his name."

"You just know the first name," Lulu answered. She waited. We gave her blank looks. "Member, me and Ferro calls him D.P." she added.

"De Pee-Pee," Pepper said, and gingerly handed the baby back to the mother.

Lulu felt his bottom, then smelled her hand. "Aw, he's just wet," she said. "You just wet, ain't you, Dardanelle Purcia? We gone have to change your diaper fore your Uncle Percy gets a look at you."

Surprised, all of us, even the baby, turned to stare at Aunt Stacia. It had never occurred to us that Lulu Mae would call her baby by our Uncle Percy's real name. Aunt Stacia frowned, then scooted her chair back from the table and started gathering the photos. "That name sho is a mouthful for one little bitty baby," she said. "Let's hope he got better sense with it than his uncle. Even if he is as cute as Purcia," she added. And we all laughed.

Before Lulu Mae went off to Oz for a loaf of bread, the three of us could coax our Uncle Percy into doing just about anything we wanted him to do. Part of it was bribery. Part of it was because our uncle was a pushover, pure and simple, so even if we had some dirt on him – which was fairly easy considering how handsome he was and how the women were always flocking to him – we only relied on bribery when we were in a real bind. We had used bribery twice: once to make Uncle Percy take us to the Project dances, and then to make him teach us how to drive his Thunderbird. But we never really needed bribery when it came to dancing. Before Lulu

Mae ran away from home, a day didn't go by without us rolling back the living room rug and turning the Motorola up to full volume. When we first came to live with Aunt Stacia, we only listened to rock and roll. "Why you always got ta turn on thees loud R-and-B stuff?" Uncle Percy would ask. And we'd remind him that the white disc jockeys only played soupy music that didn't have anything to do with black folks. "They don't know diddly bout songs like like 'Dancing in the Street,' 'Stand by Me,' or 'In the Still of the Night,'" we'd say. Not that we had to convince Uncle Percy about the differences in the music white people and black people listened to. Those were the days before cross-over records, the days when the black disc jockeys on all-night party stations were the only ones playing R-and-B, when Dick Clark's "American Bandstand" didn't have everyday black folks on it any more than the crowd scenes in movies and on television did. And when my cousins and I danced the hully-gully, we didn't look like we'd just caught a bad case of the St. Vitus disease, the way those folks did on Dick Clark.

"This is what all the kids at school are doing," we'd say to Uncle Percy, then fall into something like the Slop or the Stroll.

"If you want to do someting all the black people do, then let me teach you how they dance in the Island," Uncle Percy said.

And that's how we came to learn the Island dances. Now that I think about it, watching us learn the intricacies of Island dance must have been painful for Uncle Percy.

"Mahn, don be switchin yourself round like you tryin ta find some place ta sit on the toilet," Uncle Percy would say as steel drums slammed out a rhythm on some bootleg recording of "El Cata." "Sway on the beat, mahn. Move the hips smooth. C'est non se débattre. Move like you writin on the wall and thees ting you write make you feel good."

And we'd sway and sway until our stomachs ached from tightening muscles to make those movements just right. Except Lulu Mae never got it quite right. Lulu Mae always moved too slow, with her eyes half-closed and her face wrinkled up more than old lady Streeter's neck, and I'm here to tell you, Miz Streeter's neck looked like she'd folded it up every night and forgot to iron out the wrinkles in the morning. And when Lulu was trying to remember something complicated, like the Cuban mambo STEP-STEP HIP-TO-HIP BRUSH-BRUSH-SLIDE, her eyes would bug out behind those thick glasses like the headlights on a Chevy. Uncle Percy would stare at her and shake his head.

"Lulu, sweet chile, why you look like somebody who got stuck wit some frog they tryin ta catch for the jumpin contest? And the frog jerkin its head ever-which-a-way and makin some frog-leg moves like it's gone ta wrench the backside from its po head." But Uncle Percy could see Lulu Mae got mad when he picked on her, so he'd laugh and tell us all to "study up on the meanin of thees rhythm what you movin your body for. Ain't you got no sense of why you got ta make the body go thees way and that?"

One day Uncle Percy just plain got tired of looking at us half-step as Lord Invader sang the beauty of *"goin-down-Rockaway,"* with a chorus of steel drums sounding like sea shells tumbling across a coral beach. Uncle Percy groaned as we did something that was a cross between a diddy-bop walk and a boogie break. "Mahn, you doin too much rock and roll stuff," he said. "Some kinda la ripopée. You tryin ta dance like you in a back-up group wit Ray Charles or somebody?"

We shook our heads: No. We'd already tried Doo-wah. Who in the neighborhood hadn't? Everyone had recordings of Mary Wells, the Marvelettes, the Shirelles, and the Chantels. Project kids were as faithful at practicing some kind of routine as any choir member practicing gospel songs. Except for Doo-wah groups singing came second to the routine and a special outfit: sequined dresses, pointy-toed shoes, beehive hairdos, six coats of lipstick, and eyelashes a mile long. We had to be at least as cool as the Chantels, or the Shirelles. We practiced all the time. At school, we diddy-bopped in front of the lockers, and in the summertime, we used the hedgerows and sidewalks as a stage for our practice of synchronized back-up lyrics, while fireflies added their flickers of light. My cousins and I had our routine down pat by the time we were thirteen. We wore identical cardigan sweaters – buttoned up the back – three layers of stiff crinolines under our skirts, high-high pink satin heels, and matching pink gloves – because a good doo-wah was as much hands as feet.

Our special routine was a Doo-Wah-Shoop: DOUBLE FIST-TURN-STEP-STEP – SLIDE-KICK . . . CLAP-CLAP-CLAP-AIR-PLANE-WINDMILL . . . doo-ooh-wee-ahh. It was so cool, we added bubble gum to a step-clap-clap beat, timing the bubbles so they popped out right on the musical cue. It was better than those dumb hoola hoops the Greenlee girls had, but I have to admit, after all those doo-wahs, our Island dancing looked more like crabs scuttling sideways than sweet calypso.

Uncle Percy said, "Lord Invader don be asking for no mop for you ta scrub the floor, mahn. Thees music it comes from Afreeka through the Islands. It is how we go back from here ta the old country where the people have the Afreekan way." Then he pulled out a big piece of butcher paper he'd brought home from the post office where he worked at night, and drew circles that were supposed to show us how the steel drums were hammered into patterns for musical notes. But seeing our ignorance, Uncle Percy's lesson on steel drums shifted to a lesson on how slave trade routes moved from Africa to the Islands to America.

"It is all in the music," he told us. "The drums tell you how thees ting goes. On the steel drum you got some notes round the circle and one note always in the middle. You got only five notes wit the bass pan, but how many you got wit the ping-pong pan, huh?" We giggled. Uncle Percy stared at us.

I guess he started with me because I just couldn't stop giggling. "Maresa, why you tink it so funny when I say ping-pong pan?" he asked. I shrugged and tried to swallow my laughter, so he moved on. "And you, Miz Lulu... you tink thees music is funny? Maybe you, Pepper? Thees is funny to you too, huh?" His face didn't say funny at all.

"No, we don't think it's funny," we told him, sobering up like good little chickens. "Un-un." "No way." "No, not us."

Our protests did not fool Uncle Percy. "You see, thaat is the problem wit childrun today. You make a joke for everyting. Thees music is serious. On thees drums we have the history of the black people. All the notes here... Movin in and out like our people been moving when they took the slaves outto Afreeka." He pulled his finger around the rim of a circle. "The music is from Afreeka." When you hit the drum here—it goes, cleep... " He patted the edge of the circle. "... you get the big notes. Then you go round ta get a different sound. Dink... " He moved from the outer rim to a smaller circle drawn nearer the center. "One sound here... and one sound there. But no matter where you hit the drum, you tell about when the Mahn take us outto Afreeka and the ships move cross the big ocean. All that we know is here in the drum." Uncle Percy ran his finger around the rim of the circle. "It is the old country and many centuries of the black people. The song and the dance. But when thees ships move ta the Islands, we maybe loss some tings." His hand traced the circle again. "Then the Mahn he bring us here in thees country." Uncle Percy pulled his hand dead center of the circle. "Here the Mahn take everyting. No song. No dance. No place where we can go. You see, it is very far away from Afreeka. They tink we forget, mahn. But we remember."

"Percy, how come you acting like you know so much?"

Aunt Stacia asked him. "The way you tell it, none of us know nothing less'n we from the Islands. Why you always got to be syndicating bout them Islands? We was all slaves out there in them fields, Aye-lands or no Aye-lands."

"Woman, you listen up ta what I been sayin. I know the Mahn have us all in slavery. But I tell thees childrun bout the Islands cause many great mahn come from thaat place. That is where the great Marcus Garvey come from. And the poets like Countee Cullen and Nicolàs Guillèn. And even thees boy, thees Harry Belafonte, who come over here singing thaat day-o calypso stuff with his shirt open down ta the navel. Thay all come from the Islands, mahn."

Aunt Stacia grunted, "Humph... If they so great, how come they always got to be coming FROM them Aye-lands? And how come you ain't got no women come from them great Aye-lands?"

"What I want to know bout some Island woman? I got mah woman right here... eh, mon 'e chou?" he'd laugh, teasing Aunt Stacia with his best cat-eyed look. "I just tell thees childrun what I know bout the Island music and how ta look for why it comes ta be played thaat way. They got ta know what the music can do for the black people."

"I ain't worried bout what the music do for black people," Aunt Stacia said. "I'm worried bout what them players gone do to these girl childrun."

Aunt Stacia had good reason to be worried. I never figured out exactly why Aunt Stacia put up with our foolishness. At the time, I thought she did it because she'd had no children of her own. Later, I decided she was either crazy or a saint. Certainly the three of us gave her enough reasons to achieve sainthood, sneaking out of the house on Saturday night to go to the Project dances when we didn't have permission. "Why don't y'all go to some of them high school dances," Aunt Stacia said when she finally found out where we were going, but by that time, it was too late. We had al-

ready met boys name Eduardo, Tiño, Henri, and Rafael.
And of course, Taliàferro and Joaquim. All of them from
the Projects.

The Projects were called the War Zone, and kids who
went to the vocational high school, right next door to the
Projects, were known as the Warriors and the Bloods. Most
of them came from families that had moved from the South
or the Islands during the war, when factory work was available. Aunt Stacia said Grandma Vernida used to tell her
what it was like before the city tore down the tarpaper
shacks in the flatlands and built the Projects. She said
Grandma Vernida had even seen black folks jumping off
the trains down in the flatlands, folks who had set up house-
keeping almost on the same spot where they'd jumped from
the train. When the war was over and the city put up the
Projects, some of those folks got stuck there. My cousins and
I went dancing in the Projects, but we were always happy we
had some place else to go when the dancing was over.

But those Project boys didn't mess around when it came
to dancing. Those boys were hip even though the dances
were nothing more than sock hops. The three of us had ruined many a pair of socks until one summer when Aunt
Stacia caught us hiding our dirty clothes in the basement,
and made us wash everything until the Project dirt was out
of them. After that, we wore dancer's slippers with clunky
heels and soft leather soles, and the boys thought we were
uptown Puerto Ricans moved in from Spanish Harlem.
They were the ones most likely to have come from Spanish
Harlem, but uptown they were not. Project boys were different from the ones in our neighborhood. The boys we
grew up with were stuck-up and thought they were cute because they belonged to the right clubs and the right church,
because they went to camp in the summer, wore letter
sweaters, and played basketball at the Y in the winter. Project boys hung out on the street corner and wore leather

jackets. They usually went to the vocational high, and their families were the ones left without jobs when the war ended, and the factories and railroad yard cut back on workers. If those boys had jobs after school, they were likely to be cleaning up at the gym where the white boxers trained, running numbers for the local gamblers, or helping their mothers clean houses out in the ritzy Belmont District. When Ferro and Jock got their first gig dancing at the Club Riviera, everybody in the Projects said they'd gone big-time, and crowded around them when they dropped by the Project dances for old times' sake. The one thing you could count on in the Projects was some cool dancing partners on Saturday night.

No matter what those boys looked like in school with their ratty clothes and chewed-up pencils, when they hit the dance floor, they turned into Belafonte, Piro, and Cuban Pete, all rolled into one. Out there on the dance floor, with the rhythms of a steel band singing like palm trees kissing each other at the edge of an ocean, those boys were hot, their open shirts framing chests so hard and muscular, they seemed carved from stone. In the seventh grade, a museum trip to see marble statues had given me and my cousins a first-time look at a man's naked body, all long-limbed with muscles stretched flat across broad chests, and penises, like budding flowers, cradled in the nests of thighs. There, we were wide-eyed, little black girls staring at sights our church-going mothers absolutely had forbidden us to see. We were giggly, shoving and elbowing each other, afraid to touch the smooth marble, the out-thrust hip so inviting our fingers itched to press against it. We didn't know much more by the time we started going to the Project dances, but we pushed against those boys and imagined the statues. On the dance floor, their skin glistened with beads of sweat that winked like jewels in the dim light, and we were like little kids learning what the word "hot" really meant – sticking out our hands just to see if the touch really would burn our fingers. Let me tell you, it did. And that was all the more reason to go back for more.

Dancing with the Dardanelles was like stepping onto concrete in the summer in bare feet. It was so hot, we had to move. When those boys danced, they grabbed us and hung on until the last note. Some of the little kids playing in the street near Aunt Stacia's house had Gumby dolls that kept whatever shape they were bent into. That's how we acted when the Project boys grabbed us, especially Ferro and Jock. Like the other boys from the Projects, they wore their hair glued down by Brylcreme and water. They were boys with no shoulders and biceps as big as Popeye's. Boys with hard chests, and tight pants covering an ass like a fist. Boys with bean breath and eyes like liquid. Boys who slid by and asked us to dance like they were snitching something off a rack while looking the other way, looking cool. They used their hands like they were driving stock cars: one hand clutching a chunk of some girl's butt, the other low down at her side to shove her in gear. The phonograph's blast of the drummer's first beat was the flag to tell them they were off and running. Jock could move his hips so I'd forget to listen for the sound of the congas. And Jock loved to dip. Ferro did too, but Ferro would bend my body down from the small of my back, and at the same time, pump me onto my toes and off center until one hip was brought up to meet his oncoming hip. And that was just a mambo spin. But don't get me wrong, the Project boys weren't into belly-rubbing grope-and-grind like at the high school dances where church boys waited until the lights were low, and copped a feel in the middle of the huckle-buck.

All of the Project boys were smooth, completely Island like Destinè and Prado. The floor was always packed tight with bodies, and when some boy locked you in a dance, your very bones picked up the Latin heat of drums until, like the air in the room, nothing moved before the drummer moved. The problem was that sometimes, at the end of the dance, the very same boy who had moved his hips like you were the last uncharted continent he wanted to march into, would turn on his heels and walk away—no word, just a glimpse of him trucking toward some other unexplored territory. So we learned to do that too—dance all close with them, then turn it off as soon as the music ended. Lulu had learned that lesson too well. She had walked out of our lives, past that grocery store, and into unknown territory with the Dardanelles.

We were sitting on the porch, and Aunt Stacia was singing to Lulu's baby, who was fretting for a nap: *"Go tell Aunt Rosie... Go tell Aunt Ro-oh-sie... Go tell Aunt Rosie, the old gray goose is dead. The one she's been saving to make a feather bed."*

She was sitting beside Lulu Mae, the baby between them on a pallet in the porch swing. We had finished up the breakfast dishes, and had come outside to wait for Uncle Percy to wake up. It was one of the last few days of good weather when the wind still carried enough summer heat to make being outdoors tolerable. The shadows of leaves from the hickory tree dappled the baby's bare back with patterns, like the birds and flowers on the crib blanket Aunt Stacia had dug out of the attic and given to Lulu—"In honor of Grandma Vernida's first great-grandbaby," she'd said. But Aunt Stacia hadn't invited our neighbors, Dee Streeter and Corella Holmes, onto the porch to see the baby. Those old ladies had been sniffing around the edges of the yard since we'd come outside. I saw them watching and nudged Pepper.

She laughed. "I guess they want to meet Pee-pee."

"I told you me and Ferro calls him D.P.," Lulu said, and brushed a fly away from her child's head.

"How come you didn't bring that baby's daddy over here with you?" Aunt Stacia asked Lulu.

Lulu didn't answer, so I said, "I think Danny P. sounds better than P.P. Don't you, Aunt Stacia?"

"Lulu Mae, I asked you a question," Aunt Stacia said. "How come you didn't bring that chile's daddy home with you?"

"He's coming," Lulu told her.

"When?" Aunt Stacia asked.

Lulu let the whisper of leaves in the hickory tree answer Aunt Stacia's question. For a moment, she was the old Lulu again and the three of us were sixteen, sitting on Aunt Stacia's front porch waiting for evening when we could sneak out of the house. Lulu had her eyes half-closed so we could see more of the rim of her glasses than her face. Pepper was sitting beside me on the steps, a stalk of sweetgrass stuck in the gap between her front teeth, and I was chewing on a flower petal I had pinched from a bloom in the clump of marsh poppies growing near the porch. The flower was one of those big cheesy ones that we had liked to eat when we were kids. Except we were no longer kids, and Aunt Stacia was still waiting for Lulu to tell her where Ferro Maitland was.

"What's that baby's last name?" Aunt Stacia asked Lulu.

We knew she was asking if Lulu and Ferro were married, but Lulu evaded the question. "Ferro says it don't matter what we call him long as he ain't got no family but us. I went off to the Projects and met Ferro's folks yesterday fore I come here."

The sheer boldness of her actions stunned me and Pepper. Lulu had always been one with the downcast eyes and whispers, waiting on someone to tell her she was doing right. But not anymore.

"What's that got to do with the price of potatoes?" Aunt Stacia asked her. "We family, too."

"Ferro ain't met Mama yet," Lulu answered. The porch swing creaked as gently as her breathing. "I ain't gone ask him to come here till he can do that."

Aunt Stacia sort of moaned and sighed, "Oh chile... "

"That's how come I waited till Saturday," Lulu continued.

"I figured you could call Mama. Everybody still come over on Saturday, don't they?" She didn't pause long enough for anyone to answer her. "if my mama's gonna be here at all, it's gone be on Saturday. You go on and call her, Aunt Stacia. I'll wait."

Pepper snapped off her sprig of sweetgrass, and I snatched the last petal from the poppy I was holding. My cousin and I looked from Lulu to Aunt Stacia to Lulu again. For the first time, I saw Aunt Stacia wasn't doing so well in this standoff. Lulu was staring straight at Aunt Stacia, who was looking down at her lap where her hands rested, curled up like the leaves get when the first chilly rains of autumn hit them. And here it wasn't even October yet. None of that seemed to faze Lulu. She just rocked that porch swing like she had all the time in the world, and at that point, I saw the new Lulu as she was. It occurred to me that I'd been missing something about her all morning. Unlike the Lulu Mae of two years ago, this Lulu never hesitated to demand answers. This Lulu took charge and didn't wait for anyone to ask her opinion. This Lulu had maps of towns in her head that we had not learned the names of yet. And she had done something that women in my family had yet to do – she had left home and returned. She no longer needed their version of the world and its sins. But there was no way the Lulu we saw would pass our mothers' inspection. Even without that baby, the crucifix she had hanging around her neck would raise their hackles. That alone would surely make Aunt Bernice rant about Lulu's fall from grace.

In the past, Aunt Stacia had tried all sorts of tactics with Aunt Bernice. If any of her other sisters didn't show up one week, by the next week, Aunt Stacia would force them to visit on the pretext of helping her bake a cake for the ladies of social club, or finish sewing one of us a dress she was perfectly capable of finishing herself in an afternoon, if left alone. And when they did show up, Aunt Stacia would nag us to clean our rooms so our mothers could see how well-behaved we'd become once we'd left their houses. But it was a kind of conspiracy that had worked out fine for me and Pepper, who wanted our mothers to see us having a wonderful time away from home. And it had worked for Aunt Stacia, who had never quite forgiven her older sisters for abandoning her to take care of their mother, my Grandma Vernida. In fact, the conspiracy of guilt had worked with everyone but Aunt Bernice. She had had fifty dozen reasons for not coming by, and fifty different ways of juggling those reasons to make it seem like she really was unable to make the trip. So when Lulu Mae sat on that porch defying Aunt Stacia to call her mother, it was as if she'd forgotten all the times Aunt Stacia had tried to get her sister to visit like everyone else. Lulu sat there looking like she'd carved a whole new set of rules to live by, and one by one, she was telling us what they were. So we were grateful when Uncle Percy interrupted.

"Why you all come outside thees mornin?" he asked. "I come down for some coffee and mahn, I don't find nobody in the kitchen."

He was still standing inside the house, so he hadn't seen Lulu. Although he was half-hidden by the screen door, I could tell his face was rumpled with sleep. It may have been past noon, but for Uncle Percy, who worked the graveyard shift at the post office, it was early morning. And in Uncle Percy's mind, walking out of the house meant you were on your way somewhere. Like Aunt Stacia sometimes said, "Purcia was on his way out of this town when I met him, and he still think you don't step out the house less you gone travel." The idea of sitting on the porch on any morning made no sense to Uncle Percy, and that morning, my uncle didn't yet know that Lulu Mae had ended her travels on his porch.

Uncle Percy shoved open the door and asked, "Stacia, why you got ta be sittin wit thees girls? Don't you know my stomach is cryin for some food when I get outto the bed?"

That's when he saw Lulu. "Sacré bleu! Is it a ghost? What it is the cat drag here? Is thees Lulu Mae I'm seein? Maybe my old eyes trickin me. C'est bon comme la vie. C'mon, chile, ta your Uncle Percy."

Watching Lulu rush into Uncle Percy's arms really wicked off Pepper. "She oughta sit herself down," Pepper muttered as Lulu jumped out of the swing so fast, she woke up the baby. Hearing D.P.'s cry sent Uncle Percy into another round of: "What it is I see here?"

He pulled himself away from Lulu and picked up the baby. "What it is here? Mahn, what is thees?"

"You know what it is," Aunt Stacia told him. "Somebody think you be wanting a baby round here the way you carrying on." She was looking more at the old women next door than she was Uncle Percy. When they saw Aunt Stacia eyeing them, they grinned and waved, but it did them no good. Aunt Stacia was having too many problems with family to add Corella Holmes and Dee Streeter to her list.

"Put that baby down, Percy. You holding him up like he's some kinda trophy you done won."

"Oh, he is a champ alright," Uncle Percy laughed. And D.P. came through like a champ. He burped a dollop of sour milk and gurgled at his uncle. "Stacia, give me someting for ta wipe thees babee. He is so happy ta see his Uncle Percy, it make his stomach dance."

Pepper said, "That does it," and stomped into the house. I was going to follow her, but Aunt Stacia asked me to help get stuff for the baby. So I stayed there while Lulu rummaged around in her diaper bag. But I still had it on my mind to get away from that porch as soon as possible. That is, until Uncle Percy said, "Well now, Lulu, you tell me all you been doin." Hearing that, I thought I'd stick around for a bit.

"They tell me you goin on the stage now," Uncle Percy added. "It ain't so good ta be movin about when you got a babee."

Lulu said, "We don't move that much, Uncle Percy. Before the baby, we was in New York and Tampa. And we was over round Maryland and Virginia some too. But that was before we went to the Islands."

"You been over in them Islands?" Aunt Stacia asked.

Lulu laughed. "Of course we have. I told you that, Aunt Stacia. Member them pictures we took on the beach? That was the Islands. You member, Maresa?"

I shrugged. "Yeah... I remember... Some... "

"Too many things to be remembering," Aunt Stacia said. She was watching Uncle Percy play with Danny P. like he'd never seen a baby before. "I got enough trouble keeping up with things going from day to day," she added.

"Lulu, when you go ta the Islands, you go ta the French or the British?" Uncle Percy asked.

"Naw, we didn't get to where you was born, Uncle Percy. There was too many Maitlands for me to meet, so we only went to one place. And when the baby come, all of them wanted to see me all over again. I musta met a hundred Maitlands out on that Island."

"Well, now thees baby got ta meet the Portugals and the Garrisons and the Masons and the Hayes and the Ropers."

Uncle Percy bounced D.P. every time he called out a family name. But we noticed he'd left Lulu's until the last.

"I bet your mama got a big smile on her face seein her fine grandbabee, eh Lulu?" The baby cooed, eyes big as his mother's.

Aunt Stacia tried to hush Uncle Percy, but Lulu answered in a loud voice, "I don't know what Mama got on her face. I ain't seen Mama for more'n two years and Mama ain't seen this baby a'tall, Uncle Percy. You member the last time she was over here."

I watched Uncle Percy stop jiggling the baby and turn to Lulu. He frowned at her and I could see he actually was trying to remember the last time Aunt Bernice had visited. I thought: *"He should be remembering the last time Lulu Mae ended her visit."* But I wasn't going to say anything. I'd had enough "you remember" to last me longer than that day.

Uncle Percy said, "What you be tellin me, chile? You better take thees babee ta see his grandmama."

"Not if she don't want to see me," Lulu said.

"Percy, Bernice won't talk to the chile."

And Lulu added, "When I called her, she said: 'The voice sound familiar but I just can't place you.'"

Uncle Percy handed D.P. to his mother. "I don understand your people, Stacia. What is the matter wit thaat woman? This be her flesh and blood." Aunt Stacia shrugged. "I don know bout your sisters, Stacia. I don know why they be actin so funny." He stood up. "But I don like it. I don mind when the childrun come here, but mahn, it ain't right ta be leaving them like don nobody care."

This time, Aunt Stacia managed to signal Uncle Percy to be quiet. He saw it, but it didn't really stop his train of thought.

"Ahh... what it is I say? Your sisters make me boil, Eustacia. Sometimes I come ta be fairly disgusted wit them women," he said. "Bernice gone ta bring herself here for ta see her grandbabee or my name ain't never been Purcia Por-tugal."

"Percy, you stay out of it," Aunt Stacia called as my uncle walked down the stairs. "Percy, you hear me?" she repeated. The old ladies next door stopped looking at us out of the corners of their eyes, and turned to face our house straight-on. So Aunt Stacia waved at them. "Damn," she whispered. "Now I got to talk to them old biddies." Then she called out, "Percy... "

"Je vais lui foutre un galop," Uncle Percy answered, knowing how he frustrated the neighbors when he spoke French – "Like the Islands."

"Percy, you don't need to bring nobody here. Stay out of

it," Aunt Stacia repeated, but Uncle Percy was already at his car. "Lulu, you coulda handled this some other way," Aunt Stacia told my cousin.

Lulu smiled. At least, that is the way it looked from one angle. From the other angle, without her glasses clouding the view, it was more of a smirk than a smile. Lulu kept that half-smile in place until Aunt Stacia turned to greet her neighbors, waving "Hello" as if she had just that moment recognized the two of them.

Then Lulu said to me, "C'mon. Let's go see what Pepper's doing upstairs."

While Aunt Stacia walked to the gate to deal with old lady Streeter and Holmes, I followed Lulu into the house. Even with that baby in her arms, she walked with her back straight and her rear end swaying as if she had done nothing all her life except dance with the Dardanelles. In a way, she seemed to have taken on some of Ferro's characteristics, the chameleon look he had when one minute, he was the youngest partner in the Dardanelles, and the next, he was upstaging Jock with every move. That's the look I'd been seeing in Lulu all morning. Pepper used to say that, glasses or no, Lulu looked like she was trying to see through water and fight her way clear of it. Now it occurred to me that the real Lulu had floated to the surface and shed the cover of water the way trees shed their leaves for winter. Maybe she wasn't as twig-thin as she'd been before she'd had the baby, but she seemed to have turned as hard-edged as tree limbs did in winter. Even her walk suggested the sway of trees in the wind. It made me feel like I was sixteen and silly all over again. It was as if I had stayed in one place while Lulu had moved on without me. I didn't like that feeling. I wanted the old Lulu back, the one who'd snuck out of the house on Saturday nights, and acted as dumb as me and Pepper.

Nobody had told us dumb was only a look, so we had taken it on as serious business. We wore satin skirts, the material from Woolworth's and the pattern from Butterick, slinky-straight and extra tight. Pepper wore hers with a side slit cut clear up to her thigh. And I'm here to tell you, Pepper had some thighs on her – "thunder thighs," we called them. Me? I added three layers of flounce to the bottom of my skirt, and every time I tripped across the floor, I looked like I was going to audition for a part in some movie about flying off to Rio de Janeiro, or some place. And I looked like I was ready to fly all by my lonesome. But in those days, Lulu was the one who seemed to be only half there. She'd take off her glasses, and without them, she was so nearsighted, her eyes were wide with the strain of seeing past anything that wasn't right in front of her nose.

We'd always tried to time our arrival at the Club Riviera to coincide with the last part of the R-and-B set. The Riviera was part bar, part club, with live music nights on Fridays and Saturdays when the R-and-B dance band traded off sets with the steel band. In those days, some white folks might have known about the Ink Spots and Nat King Cole, but none of them could have identified King Creole's Calypso Band, Perez Prado, or Lord Invader. At the Riviera, the R-and-B warmed up folks for some righteous steel drum Latin beats. That music transformed the Riviera into Club Havana straight out of Cuba, or the Folies Bergère, where everyone knew Josephine Baker could rhumba meaner than anything seen outside of the Islands. I say this because for us, that place was magic and we were unbelievably shy, shy the way black girls could be when they had bought into that racist crap about how being black made them automatically cool and in the know about sex and all that goes with it – and that, in turn, made them run a bluff they couldn't put down for fear of finding out just how little ground was under their feet. In those days, we ran that bluff by sitting at a back table at the Club Riviera. Both of the Riviera bands were hot, and by the time they really started cooking, with the crowd clapping their hands, and screaming "aRRRiba!" in an ear-splitting trill of *R*'s jitterbugging out of everybody's mouth,

King Midas would yell: "Ladies and Gents, and all those who ain't – It's SHOW TIME at the Club Riviera." And then we'd get the Dardanelles. To us, they never seemed to stand still, partly an illusion of the chandelier ball spinning above their heads, and partly because we knew they were going to come over and pick one of us for a dance. My cousins and I would scream louder than anyone else. By the time that band turned up the heat on those steel drums, timbales, and congas, they were glistening with sweat and so were we. And all the time, we swore we were cool, shaking our hips like we could wear out a dress from the inside.

"Looking sixteen and going on thirty ain't too bad." That's what Bruno had said the first time he served us. Bruno was the bartender, and he called out the names of drinks as if they were words in a scat-man's song: *"gin-mill-double-fizz, Johnnie-Walker-Red-and-milk, C.C.-coming-up-on-seven"* – whatever the traffic would bear. The traffic at the Riviera would bear most anything, and Bruno presided over his menagerie of bottles, bar stools, and plate-sized tables – their candles trapped in tiny red-lacquered cages – while a revolving ball coated in slivers of glass sprinkled pin-points of light over the miniature stage and dance floor. At first, we let Pepper order for us. "A Manhattan, straight-up," she'd purred, her voice pitched real low trying to imitate movie stars in films where men were Belafonte-cool and danced with women, like Dorothy Dandridge, who always had husky voices. Pepper had practiced smoking, so she'd tried her Bette Davis trick of blowing out a match without taking the cigarette from her mouth. At home, Lulu and I had applauded when she finally had learned to kill the match without showering us with sparks from the cigarette. But Bruno hadn't been impressed one little bit.

"You got a choice," he'd told us. "Canada Dry with or without the cherry."

It wasn't the kind of statement that invited a challenge, so we went for broke. All of us had said, "Cherry," except

Lulu. She'd said, "No cherry, thank you," in a small voice, and all the time looking down in her lap.

I saw Bruno smile. "Take your glasses off, kid," he'd told Lulu.

She'd grabbed her specs as if she thought Bruno would snatch them away from her. "I can't see without my glasses," she'd mumbled.

Bruno had grunted. "In here, you ain't missing much. Besides, some cats like thinking a chick can't move less they got the lead. Get it?" He'd grinned. Lulu had grinned back, but all of us got it.

From that point on, Bruno served our Virgin Marys in tall glasses, cherries on top, while Lulu got hers in a champagne glass, a half-slice of lime clinging to the side. From that point on, whenever she was in the Riviera, Lulu took off her glasses and left one eye shadowed by a flower she'd pinned in her hair. But you can't go from playing Dorothy Dandridge out of Porgy and Bess to actually being Dorothy Dandridge, and it seemed to me that Lulu Mae had drifted home from the Dardanelles thinking she really was somebody's idea of Dorothy Dandridge. The problem was that nothing had changed except what was in her head. While Lulu Mae had been busy forgetting the way home, all we had was a memory of her. That's why she didn't need to keep getting on everyone's nerves by saying: "You remember?" What we remembered was already enough to get on our nerves.

I found Pepper sitting up in her bed when I got to the room. She had left my bed untouched, but Lulu's bed, the one we'd been using to hold our dirty clothes, was piled high with clothes, books, shoes, and whatever else Pepper could find to cover it.

"Where's that heifer?" she asked. Then she punched the pillow like it was a catcher's mitt. "Where's Miz Thang?"

"Down the hall putting the baby to sleep in Aunt Stacia's bed."

"I'm sick of her," Pepper said. "Coming in here like she knows everything and we don't know nothing. Talking bout: member this? Member that? What she think I am? The Encyclopedia?"

"Just let it rest," I said. "Let it rest." Then I plopped down on my bed and tried to clear my head of everything that went with thinking about Lulu and her baby. That was difficult. I realized life had been a lot easier before 7:00 A.M. when Lulu had rung that doorbell. "What are we gonna do?" I asked Pepper.

She stopped filing her nails long enough to glare at me. "Why do WE have to do anything? WE didn't run off nowhere. You didn't see me slipping outta here and getting myself preg-nut, did you?" The angle of her nail file was directly in line with the light filtered past the hickory tree. I shook my head, No, meaning none of us could slip out of the house. The tree limb we'd used had been cut clean down to the trunk by Uncle Percy the year Lulu ran away. There was a scar on the cross section of trunk where the limb had been sealed with tar, and the center glowed yellow-brown, like skin in the sunlight.

"WE ain't gone do diddly-squat," Pepper said.

I said, "I guess not," and closed my eyes, trying to take my own advice about resting. It still wasn't easy. The very air betrayed me. The room smelled like me and Pepper: her Bluegrass cologne and the Chanel No. 5 my father sent me every Christmas. There was still a faint aroma of Bergamot Hair Oil, Noxzema, and Pepper's ever-present bottle of Witch Hazel for her pimples. But underneath it all, I picked up the scent of Lulu's Cuticura Ointment and Avon Magnolia Blossoms, although we'd packed away Lulu's stuff long ago. Even the extra desk was sitting in the hallway, and her bed, under the mass of stuff Pepper had put on it, was made up like a sofa. But despite our cleanup, Lulu had never left that room. We'd just been faking it, and we would have kept faking it, even with her return, if she hadn't walked into the room and pretended to ignore all the stuff Pepper had piled on her bed.

Lulu sat herself on that pile without even bothering to look at what might be under her. "I wish I coulda brought my Queen Esther dress for you to see," she said, "cept it's too big to fit in that little old suitcase. I ate so much, I put on a little weight after the baby, you know." She showed us her dimpled knees. "Couldn't seem to stop eating. But what I really missed was them bags of caramel corn we useta get from Sears. Girl, sometimes I swear I could member just how that stuff smells when you first get off the elevator. You know, right there by the shoe department. I can't wait to pick up a bag. I know the stuff's fattening, but Ferro likes me a little on the plump side though. What you think? You member how I was always trying to keep from putting on too much weight, an . . . "

Without opening my eyes, I interrupted. "Lulu Mae, if you ask us to remember one more thing, I'm gone wring your neck."

"Girl, you ain't changed a bit," she said. "You was always running off at the mouth.

"You know, she don't even listen to her ownself," Pepper said.

"You can't listen when your lips be flapping," I muttered.

"And I still have trouble membering all the words to songs," Lulu said. "It's the same as when we useta go to the Club Riviera. Even before that. Y'all remember how I useta sing: *'granite Jesus if you please?'* I thought Jesus was made outta some kinda stone."

The bed creaked as Pepper stood up on it. When I opened my eyes, she was poised to throw the pillow at Lulu's head. I yelled, "Pepper, don't you do that! Let me!"

Lulu sort of half-covered her head. "This is just like old times," she giggled.

I groaned. Pepper let the pillow fly and yelled, "Will you shut up with the old times, for Chris'sake?"

The pillow knocked Lulu's glasses cockeyed across her nose, but her hurt look was not about her glasses. "I thought y'all would be glad to see me come home." Pepper grunted and fell back onto the bed. I plopped down again too. We were about to be had. Lulu had put on her chameleon look – the "what-about-li'l-old-me?" expression. That was the look she'd used when the Dardanelles bounced onto the floor after King Midas warmed up the crowd with a couple of easy pieces, like "Stardust Mambo," or "Goza Cha-cha-cha." It was the look that got Ferro's attention when the boys were ready to pick partners from the audience for their demonstation number. Pepper would say, "He just talked to her cause she was sitting there looking like she just been sucking her thumb." It had worked with Ferro. Now Lulu was trying it on us. Why not? It was what she remembered, and we'd done nothing to set her straight on how we'd changed.

"You didn't even write," I said.

Lulu settled her glasses back onto her nose and whispered, "I guess I just forgot."

Pepper sat up in the bed. "Ohh mahn, leesten ta thees girl, eh? Thaat boy screw her so good she forget how ta read and write."

"Naw, we was busy," Lulu said. "It's like I told Uncle Percy, we played clubs from here to the Islands and back. It didn't have nothing to do with sex. Besides, y'all had boyfriends. I mean, I know y'all ain't still virgins."

I looked at Pepper. We both knew that was a question, but it wasn't one we were about to answer. "What makes you think we'd tell you about it, Miz Rusty Butt?" Pepper snapped.

"I was always talking bout y'all," Lulu whimpered. "Ferro didn't like it that I was talking bout y'all so much. He said... "

"Lulu, has it ever occurred to you that we don't give one diddly-damn about what Ferro likes and don't like any-

more? We ain't been to the Projects since the riots. We don't
even go to the Riviera. We listen to jazz now."

Teary-eyed, she stared at Pepper. "But you useta..."

I sat up so abruptly she stopped mid-sentence. "Lulu Mae
Roper, you can't just waltz in here and expect to take up
where you left off like we just been waiting for you to come
home so's we can finish the next sentence. And it won't do
you one bit of good to be telling us to remember stuff all the
time. I spect we remember better than you do anyway. But
that don't matter. We just ain't the same folks as when you
left. Like Pepper said, we listen to jazz now, and go over to
the Y to go swimming. And Aunt Stacia was sick all last winter. And my mama had an operation." Lulu opened her
mouth as if to say something, but I held up my hand to stop
her. "What I'm trying to say to you, Lulu Mae, is we been living while you been Lord-knows-where. You didn't tell us
where you was going, even though we were supposed to be
telling each other everything. So now that you are back,
don't be trying to play catch-up."

Lulu was really crying by that time. "I don't know what to
do."

"You can start by saying: 'I'm sorry,'" I told her.

"Then you can get your butt off my clothes," Pepper said.

We let her cry for a while – there was no reason to let Lulu
think it only took a few tears to turn us around – then we listened as she told us stories about the Island, and clubs
where she and the boys had danced. Before long, she was
teaching us a few new dance steps – "the paz," she said, her
French just as bad as it had always been – and we found out
Lulu had learned to let herself go loose, arms and legs moving against the rhythm of her body until she looked like
cloth falling away from the bolts of material Aunt Stacia unfolded when she was ready to lay out a pattern for a dress.
Pepper and I tried to follow her when she told us how folks
danced "more the Afreekan way" in Jamaica, Bermuda, the
Bahamas, and all those Islands laying south off the Florida

Keys. And Pepper and I welcomed the old Lulu home while asking the new one, Queen Esther herself, how we could get to those places, seeing as how by the end of the year, we would have outgrown Aunt Stacia and everything else in our hometown. But whenever Lulu got too big-headed about being the first one out the door, we pulled her up short. We might have been having trouble forgiving her for abandoning us for a life that had made her grow up faster than we had, but as long as she was in that room, she was still the same old Lulu, and the three of us were still subject to the same failures, the same rules and regulations that had brought us all to Aunt Stacia's house.

A noise in the hall made us remember that's where we still were. Aunt Stacia was standing in the doorway, holding the baby. Danny P. was only half awake, rubbing his eyes with the backs of his hands, his mouth open in that oval shape babies get when they know somebody's going to take care of them even if they can't speak for themselves.

"Lulu Mae, what was this baby doing by his lonesome?"

Pepper and I grinned and gave each other the high-five sign. Once again, Lulu's forgetfulness was catching up with her.

"I made him a pallet," she told Aunt Stacia. "He was alright when I left."

Aunt Stacia grunted. "This baby ain't like a package you can wrap up. He ain't on loan, and you can't be walking off and leaving this chile like you done forgot a bundle of laundry somewhere. Don't you be leaving this baby by himself like that."

Lulu looked down at the floor. "Yes ma'am," she said.

Aunt Stacia saw me and Pepper grinning like Cheshire cats. "Everything alright in here?" she asked.

"Yes ma'am," we said in chorus. "Everything's fine."

"Well, you might as well get on downstairs. We done be having company. Your mama's on her way here, Lulu Mae."

Even though she was still standing up, I could see Lulu

slump a little. Pepper and I moved closer to her. Not touching. Just there.

"I don't know how Percy did it," Aunt Stacia said. She was looking more at Danny P. than at us. The baby stuck his head in the soft crook of Aunt Stacia's neck. "He's bringing her over soon as he stop by for Zenobia and Lil'June."

"Aunt Bernice is coming here?" I asked.

Aunt Stacia nodded her head. "That's what I said. And maybe you best call the baby's daddy, Lulu. Ain't no reason to put it off, I guess. I don't even know if we got enough food for everybody."

"I can run down to the store and pick up something," Lulu Mae offered.

In chorus, all of us, including Aunt Stacia, yelled, "NO!"

The baby yelped, and Lulu's eyes grew wide. Then we all realized what we'd been thinking and began to laugh. Little Danny P. clapped his hands with delight at the noise we made.

DENNIS McFARLAND

Nothing to Ask For

Inside Mack's apartment, a concentrator – a medical machine that looks like an elaborate stereo speaker on casters – sits behind an orange swivel chair, making its rhythmic, percussive noise like ocean waves, taking in normal filthy air, humidifying it, and filtering out everything but the oxygen, which it sends through clear plastic tubing to Mack's nostrils. He sits on the couch, as usual, channel grazing, the remote-control button under his thumb, and he appears to be scrutinizing the short segments of what he sees on the TV screen with Zen-like patience. He has planted one foot on the bevelled edge of the long oak coffee table, and he dangles one leg – thinner at the thigh than my wrist – over the other. In the sharp valley of his lap, Eberhardt, his old long-haired dachshund, lies sleeping. The table is covered with two dozen medicine bottles, though Mack has now taken himself off all drugs except cough syrup and something for heartburn. Also, stacks of books and pamphlets – though he has lost the ability to read – on how to heal yourself, on Buddhism, on Hinduism, on dying. In one pamphlet there's a long list that includes most human ailments, the personality traits and character flaws that cause these ailments, and the affirmations that need to be said in order to overcome them. According to this well-intentioned misguidedness, most disease is caused by self-hatred, or rejection of reality, and almost anything can be cured by learning to love yourself – which is accomplished by saying, aloud and often, "I love myself." Next to these books are pamphlets and Xeroxed articles describing more unorthodox remedies – herbal brews, ultrasound, lemon juice, urine, even penicillin. And, in a ceramic dish next to these, a small, waxy envelope that contains "ash" – a very fine, gray-white, spiritually enhancing powder materialized out of thin air by Swami Lahiri Baba.

As I change the plastic liner inside Mack's trash can, into which he throws his millions of Kleenex, I block his view of the TV screen – which he endures serenely, his head perfectly still, eyes unaverted. "Do you remember old Dorothy Hughes?" he asks me. "What do you suppose ever happened to her?"

"I don't know," I say. "I saw her years ago on the nude beach at San Gregorio. With some black guy who was down by the surf doing cartwheels. She pretended she didn't know me."

"I don't blame her," says Mack, making bug-eyes. "I wouldn't like to be seen with any grown-up who does cartwheels, would you?"

"No," I say.

Then he asks, "Was everybody we knew back then crazy?"

What Mack means by "back then" is our college days, in Santa Cruz, when we judged almost everything in terms of how freshly it rejected the status quo: the famous professor who began his twentieth-century-philosophy class by tossing pink rubber dildos in through the classroom window; Antonioni and Luis Buñuel screened each weekend in the dormitory basement; the artichokes in the student garden, left on their stalks and allowed to open and become what they truly were – enormous, purple-hearted flowers. There were no paving-stone quadrangles or venerable colonnades – our campus was the redwood forest, the buildings nestled among the trees, invisible one from the other – and when we emerged from the woods at the end of the school day, what we saw was nothing more or less than the sun setting over the Pacific. We lived with thirteen other students, in a rented Victorian mansion on West Cliff Drive, and at night the yellow beacon from the nearby lighthouse invaded our attic windows; we drifted to sleep listening to the barking of seals. On weekends we had serious softball games in the vacant field next to the house – us against a team of tattooed long-haired townies – and afterward, keyed up, tired and sweating, Mack and I walked the north shore to a place where we could watch the waves pound rocks and send up sun-ignited columns of water twenty-five and thirty feet tall. Though most of what we initiated "back then" now seems to have been faddish and wrongheaded, our friendship was exceptionally sane and has endured for twenty years. It endured the melodramatic confusion of Dorothy Hughes, our beautiful shortstop – I loved her, but she loved Mack. It endured the subsequent revelation that Mack was gay – any tension on that count managed by him with remarks about what a homely bastard I was. It endured his fury and frustration over my low-bottom alcoholism, and my sometimes raging (and *en*raging) process of getting clean and sober. And it has endured the onlooking fisheyes of his long string of lovers and my two wives. Neither of us had a biological brother – that could account for something – but at recent moments when I have felt most frightened, now that Mack is so ill, I've thought that we persisted simply because we couldn't let go of the sense of *thoroughness* our friendship gave us; we constantly reported to each other on our separate lives, as if we knew that by doing so we were getting more from life than we would ever have been entitled to individually.

In answer to his question – was everybody crazy back then – I say, "Yes, I think so."

He laughs, then coughs. When he coughs these days –

which is often – he goes on coughing until a viscous, bloody fluid comes up, which he catches in a Kleenex and tosses into the trash can. Earlier, his doctors could drain his lungs with a needle through his back – last time they collected an entire liter from one lung – but now that Mack has developed the cancer, there are tumors that break up the fluid into many small isolated pockets, too many to drain. Radiation or chemotherapy would kill him; he's too weak even for a flu shot. Later today, he will go to the hospital for another bronchoscopy; they want to see if there's anything they can do to help him, though they have already told him there isn't. His medical care comes in the form of visiting nurses, physical therapists, and a curious duo at the hospital: one doctor who is young, affectionate, and incompetent but who comforts and consoles, hugs and holds hands; another – old, rude, brash, and expert – who says things like "You might as well face it. You're going to die. Get your papers in order." In fact, they've given Mack two weeks to two months, and it has now been ten weeks.

"Oh, my God," cries Lester, Mack's lover, opening the screen door, entering the room, and looking around. "I don't recognize this hovel. And what's that wonderful smell?"

This morning, while Lester was out, I vacuumed and generally straightened up. Their apartment is on the ground floor of a building like all the buildings in this Southern California neighborhood – a two-story motel-like structure of white stucco and steel railings. Outside the door are an X-rated hibiscus (blood red, with its jutting, yellow powder-tipped stamen), a plastic macaw on a swing, two enormous yuccas; inside, carpet, and plainness. The wonderful smell is the turkey I'm roasting; Mack can't eat anything before the bronchoscopy, but I figure it will be here for them when they return from the hospital, and they can eat off it for the rest of the week.

Lester, a South Carolina boy in his late twenties, is sick,

too — twice he has nearly died of pneumonia — but he's in a healthy period now. He's tall, thin, and bearded, a devotee of the writings of Shirley MacLaine — an unlikely guru, if you ask me, but my wife, Marilyn, tells me I'm too judgmental. Probably she is right.

The dog, Eberhardt, has woken up and waddles sleepily over to where Lester stands. Lester extends his arm toward Mack, two envelopes in his hand, and after a moment's pause Mack reaches for them. It's partly this typical hesitation of Mack's — a slowing of the mind, actually — that makes him appear serene, contemplative these days. Occasionally, he really does get confused, which terrifies him. But I can't help thinking that something in there has sharpened as well — maybe a kind of simplification. Now he stares at the top envelope for a full minute, as Lester and I watch him. This is something we do: we watch him. "Oh-h-h," he says, at last. "A letter from my mother."

"And one from Lucy, too," says Lester. "Isn't that nice?"

"I guess," says Mack. Then: "Well, yes. It is."

"You want me to open them?" I ask.

"Would you?" he says, handing them to me. "Read 'em to me, too."

They are only cards, with short notes inside, both from Des Moines. Mack's mother says it just makes her *sick* that he's sick, wants to know if there's anything he needs. Lucy, the sister, is gushy, misremembers a few things from the past, says she's writing instead of calling because she knows she will cry if she tries to talk. Lucy, who refused to let Mack enter her house at Christmas time one year — actually left him on the stoop in subzero cold — until he removed the gold earring from his ear. Mack's mother, who waited until after the funeral last year to let Mack know that his father had died; Mack's obvious illness at the funeral would have been an embarrassment.

But they've come around, Mack has told me in the face of my anger.

I said better late than never.

And Mack, all forgiveness, all humility, said that's exactly right: much better.

"Mrs. Mears is having a craft sale today," Lester says. Mrs. Mears, an elderly neighbor, lives out back in a cottage with her husband. "You guys want to go?"

Eberhardt, hearing "go," begins leaping at Lester's shins, but when we look at Mack, his eyelids are at half-mast—he's half asleep.

We watch him for a moment, and I say, "Maybe in a little while, Lester."

LESTER SITS ON THE edge of his bed reading the newspaper, which lies flat on the spread in front of him. He has his own TV in his room, and a VCR. On the dresser, movies whose cases show men in studded black leather jockstraps, with gloves to match—dungeon masters of startling handsomeness. On the floor, a stack of gay magazines. Somewhere on the cover of each of these magazines the word "macho" appears; and inside some of them, in the personal ads, men, meaning to attract others, refer to themselves as pigs. "Don't putz," Lester says to me as I straighten some things on top of the dresser. "Enough already."

I wonder where he picked up "putz"—surely not in South Carolina. I say, "You need to get somebody in. To help. You need to arrange it now. What if you were suddenly to get sick again?"

"I know," he says. "He's gotten to be quite a handful, hasn't he? Is he still asleep?"

"Yes," I answer. "Yes and yes."

The phone rings and Lester reaches for it. As soon as he begins to speak I can tell, from his tone, that it's my four-year-old on the line. After a moment, Lester says, "Kit," smiling, and hands me the phone, then returns to his newspaper.

I sit on the other side of the bed, and after I say hello, Kit says, "We need some milk."

"OK," I say. "Milk. What are you up to this morning?"

"Being angry mostly," she says.

"Oh?" I say. "Why?"

"Mommy and I are not getting along very well."

"That's too bad," I say. "I hope you won't stay angry for long."

"We won't," she says. "We're going to make up in a minute."

"Good," I say.

"When are you coming home?"

"In a little while."

"After my nap?"

"Yes," I say. "Right after your nap."

"Is Mack very sick?"

She already knows the answer, of course. "Yes," I say.

"Is he going to die?"

This one, too. "Most likely," I say. "He's that sick."

"Bye," she says suddenly—her sense of closure always takes me by surprise—and I say, "Don't stay angry for long, OK?"

"You already said that," she says, rightly, and I wait for a moment, half expecting Marilyn to come onto the line; ordinarily she would, and hearing her voice right now would do me good. After another moment, though, there's the click.

Marilyn is back in school, earning a Ph.D. in religious studies. I teach sixth grade, and because I'm faculty adviser for the little magazine the sixth-graders put out each year, I stay late many afternoons. Marilyn wanted me home this Saturday morning. "You're at work all week," she said, "and then you're over there on Saturday. Is that fair?"

I told her I didn't know—which was the honest truth. Then, in a possibly dramatic way, I told her that fairness was not my favorite subject these days, given that my best friend was dying.

We were in our kitchen, and through the window I could see Kit playing with a neighbor's cat in the backyard. Marilyn turned on the hot water in the kitchen sink and stood still while the steam rose into her face. "It's become a question of where you belong," she said at last. "I think you're too involved."

For this I had no answer, except to say, "I agree" – which wasn't really an answer, since I had no intention of staying home, or becoming less involved, or changing anything.

Now Lester and I can hear Mack's scraping cough in the next room. We are silent until he stops. "By the way," Lester says at last, taking the telephone receiver out of my hand, "have you noticed that he *listens* now?"

"I know," I say. "He told me he'd finally entered his listening period."

"Yeah," says Lester, "as if it's the natural progression. You blab your whole life away, ignoring other people, and then right before you die you start to listen."

The slight bitterness in Lester's tone makes me feel shaky inside. It's true that Mack was always a better talker than a listener, but I suddenly feel that I'm walking a thin wire, and that anything like collusion would throw me off balance. All I know for sure is that I don't want to hear any more. Maybe Lester reads this in my face, because what he says next sounds like an explanation: he tells me that his poor old backwoods mother was nearly deaf when he was growing up, that she relied almost entirely on reading lips. "All she had to do when she wanted to turn me off," he says, "was to just turn her back on me. Simple," he says, making a little circle with his finger. "No more Lester."

"That's terrible," I say.

"I was a terrible coward," he says. "Can you imagine Kit letting you get away with something like that? She'd bite your kneecaps."

"Still," I say, "that's terrible."

Lester shrugs his shoulders, and after another moment I

say, "I'm going to the K-mart. Mack needs a padded toilet seat. You want anything?"

"Yeah," he says. "But they don't sell it at K-mart."

"What is it?" I ask.

"It's a *joke*, Dan, for Chrissake," he says. "Honestly, I think you've completely lost your sense of humor."

When I think about this, it seems true.

"Are you coming back?" he asks.

"Right back," I answer. "If you think of it, baste the turkey."

"How could I not think of it?" he says, sniffing the air.

In the living room, Mack is lying with his eyes open now, staring blankly at the TV. At the moment, a shop-at-home show is on, but he changes channels, and an announcer says, "When we return, we'll talk about tree pruning," and Mack changes the channel again. He looks at me, nods thoughtfully, and says, "Tree pruning. Interesting. It's just like the way they put a limit on your credit card, so you don't spend too much."

"I don't understand," I say.

"Oh, you know," he says. "Pruning the trees. Didn't the man just say something about pruning trees?" He sits up and adjusts the plastic tube in one nostril.

"Yes," I say.

"Well, it's like the credit cards. The limit they put on the credit cards is... " He stops talking and looks straight into my eyes, frightened. "It doesn't make any sense, does it?" he says. "Jesus Christ. I'm not making sense."

WAY OUT EAST ON University, there is a video arcade every half mile or so. Adult peepshows. Also a McDonald's, and the rest. Taverns – the kind that are open at eight in the morning – with clever names: Tobacco Rhoda's, the Cruz Inn. Bodegas that smell of cat piss and are really fronts for numbers games. Huge discount stores. Lester, who is an expert in these matters, has told me that all these places feed on addicts. "What do you think—those peepshows stay in business on the strength of the occasional customer? No way. It's a steady clientele of people in there every day, for hours at a time, dropping in quarters. That whole strip of road is *made* for addicts. And all the strips like it. That's what America's all about, you know. You got your alcoholics in the bars. Your food addicts sucking it up at Jack-in-the-Box —you ever go in one of those places and count the fat people? You got your sex addicts in the peepshows. Your shopping addicts at the K-mart. Your gamblers running numbers in the bodegas and your junkies in the alleyways. We're all nothing but a bunch of addicts. The whole fucking addicted country."

In the arcades, says Lester, the videos show myriad combinations and arrangements of men and women, men and men, women and women. Some show older men being serviced by eager, selfless young women who seem to live for one thing only, who can't get enough. Some of these women have put their hair into pigtails and shaved themselves— they're supposed to look like children. Inside the peepshow booths there's semen on the floor. And in the old days, there were glory holes cut into the wooden walls between some of the booths, so, if it pleased you, you could communicate with your neighbor. Not anymore. Mack and Lester tell me that some things have changed. The holes have been boarded up. In the public men's rooms you no longer read, scribbled in the stalls, "All faggots should die." You read, "All faggots should die of AIDS." Mack rails against the moratorium on fetal-tissue research, the most promising avenue for a cure. "If it was Legionnaires dying, we wouldn't have any moratorium," he says. And he often talks about Africa, where governments impede efforts to teach villagers about condoms: a social worker, attempting to explain their use, isn't allowed to remove the condoms from their foil packets; in another country, with a slightly more liberal government, a field nurse stretches a condom over his hand, to show how it works, and later villagers are found wearing the condoms like mittens, thinking this will protect them from disease. Lester laughs at these stories but shakes his head. In our own country, something called "family values" has emerged with clarity. "*Whose* family?" Mack wants to know, holding out his hands palms upward. "I mean we *all* come from families, don't we? The dizziest queen comes from a family. The axe-murderer. Even Dan *Quayle* comes from a family of some kind."

But Mack and Lester are dying, Mack first. As I steer my pickup into the parking lot at the K-mart, I almost clip the front fender of a big, deep-throated Chevy that's leaving. I have startled the driver, a young Chicano boy with four kids in the backseat, and he flips me the bird – aggressively, his arm out the window – but I feel protected today by my sense of purpose: I have come to buy a padded toilet seat for my friend.

WHEN HE WAS YOUNGER, Mack wanted to be a cultural anthropologist, but he was slow to break in after we were out of graduate school – never landed anything more than a low-paying position assisting someone else, nothing more than a student's job, really. Eventually, he began driving a tour bus in San Diego, which not only provided a steady income but suited him so well that in time he was managing the line and began to refer to the position not as his job but as his calling. He said that San Diego was like a pretty blond boy without too many brains. He knew just how to play up its cultural assets while allowing its beauty to speak for itself. He said he liked being "at the controls." But he had to quit work over a year ago, and now his hands have become so shaky that he can no longer even manage a pen and paper.

When I get back to the apartment from my trip to the K-mart, Mack asks me to take down a letter for him to an old high-school buddy back in Des Moines, a country-and-Western singer who has sent him a couple of her latest recordings. *"Whenever I met a new doctor or nurse,"* he dictates, *"I always asked them whether they believed in miracles."*

Mack sits up a bit straighter and rearranges the pillows behind his back on the couch. "What did I just say?" he asks me.

"'I always asked them whether they believed in miracles.'"

"Yes," he says, and continues. *"And if they said no, I told them I wanted to see someone else. I didn't want them treating me. Back then, I was hoping for a miracle, which seemed reasonable.* Do you think this is too detailed?" he asks me.

"No," I say. "I think it's fine."

"I don't want to depress her."

"Go on," I say.

"But now I have lung cancer," he continues. *"So now I need not one but two miracles. That doesn't seem as possible somehow.* Wait. Did you write 'possible' yet?"

"No," I say. "'That doesn't seem as . . . '"

"Reasonable," he says. "Didn't I say 'reasonable' before?"

"Yes," he says. "How does that sound?"

"It sounds fine, Mack. It's not for publication, you know."

"It's not?" he says, feigning astonishment. "I thought it was: 'Letters of an AIDS Victim.'" He says this in a spooky voice and makes his bug-eyes. Since his head is a perfect skull, the whole effect really is a little spooky.

"What else?" I say.

"Thank you for your nice letter," he continues, *"and for the tapes."* He begins coughing—a horrible, rasping seizure. Mack has told me that he has lost all fear; he said he realized this a few weeks ago, on the skyride at the zoo. But when the coughing sets in, when it seems that it may never stop, I think I see terror in his eyes: he begins tapping his breastbone with the fingers of one hand, as if he's trying to wake

up his lungs, prod them to do their appointed work. Finally he does stop, and he sits for a moment in silence, in thought. Then he dictates: *"It makes me very happy that you are so successful."*

At Mrs. Mear's craft sale, in the alley behind her cottage, she has set up several card tables: Scores of plastic dolls with hand-knitted dresses, shoes, and hats. Handmade doll furniture. Christmas ornaments. A whole box of knitted bonnets and scarves for dolls. Also, some baked goods. Now, while Lester holds Eberhardt, Mrs. Mears, wearing a large straw hat and sunglasses, outfits the dachshund in one of the bonnets and scarves. "There now," she says. "Have you ever seen anything so *precious?* I'm going to get my camera."

Mack sits in a folding chair by one of the tables; next to him sits Mr. Mears, also in a folding chair. The two men look very much alike, though Mr. Mears is not nearly as emaciated as Mack. And of course Mr. Mears is eighty-seven. Mack, on the calendar, is not quite forty. I notice that Mack's shoelaces are untied, and I kneel to tie them. "The thing about reincarnation," he's saying to Mr. Mears, "is that you can't remember anything and you don't recognize anybody."

"Consciously," says Lester, butting in. "*Sub*consciously you do."

"Subconsciously," says Mack. "What's the point? I'm not the least bit interested."

Mr. Mears removes his hounds-tooth-check cap and scratches his bald, freckled head. "I'm not, either, " he says with great resignation.

As Mrs. Mears returns with the camera, she says, "Put him over there, in Mack's lap."

"It doesn't matter whether you're interested or not," says

Lester, dropping Eberhardt into Mack's lap.

"Give me good old-fashioned Heaven and Hell," says Mr. Mears.

"I should think you would've had enough of that already," says Lester.

Mr. Mears gives Lester a suspicious look, then gazes down at his own knees. "Then give me nothing," he says finally.

I stand up and step aside just in time for Mrs. Mears to snap the picture. "Did you ever *see* anything?" she says, all sunshades and yellow teeth, but as she heads back toward the cottage door, her face is immediately serious. She takes me by the arm and pulls me along, reaching for something from one of the tables—a doll's bed, white with a red strawberry painted on the headboard. "For your little girl," she says aloud. Then she whispers, "You better get him out of the sun, don't you think? He doesn't look so good."

But when I turn again, I see that Lester is already helping Mack out of his chair. "Here—let me," says Mrs. Mears, reaching an arm toward them, and she escorts Mack up the narrow, shaded sidewalk, back toward the apartment building. Lester moves alongside me and says, "Dan, do you think you could give Mack his bath this afternoon? I'd like to take Eberhardt for a walk."

"Of course," I say, quickly.

But a while later—after I have drawn the bath, after I've taken a large beach towel out of the linen closet, refolded it into a thick square, and put it into the water to serve as a cushion for Mack to sit on in the tub; when I'm holding the towel under, against some resistance, waiting for the bubbles to stop surfacing, and there's something horrible about it, like drowning a small animal—I think Lester has tricked me into this task of bathing Mack, and the saliva in my mouth suddenly seems to taste of Scotch, which I have not actually tasted in nine years.

There is no time to consider any of this, however, for in a

moment Mack enters the bathroom, trailing his tubes behind him, and says, "Are you ready for my Auschwitz look?"

"I've seen it before," I say.

And it's true. I have, a few times, helping him with his shirt and pants after Lester has bathed him and gotten him into his underwear. But that doesn't feel like preparation. The sight of him naked is like a powerful, scary drug: you forget between trips, remember only when you start to come on to it again. I help him off with his clothes now and guide him into the tub and gently onto the underwater towel. "That's nice," he says, and I begin soaping the hollows of his shoulders, the hard washboard of his back. This is not human skin as we know it but something already dead —so dry, dense, and pleasantly brown as to appear manufactured. I soap the cage of his chest, his stomach—the hard, depressed abdomen of a greyhound—the steep vaults of his armpits, his legs, his feet. Oddly, his hands and feet appear almost normal, even a bit swollen. At last I give him the slippery bar of soap. "Your turn," I say.

"My poor cock," he says as he begins to wash himself.

When he's done, I rinse him all over with the hand spray attached to the faucet. I lather the feather white wisps of his hair—we have to remove the plastic oxygen tubes for this— then rinse again. "You know," he says, "I know it's irrational, but I feel kind of turned off to sex."

The apparent understatement of this almost takes my breath away. "There are more important things," I say.

"Oh, I know," he says. "I just hope Lester's not too unhappy." Then, after a moment, he says, "You know, Dan, it's only logical that they've all given up on me. And I've accepted it mostly. But I still have days when I think I should at least be given a chance."

"You can ask them for anything you want, Mack," I say.

"I know," he says. "That's the problem—there's nothing to ask for."

"Mack," I say. "I think I understand what you meant this morning about the tree pruning and the credit cards."

"You do?"

"Well, I think your mind just shifted into metaphor. Because I can see that pruning trees is like imposing a limit — just like the limit on the credit cards."

Mack is silent, pondering this. "Maybe," he says at last, hesitantly — a moment of disappointment for us both.

I get him out and hooked up to the oxygen again, dry him off, and begin dressing him. Somehow I get the oxygen tubes trapped between his legs and the elastic waistband of his sweatpants — no big deal, but I suddenly feel panicky — and I have to take them off his face again to set them to right. After he's safely back on the living-room couch and I've returned to the bathroom, I hear him: low, painful-sounding groans. "Are you all right?" I call from the hall-way.

"Oh, yes," he says, "I'm just moaning. It's one of the few pleasures I have left."

The bathtub is coated with a crust of dead skin, which I wash away with the sprayer. Then I find a screwdriver and go to work on the toilet seat. After I get the old one off, I need to scrub around the area where the plastic screws were. I've sprinkled Ajax all around the rim of the bowl and found the scrub brush when Lester appears at the bath-room door, back with Eberhardt from their walk. "Oh, Dan, really," he says. "You go too far. Down on your knees now, scrubbing our toilet."

"Lester, leave me alone," I say.

"Well, it's true," he says. "You really do."

"Maybe I'm working out my survivor's guilt," I say, "if you don't mind."

"You mean because your best buddy's dying and you're not?"

"Yes," I say. "It's very common."

He parks one hip on the edge of the sink. And after a mo-

ment he says this: "Danny boy, if you feel guilty about sur-
viving... that's not irreversible, you know. I could fix that."

We are both stunned. He looks at me. In another moment, there are tears in his eyes. He quickly closes the bathroom door, moves to the tub and turns on the water, sits on
the side, and bursts into sobs. "I'm sorry," he says. "I'm so
sorry."

"Forget it," I say.

He begins to compose himself almost at once. "This is
what Jane Alexander did when she played Eleanor Roose-
velt," he says. "Do you remember? When she needed to cry
she'd go in the bathroom and turn on the water, so nobody
could hear her. Remember?"

IN THE PICKUP, ON THE way to the hospital, Lester – in
the middle, between Mack and me – says, "Maybe after
they're down there you could doze off, but on the *way* down,
they want you awake." He's explaining the bronchoscopy to
me – the insertion of the tube down the windpipe – with
which he is personally familiar: "They reach certain points
on the way down where they have to ask you to swallow."

"*He's* not having the test, is he?" Mack says, looking confused.

"No, of course not," says Lester.

"Didn't you just say to him that he had to swallow?"

"I meant *anyone,* Mack," says Lester.

"Oh," says Mack. "Oh, yeah."

"The general 'you,'" Lester says to me. "He keeps forgetting little things like that."

Mack shakes his head, then points at his temple with one
finger. "My mind," he says.

Mack is on tank oxygen now, which comes with a small
caddy. I push the caddy, behind him, and Lester assists him
along the short walk from the curb to the hospital's front
door and the elevators. Nine years ago, it was Mack who

drove *me* to a different wing of this same hospital–against my drunken, slobbery will–to dry out. And as I watch him struggle up the low inclined ramp toward the glass-and-steel doors, I recall the single irrefutable thing he said to me in the car on the way. "You stink," he said. "You've puked and probably pissed your pants and you *stink*," he said–my loyal, articulate, and best friend, saving my life, and causing me to cry like a baby.

Inside the clinic upstairs, the nurse, a sour young blond woman in a sky-blue uniform who looks terribly over-worked, says to Mack, "You know better than to be late."

We are five minutes late to the second. Mack looks at her incredulously. He stands with one hand on the handle of the oxygen-tank caddy. He straightens up, perfectly erect– the indignant, shockingly skeletal posture of a man fasting to the death for some holy principle. He gives the nurse the bug-eyes, and says, "And you know better than to keep me waiting every time I come over here for some goddam pro-cedure. But get over yourself: shit happens."

He turns and winks at me.

Though I've offered to return for them afterward, Lester has insisted on taking a taxi, so I will leave them here and drive back home, where again I'll try–successfully, this time–to explain to my wife how all this feels to me, and where, a few minutes later, I'll stand outside the door to my daughter's room, comforted by the music of her small high voice as she consoles her dolls.

Now the nurse gets Mack into a wheelchair and leaves us in the middle of the reception area; then, from the proper position at her desk, she calls Mack's name, and says he may proceed to the laboratory.

"Dan," Mack says, stretching his spotted, broomstick arms toward me. "Old pal. Do you remember the Christmas we drove out to Des Moines on the motorcycle?"

We did go to Des Moines together, one very snowy Christmas – but of course we didn't go on any motorcycle, not in December.

"We had fun," I say and put my arms around him, awkwardly, since he is sitting.

"Help me up," he whispers – confidentially – and I begin to lift him.

Marguerite Marie

"Are you worried?" asked Blue.

"No," answered Marguerite Marie. "For the one hundredth time, I am *not* worried. I am definitely not worried. No."

"Come on, Ems, not even a little bit worried?" asked Blue.

Blue was making angel wings in the sand with her nicely rounded white feet. She wasn't looking into her sister's eyes, and Marguerite Marie was glad of that.

"No," said Marguerite, crumpling and releasing the nylon ruffle on the edge of her magenta swimsuit. "Not even a little. Don't you remember the night she left us off at the movies and didn't come back till two shows later? That was sure longer than this."

Blue stopped moving her angel feet.

"Yeah," she said, "and that time she gave us a dollar each in case we needed food or a bus home. This time she only gave us fifty cents each for ice cream."

Marguerite clenched her fist inside her sweatshirt pocket. Her hand was gritty with sand and sweat.

"Right," said Marguerite Marie because it was the older sister's job to be very sure, just like it was the younger sister's job to ask the scary questions and expect answers that made her feel warm and good inside. Even if the sisters were only half sisters. And even if the older sister was only twelve years old. And even if the sweat on the hand of the older sister was the sweat of worry and fear and not the sweat of the afternoon heat of the beach.

"I'm going in," announced Blue.

"Wait, hide your quarters in your shoe."

Blue tossed them into the toe of her transparent pink jelly shoes, and ran off toward the water, her golden legs pumping, spitting sand behind.

"You stay right in front of me while you're swimming, you hear?"

Blue let her arms fly out, hands waving, to say she had heard.

Marguerite slid along the bed quilt that served as the girls' beach blanket. It was a picture quilt made by Marguerite's black granny somewhere in Louisiana, and it showed a farmhouse and a tree and a man and a lady on the top half. On the bottom were rows of brown sticks with white puffs attached to the tops and black people with colorful pieces of material in their heads, standing beside the brown sticks. Momma had thrown the quilt into a closet when Granny first sent it, and later used it, decoration side down, as a rug for everyone to walk on. Marguerite had taken it to the laundromat one day, washed it clean, brought it home, and hid it till Momma promised to let her have it for herself.

"Why you want to be reminded of your black half by sleeping under that thing is beyond me," her mother had said. "You'd think the mirror would be enough."

"Then why'd you let him be my daddy?" Marguerite had yelled, clutching the quilt so that she wouldn't topple over from anger.

"Pure mistake. All the more because it made for your poor sister, Josephine, being born blue. It doesn't ever do to mix. Marguerite Marie. Oh, if I could start over, if only your poor mother could start over right now and forever . . . "

Marguerite reached for Blue's two quarters. The jelly shoes had grown hot in the sun. They smelled like new tar, laid down in wide, healing sweeps on a summer blacktop. Someone could slip the coins right out of those shoes, steal them clean. Marguerite pushed the coins into the toe of her right sneaker, placed her own two quarters into her left sneaker, rolled her sweat shirt up, and set it, pocket side to the quilt. Then, she unfolded her long, dark legs and scanned the ocean. Blue was hopping around in the water with what looked like a family. Two kids younger than Blue, about five and seven, and a father playing monster, playing whale, playing man under the bed.

Marguerite kept a sharp, curious eye on him. What kind of a man would hang around with the children he fathered when he could be off seeing the world like her daddy? Like Blue's daddy? Marguerite walked down toward the water. She held on to the ruffle of her bathing suit, rolling it between her fingers, letting it unfurl, quick as a whisper, and then forcing it into a slick curl again.

She saw the man smiling at Blue, lifting her up and up into the air. It seemed like Blue was part of his family now, instead of belonging with her own sister.

"Josephine!" shouted Marguerite. "You get out, now."

Blue looked over at Marguerite. So did the man.

"Who's that?" he asked. "Your nanny?" He opened his mouth wide when he laughed.

That was how Momma let it be known sometimes. By a quiet "No, not *both* of them," in response to a curious stranger. Sometimes by even less than that. By a turn of the eye, twist of the neck in denial. People were ready to believe that Marguerite Marie couldn't belong, because she shouldn't belong.

Blue frowned, pinching in her skin frosted with hair so light it could hardly be defined as an eyebrow. To Marguerite's satisfaction, she saw the defiance and loyalty roll in across Blue's features and put up her mouth.

"She's my sister," said Blue. "Come to tell me my mother's waiting for us."

Blue stomped through the last few feet of water to the shore, raising lacy ruffles of seawater around her ankles. Everything Blue did came out beautiful.

If Marguerite could have chosen one thing to be, it would have been beautiful. Momma always said if you weren't born rich, you had to be either beautiful or smart to make your way, and that, for a woman, beautiful was better. Like Eva, who lived upstairs from them and was an executive secretary to a very important man, downtown. Eva bought her clothes according to what was new these days and she fitted her body to them like taffy into wrappers. Eva's gold frosted hair curled itself long and slow, not short and skimpy, and she said she could use any office machine in the world that any man could explain to her once. A beautiful and important executive secretary was everything Marguerite ever wanted to be, even though English and Spelling were impossible mysteries to her, and clothes, no matter how new, seemed to hang like bed sheets across her bones.

"Is she back yet?" Blue asked.

"Not yet."

"Ems, I'm worried again."

"Don't, please," said Marguerite. "Let's use our ice cream money now."

"I wanna go back in. It's fun."

"No, you're not. No." Marguerite set her mouth the way she remembered Momma doing it, pulling the corners up and wide apart like an elastic band, shaking her head in a warning like the high branches of a tree just beginning to move in a storm wind.

Blue thumped her pearly toes into the sand.

"I'm going."

"You are *not*." Marguerite grabbed at Blue's fine blond curls with her dark, thin hand. She gave the curls a tug.

"You will *listen!*"

Marguerite felt lines of heat move up her hand as Blue scratched it hard. Marguerite let go, raising her hand to strike, but she forced her arm down instead, and hit her own leg with a smack that swelled and stung, absorbing heat from the air around.

"You are not my Momma!" yelled Blue.

"When Momma is gone, I am your Momma," Marguerite shouted. "And you will come along with me."

Blue mumbled something, but she started moving toward the store that occupied the bottom floor of the big white house with dark green shutters at the edge of the beach. She ambled ahead like a horse, trotting quickly for a moment, then bending her knees, dragging her feet in the sand, and trotting again, sulky and disgruntled.

Marguerite didn't care how her sister came along, as long as she did.

"I'm pretending I'm walking through fairy dust," Blue sang. "And every step is a wish and every wish is a bird and every bird flies to Momma on her bus to wherever she is going and tells her to come back to us."

Marguerite was wishing that she could wish like Blue instead of living in the air she lived in, that thundered dangers at her. She wished she didn't know that wishes don't turn into birds and that people can come to an end of things.

"If Momma's on some bus, it's taking her to Penney's to get a new blouse or to the Stop & Shop to get us some hot dogs for supper," said Marguerite.

"Did she give you any more money than fifty cents?"

"No," said Marguerite. "She did not."

"I'm getting a lime popsicle, then."

"It'll only drip green all over your legs and be gone in three minutes in the sun. I'm getting a small Coke so I can sip it all afternoon."

"You're smart," said Blue, but Marguerite knew that Blue would get the lime popsicle anyhow, and then beg for the last sip of *her* Coke, later on. And get it, too.

MR. D'ANGELO KEPT ALL sorts of treasures in his store at the edge of the beach. He had seashell bracelets and glass balls filled with water that sprinkled sequins on a lighthouse when you tipped them. He had decks of cards as small as matchbooks and pieces of coral in pinks and greens and boxes made of cedar wood that said Rock Point Beach on them in black letters, and small, polished stones for a nickel apiece. Sometimes Mr. D'Angelo gave out free pieces of bubble gum to the kids. Marguerite never accepted his gifts. She would whisper to Blue about candy and strangers, but Blue would turn her face away just enough so as not to be able to read her sister's warnings. Blue would thank Mr. D'Angelo sweetly. Marguerite tried not to like Mr. D'Angelo, but she always felt like smiling at him, and staying in his house-store a moment longer and asking him to offer her the gum so many times that she would have to accept it.

"Well, hello, girls," he said when he saw them. He had been straightening out the piles of baseball cards that the boys had left a mess. Mr. D'Angelo gave a little bow, so that Marguerite could see the bald spot on the very top of his head, sitting like a full moon in a gray sky. He was wearing a yellow shirt decorated with turquoise palm trees that stood under pink suns. Underneath tan shorts, his chubby legs squirted out and down, stuffed at the ends into brown leather sandals. Mr. D'Angelo looked the way Marguerite imagined Santa Claus would look on summer vacation.

"Today is a good luck day," said Mr. D'Angelo. He scratched the very top of his head with the tip of his little finger, waiting for the girls to respond.

"Why do you always scratch right on top?" asked Blue.

"Do I? I guess to make sure my head is still there."

Blue laughed, shrugging her shoulders and pointing her chin up at him.

"So, girls, do you need some good luck?"

"Oh, yes," said Blue, shaking her head as though it sat like a plaster doll's head on a spring. "We need *extra* good luck because..."

Marguerite caught one of the bouncing curls and pulled it.

Mr. D'Angelo turned his head toward Marguerite and straightened up. The two were of similar height, she, thin and tall, he plump and short.

"Well, Little Momma. Your baby almost told a tale? Hmmm? Are you girls in trouble?"

"No," said Marguerite, trying not to look him in the eye. She rolled the ruffle on her suit, letting it out, rolling it in, afraid he would see, underneath the fearless glaze of her dark eyes, the tears forming, ready to burst their crystal shapes and fill out into hot, plump drops that would give her away.

"Yes," said Blue. "Yes, we are. Our mother is gone."

"What!"

"She's lying," said Marguerite. "She's not gone. It's just that Josephine had a fight with her this morning and Momma always talks about starting over and everything, especially when we have a fight. She dreams about what it would be like without us to weigh her down, what wonderful chances she would have and now Josephine feels bad about the fight, that's all."

"Are you sure?" Mr. D'Angelo leaned in towards Marguerite, who backed away an equal distance.

"She just went shopping for our supper," Marguerite continued. "Could I please have a small Coke?"

Before she could protest, Marguerite felt Mr. D'Angelo slip one of the small, polished stones into her hand.

"Free today," he said. "For good luck."

Marguerite closed her hand around the cool, smooth piece. She wanted that feeling at the center of herself.

"Where do you live?" Blue asked. She tugged on his Hawaiian shirt.

"Right here. On the top of this store is my house."

"Do you have any children?"

"Oh, yes, but they're all grown up now, and they have houses of their own to live in."

"Josephine Emily! If you dare to ask another question, you will not get to use your money this afternoon at all!"

Blue turned her face away from Marguerite's.

"May I have a lime popsicle, please?"

Mr. D'Angelo slipped a good luck stone into Blue's hand as well, and took a lime popsicle from the big square freezer at the back of the store. He handed Marguerite her Coke.

"That's ninety-five cents all together."

Marguerite dropped the four quarters into his hand.

"Please keep the extra five cents to pay for my good luck stone."

"It was a gift, Little Momma. It will hurt my feelings."

Marguerite was already leading the dripping Blue out of the store.

"That way," she called over her shoulder, "it will really be mine."

"She's not coming back this time," said Blue, as they walked back to the quilt. "We have to figure out something to do."

"Don't sit on my quilt till you've finished your popsicle. Then go wash off all the sticky stuff."

"She's not coming back. Admit it." Blue licked at the chartreuse rivers that ran like veins across the top of her hand.

"She told us to wait for her and that's what we're going to do," said Marguerite, focusing on her sister again. "How about if I go to the top of the beach every half hour and meet the buses that come."

"I have my own plan." Blue twirled her sticky green index finger in her gold curls the way she always did when she was proud of herself. "I'm going to baby-sit little kids for a quarter or a dime so their Mommas can go in swimming. Then we can get hamburgs or hot dogs at Mr. D'Angelo's for supper."

"You can't do that," said Marguerite.

"Why not?"

"You just can't. That's all."

Blue crossed her arms and crunched them into her chest. She put on her adorable anger act.

"If you don't let me do it, I'll run away. I'll sneak off when you don't know it and start over again like Momma did and leave you all alone with nobody to boss. You'll never find me, I swear it, cross my heart."

Marguerite felt the dangers falling out of the air again, thumping onto the sand around her, writhing in and out of her toes, twining up her legs. The danger of being alone forever crawled up her bony chest and wrapped itself around her neck.

"You must never do that!" The words hissed out of her closed throat on a thin stream of air.

"I'm going to do my plan, then."

Marguerite felt the pressure of Blue's arms around her waist and the glancing pull of Blue's fine, sticky hair across her shoulder.

"I would never really leave you," said Blue, and she bounded off toward the water like a kite in an unpredictable wind.

Between buses, Marguerite kept a sharp eye on Blue, who had collected $2.75 by the time the flat, gray clouds rolled across the lowering sun and sent most of the families home for dinner. The mothers had given her quarters instead of dimes and the little ones she had watched over had hated to see their Mommas come back out of the ocean. Blue was so charming you could learn to love her in two seconds flat.

Marguerite had watched five buses arrive, let off their loads and lumber away, roaring over the road that led to town. The passengers got off carrying beach blankets and pails, wearing bathing suits and sandals. None of them wore heart-shaped sunglasses with red frames and a black T-shirt that said "Foxy" in sparkly letters. None of them carried a reluctant recognition for her in their eyes underneath the dark of the glasses. The last two buses, more people got on than got off.

The rain that came about seven in the evening sent everyone rushing with shirts and blankets over their heads to the edge of the beach to wait for the bus to take them home. The man who had lifted Blue out of the water was carrying his own daughter, sheltering her head from the rain, just like Momma had done the time they got caught in the storm walking home from seeing *Bambi,* trying to save bus money. That was so long ago, before Blue, when it was only Momma and Marguerite, the happy, comfortable two of them in that long, cold, soaking rainstorm that didn't matter a bit inside of Momma's thin, soft arms.

Marguerite and Blue pulled the hoods of their sweat shirts up over their heads when the first big drops skidded into the sand. Marguerite expected Blue to start complaining about being hungry and tired and wet, but instead, Blue offered her a piece of bubble gum and chomped on one herself. Between the two of them, there was only the juicy spit-cracking of the gum and the thudding of the rain.

Marguerite interrupted the sounds with words.

"Where'd you get the gum?"

"Mrs. Ferguson, the lady with the twins. She gave it to me with my quarter."

"You didn't beg it, did you?"

"I *saved* it till now. Just like you would. Aren't I smart to save it?" Blue twirled her hair. "Just like you, Ems."

Marguerite suddenly couldn't bear the idea that Blue might be white and beautiful and charming and smart, all at the same time.

"You begged it, I know you did." Marguerite knew she was saying it out of pure spite, but she couldn't help herself.

"No, honest. I didn't." Blue sounded indignant.

"You begged it. Nothing will make me think different," Marguerite insisted.

"I didn't. I didn't!" Blue began thudding her soft knuckles into Marguerite's arm. The bone buzzed and ached.

Marguerite grabbed Blue's shoulders and shook her.

"You did, you little snake. You tell the truth," Marguerite shouted. "You just go off and do what you want to, no matter what I tell you. You just go off like that and leave me!"

Blue's face was shaking and chattering in front of her like an old movie. No, it was saying, no, no, no.

Marguerite flung it away and started stomping the sand, hitting and twirling, watching the beach and Blue and the bus stop and Mr. D'Angelo's whirl by and by and by until all of her thumped crazily onto the quilt. She collected her arms and legs into herself and sat there.

Blue brought her face in close and talked in slow motion. "We got to go, Ems."

"She told us to wait," Marguerite said before she had to close her throat down against the heavings that rose inside and dissolved against the barrier. She built a careful fence around her brain, and thought of nothing and nothing and nothing again.

Blue stood up and forced her jelly shoes on over her squeaky, wet feet. She bent down again and Marguerite felt each sneaker grate over her sandy, brittle toes and snap up over her heel.

"I have a plan," said Blue. "Let me do my plan."

Marguerite meant her voice to be definite, but it whispered itself and flew away on the wind like a boat whistle in the night.

"When Momma's gone, I'm the Momma."

Marguerite felt Blue roll her off the bed quilt. She watched Blue bunch up the material and hike it under her arm. She felt Blue's hand slip into her own and pull her to a stand.

"And when Momma's gone forever," said Blue, "we're just sisters again."

When Blue said that, the fence broke down in Marguerite's brain and the barrier she had set up against the retching gave way. Her throat was moving in horrible rhythm, and Blue was keeping time to it with her words, "It's okay, it's okay," and with her feet, which were moving them slowly toward the house at the edge of the beach.

Marguerite's throat quieted for a while. Some words, bumpy and irregular, raw and thin, rose and escaped.

"I been keeping something," said Marguerite to her sister. "Momma gave it to us before she left."

"What is it?" asked Blue.

Marguerite drew a thin, rumpled twenty dollar bill from her sweat shirt pocket and held it out in front of them. It snapped and flew in the storm wind of the evening beach like a tiny ship's flag on a ten-thousand-mile sea.

PAMELA PAINTER

New Family Car

A SNOW DAY for Emily's high school and my car's transmission problems have marooned us inside, unexpectedly
together. Emily and her friends are sprawled on beanbag
chairs in the adjacent dining room, which has no dining
table, only stereo equipment, an exercycle and books. I can
see them — five in all — through the archway across from
where I'm stretched out on the couch grading freshman
comp papers. Two pizzas are baking in the oven.

I'm still in my bathrobe, no bra, even though it is late afternoon and soon I'll have to turn on a light. A cup of cold
tea beside me on the floor makes me want a glass of white
wine. The comp papers are weighing flat and heavy on my
chest, along with the news that Arnie is moving out. I
haven't yet told Emily.

Their voices come to me like a radio at low volume till I
hear Zack ask Becka, "So where are your parents?" Since
when did kids care where their parents were — except to decide at whose house to throw the all-night party? Now I'm
listening in.

"Mom's here. Dad's in L.A.," Becka says. Becka is the new
drummer in the band Zack's putting together. Emily says
their gigs have increased since she joined up. Zack is Emily's
boyfriend.

"No shit! L.A.," he says.

"You can have it," Becka says. "It's mostly Mexicans, hot pavement, cars, and smog."

"Don't you ever go back?" Taj asks. ("Taj as in Taj Mahal," Emily said.) Taj is their songwriter and singer – vocalist, they call her. Emily is French-braiding Taj's long blond hair, something she refuses to do for me. I watch the fat braid curve slowly over the crown of Taj's head. "You know," Taj prompts. "Go out to see your dad?"

Becka shakes her mowed head. She has a half-inch growth of auburn hair under an equally short lawn of matte black. Not one of her six earrings matches. She tells them her dad has this two-year-old kid and treats Becka like a baby-sitter. "As soon as I arrive, he and Fay whip out a list of new restaurants they want to try. One night they came back stoned and he told Fay to drive me home like I was a sitter from the neighborhood. I don't even know how I'm related to the kid – first he married this woman – after divorcing Mom – and they fought all the time. Then they got a divorce. Then they had a kid. They're still divorced, but now they're living together again."

"You got a half sister," Zack says, cradling his guitar. "Thank God my parents are divorced. But Dad still rants and raves about Mom all the time. I agree with him just to shut him up. He says she buys purses like Marcos's wife bought shoes. Once he tried to get me to count them."

"That's really sick," Emily says. She goes over to Zack and kneads her fingers in his curly hair and he reaches up and pulls her in close for a kiss. Please keep it light. I turn my head to watch the snow swirling heavily against the windows, no pattern to its falling. Arnie is probably in his new apartment assembling bookshelves and unpacking his share of dishes, pots and pans.

"You gotta shut them down sometimes," Franco says. He's a lanky kid with a black mohawk, the band's leader. "I just hold up my hand and say, 'Hey, Mom, I've heard it before.'" He scratches his mohawk with a pencil – somehow, it resembles Taj's braid. He says his father used to drink straight vodka all day from a brown coffee mug. "I give him credit for going off the booze, but now he's cheating on Karen just like he did on my mom. She's dumb for sticking around. But I'm not about to get involved."

Involved, I think. Franco, my boy, you are involved. I remember saying to a friend that we're traumatizing our kids with all these divorces and recouplings, and he said, No, we're just giving them emotional information.

Becka is talking. She says the problem is you never know how to treat stepparents. "Fay always wants to play serious makeup with me. Mud packs, manicures. Last time there I said what she really needs is a two-tone punk cut like mine. Now she doesn't bug me anymore."

Zack rolls his eyes in sympathy and says his father was living for a while with an old high school girlfriend named Jeanette who'd named her daughters Lynnette and Fayette. "I told her if she had a son they could name him Crockette. She didn't think it was funny. 'Funny' to them is this game they play at dinner." Zack puts down his guitar to demonstrate. "First night I'm there, Fayette burps and suddenly everybody's laughing and pointing at me. I look around the table and they're all sitting with a thumb poking into their foreheads. 'You're last,' Lynnette said. 'That means you have to eat it.'" Zack burps and I rise up on my elbow to watch him smash his thumb against his forehead. "I *refused* to play," Zack says. "I 'ate it' every time. Dad finally smartened up and moved out."

"Gross." Emily pauses, braiding again, her hands holding the blond strands of Taj's hair like reins. She says she remembers when Arnie moved in. I lie back down and close my eyes, not sure I can take it. She says, "Suddenly there was this stranger in the bathroom trimming his toenails. I could hear it in my bedroom two doors away. His tennis shoes smell like rotten eggs."

She's right. Arnie's tennis shoes reek. He used to count on me to tell him when to buy new ones. I haven't had the nerve to do that for a while. And he hasn't suggested I take off a little weight either. Unexpectedly, tears well up in my eyes and I need to blow my nose, but that would expose my couch-cover. I turn my face into the cushion and sniff softly and fast.

"You think you got it bad," Franco says. "My mom's living in this humongous loft with this painter who's ten years younger. He listens to Philip Glass all day and cooks in an old black wok – everything tastes like fried shrimp. When I sleep over this guy borrows my clothes. I wake up late and there he is, working in my shirt or jeans." He points to black splotches on his Levis.

"At least you don't have to live there full time," Zack says. "Anyway, it probably won't last." I go back to reading an essay on a pet raccoon for the third time.

"Trouble is all those divorces really mess up the photograph albums," Emily says. And here it comes. My pen freezes on the page. "Mom butchered ours. There's only about two pictures left of Dad in all twelve albums."

I glance at the albums lined up on the shelf beside the fireplace. I'd always wondered if Emily or Greg noticed – heads missing, hands emerging from uneven borders.

But Emily isn't finished. She goes on to reveal how her father and I had to get married. Uncharacteristically, I'm speechless as she continues, "Dumb, but that's what you did in Mom's day if you got pregnant. They didn't have the pill."

"No wonder they got divorced," Becka says. "Why didn't she have an abortion?"

"It wasn't legal. And anyway, you're talking about my brother, Greg. He's at school," Emily says, giving Taj's head a hard push.

Taj's shoulders shrug. "My father could have arranged it—even back then."

"What's he do?" Becka asks.

"He was a dealer. Dead now," Taj says, her tone matter-of-fact as she describes his sudden heart attack in St. Bart's.

"Tell Becka the rest of it," Zack says. Clearly he's heard this story before because, having ushered it in, he leaves to check on the pizzas.

"When I was six, Dad got me every other weekend. He used to take me on drug deals—said I was good luck." Taj pats down the length of her braid to see how far it's done. Then she describes how she helped him weigh stuff out on special scales—back then it was grass. "We put it in baggies and tied it with those wire things. He died before they invented Ziploc bags," she says. Saturdays were their big days. First they checked in at the zoo to see the bears or lions, or a hallway of snakes—just to give her something to tell her mother. Then they'd have to go make deliveries. I picture a small girl sobbing as she is dragged away from giraffes, elephants, monkeys. There's the song Taj should write.

Emily winds a rubber band around the end of Taj's braid and flips it over her shoulder. Then Emily flops down next to Zack. The beans in the chair crunch and shift. "So who's the guy answering the phone in such a sexy voice?" she asks Taj.

"Mom swears she's not getting married again, but she has guys—one just moved in, and one on the phone. I mean it's not exactly a revolving door or anything. They're OK. The time one came on to me I told Mom and he was gone that same night."

"Pervert," Emily and Becka say in unison.

"Mom's bottom line is they have to have a job. She says it keeps them busy."

"Not busy enough," Emily says. "My dad's had seven jobs in the past three years. Trouble is they don't last longer than two weeks. Now I don't ask," she says. "You meet him and he mentions Yale in the first twenty minutes. Mom says it was all downhill after Yale."

"Emily! Goddamn it, that's enough," I yell, throwing the comp papers on the floor and sitting up. "At least I never told you how low that hill was to begin with."

No one says anything.

I tighten the belt on my old chenille bathrobe, wishing I'd put on underwear and combed my hair. Where did they think I was anyway? Taking a goddamn bubble bath? I search for my flip-flops and stand up. "You ought to be out there shoveling walks, not sitting around here—"

"Mo—om," Emily says. She gives Zack a push and tells him to go check on the pizza. No one looks at me. What would they do if I announced, 'Yeah, well, another thing: Arnie and I are splitting up. He's taking his tennis shoes with him; we won't have Arnie's old toenails to step on anymore.' Would Franco shrug and say, 'Hey, these things happen'? I mean, how cool can these kids be?

"Come and get it," Zack calls from the kitchen and slams the oven door. They all exit fast. I marvel at their appetites.

AT TWELVE, THE COMP papers are finished and I'm in bed with a book, waiting for Emily to get back from Zack's house where they all fled after the pizza. I tried calling Greg at school but he wasn't in, so I missed the chance to rehearse my eleventh-hour news.

Outside, the snow stopped as the temperature fell and now, outlined with lacy frost, the small windowpanes have become black valentines. Boxes of Arnie's books and papers, three overflowing duffles, and a mountain of shoes tug at my peripheral vision. He's coming early tomorrow to move his things out, say good-bye to Emily. But first I need to tell her myself.

It's close to one when I hear her coming up the stairs. Angry with relief, I pull on my robe and go down the hall to her room. "What are you doing up so late?" she asks. Expertly, she crosses her arms in front of her and pulls the red sweater over her head in one movement. Her long hair swings free.

I sit down on the other twin bed, and my first words surprise me. "Jesus. Did you need to tell them your father and I had to get married?"

"Yeah, you're right," Emily says. "I guess I said too much, huh?" She turns her back to slide her bra around and pulls on a red nightshirt. Then she lifts her quilt and flops into bed. The wool quilt, made by my grandmother, is almost in tatters but she refuses to sleep with anything else. Her eyes are closed as she says, "I'm sorry, Mom." A little too easily. "I really am. They won't remember." And definitely too cool.

"Don't give me that shit," I say, reaching over to yank her pillow hard from under her head the way magicians do with tableclothes and plates.

Emily jerks up onto her elbow and clutches the quilt to her chest. "What are you doing. What the fuck is wrong?"

"I'm trying to talk to you," I say.

"But it's two in the morning. Can't it wait? Where's Arnie?"

I tell her then. In a calmer voice I say that last night Arnie and I agreed to split up—that he'd be coming over tomorrow morning to officially move out. To say good-bye to her.

"Oh, shit," she says, rolling her glistening eyes.

"What do you mean 'oh, shit?'"

"I mean I'll miss him," she says. Tears are running down her cheeks now, darkening her freckles. "I mean he was okay."

"Give me a break," I yell. "First you complain about him and now he's a saint."

"That bad, huh?" she says.

I nod and hug the pillow I swiped from her. "You've

probably overheard enough to know what happened."

"Yeah, I guess it's been coming."

My mouth quivers as I say, "But you don't have to make a big deal about it. I mean you don't have to announce it to your friends – 'Hey, guys, no more smelly tennis shoes,' – like you did this afternoon."

Emily points her finger at me. "You were spying on us."

"I was not. I was grading papers in the living room. I was hearing you talk. There's a difference – and I don't like my life paraded around for a bunch of kids."

"You forget. It's my life too," Emily says, lurching up. She grabs her pillow back from me and squashes it to her chest. "You ever think of that? Did you and Dad ever once think of that? Of me and Greg and what we were going through?" She buries her face in her pillow as I move across to sit on her bed. I hug her hard and soon her fingers are pressing and smoothing the soft chenille ridges of my robe where she holds my shoulders.

"Oh, Emmy, of course we thought about it. We stayed married one whole year longer, agonizing over what it would do to you and Greg. And Arnie and I talked about it, too. It isn't like we didn't try – for you." My voice is rising, catching as it soars, but I can't stop. "But I know that's not what you and your friends all think, complaining about half sisters, and boyfriends and stepparents. You think you'd have been better off if your father and I had stayed to-gether."

"What's the matter with that?" Emily says, pulling back and glaring at me. Trying not to cry harder.

"Because it wouldn't have been true," I say.

"But that – doesn't help. Don't you – see?" she hiccoughs, her chin trembling.

"So why talk about it?" I ask.

"Oh. So that's it," she says. "You're still thinking 'what will people say?' Jesus, Mom. If you're going to listen in, you have to lighten up."

"But it's like – it's like you're playing games."

"Games!" Emily's eyebrows, tiny arcs, rise.

"You're playing – I don't know." I shake my head – somehow it is all so familiar, and then I do know. "You're playing 'My-family's-more-fucked-up-than-your-family.'"

Emily's shoulders shake and suddenly she's laughing hysterically, wiping her face with both hands. "That's funny, Mom. That's really funny."

"It is *not*. It's how we used to one-up friends. Only we did it with the number of bathrooms we had, or who went on vacations to Niagara Falls – or whose family had a new car. No one ever had two cars."

"So what?" Emily says. "So now it's fucked-up families." Then she grins. "You're lucky we don't flunk out of school, do crack, or join the Hare Krishnas. Besides, some kids can't play. You know, they have dumb happy homes. Their parents have been married for twenty-seven years and they go to church on Sunday and in summer they trot off to family reunions two states away. Like NOT having a new car was for you twenty-five years ago. I mean what are these kids going to say? Nothing. So they can't play." She tugs open the little drawer in her nightstand and fishes around. "Here. You want to see something?" She pulls out a creased envelope and empties it onto the quilt between us. "See. I saved all those pieces of Dad. So that wasn't a big deal either." And there they are, ragged photographs of my first husband – small glossy heads, square torsos, bits of me. She stirs the pieces around with a wet, glistening finger.

"Oh, Emmy, I wish –"

"No. Stop. You're right. It's better this way." She scoops her dad up and dumps him back into the envelope. We're all still in pieces. "Arnie too," she says. "You going to operate on him?"

Our laughs are damp and sniffly. Then I lean over her to smooth her shining eyebrows, kiss her wet cheeks and bangs. She puts her arms up to hold me tightly for a moment, then she lets me go. I tell her I love her. When I turn off the light, her windows sparkle with the same black lacy valentines. They'll be white come morning.

"Hey, Mom," she calls out from the dark, her voice still offering too-small comfort. "So maybe it is a game, so what? At least I didn't win."

ANNICK SMITH

It's Come to This

No horses. That's how it always starts. I am coming
down the meadow, the first snow of September whipping
around my boots, and there are no horses to greet me. The
first thing I did after Caleb died was get rid of the horses.

"I don't care how much," I told the auctioneer at the Missoula Livestock Company. He looked at me slant-eyed from
under his Stetson. "Just don't let the canneries take them."
Then I walked away.

What I did not tell him was I couldn't stand the sight of
those horses on our meadow, so heedless, grown fat and un-
tended. They reminded me of days when Montana seemed
open as the sky.

Now that the horses are gone I am more desolate than
ever. If you add one loss to another, what you have is double
zip. I am wet to the waist, water sloshing ankle-deep inside
my irrigating boots. My toes are numb, my chapped hands
are burning from the cold, and down by the gate my dogs
are barking at a strange man in a red log truck.

That's how I meet Frank. He is hauling logs down from
the Champion timberlands above my place, across the right-
of-way I sold to the company after my husband's death. The
taxes were piling up. I sold the right-of-way because I would

not sell my land. Kids will grow up and leave you, but land is something a woman can hold on to.

I don't like those log trucks rumbling by my house, scattering chickens, tempting my dogs to chase behind their wheels, kicking clouds of dust so thick the grass looks brown and dead. There's nothing I like about logging. It breaks my heart to walk among newly cut limbs, to be enveloped in the sharp odor of sap running like blood. After twenty years on this place, I still cringe at the snap and crash of five-hundred-year-old pines and the far-off screaming of saws.

Anyway, Frank pulls his gyppo logging rig to a stop just past my house in order to open the blue metal gate that separates our outbuildngs from the pasture, and while he is at it, he adjusts the chains holding his load. My three mutts take after him as if they were real watchdogs and he stands at the door of the battered red cab holding his hands to his face and pretending to be scared.

"I would surely appreciate it if you'd call off them dogs," says Frank, as if those puppies weren't wagging their tails and jumping up to be patted.

He can see I am shivering and soaked. And I am mad. If I had a gun, I might shoot him.

"You ought to be ashamed... a man like you."

"Frank Bowman," he says, grinning and holding out his large thick hand. "From Bowman Corners." Bowman Corners is just down the road.

"What happened to you?" he grins. "Take a shower in your boots?"

How can you stay mad at that man? A man who looks at you and makes you look at yourself. I should have known better. I should have waited for my boys to come home from football practice and help me lift the heavy wet boards in our diversion dam. But my old wooden flume was running full and I was determined to do what had to be done before dark, to be a true country woman like the pioneers I read about as a daydreaming child in Chicago, so long ago it seems another person's life.

"I had to shut off the water," I say. "Before it freezes." Frank nods, as if this explanation explains everything.

Months later I would tell him about Caleb. How he took care of the wooden flume, which was built almost one hundred years ago by his Swedish ancestors. The snaking plank trough crawls up and around a steep slope of igneous rock. It has been patched and rebuilt by generations of hard-handed, blue-eyed Petersons until it reached its present state of tenuous mortality. We open the floodgate in June when Bear Creek is high with snow melt, and the flume runs full all summer, irrigating our hay meadow of timothy and wild mountain grasses. Each fall, before the first hard freeze, we close the diversion gates and the creek flows in its natural bed down to the Big Blackfoot River.

That's why I'd been standing in the icy creek, hefting six-foot two-by-twelves into the slotted brace that forms the dam. The bottom board was waterlogged and coated with green slime. It slipped in my bare hands and I sat down with a splash, the plank in my lap and the creek surging around me.

"Goddamn it to fucking hell!" I yelled. I was astonished to find tears streaming down my face, for I have always prided myself on my ability to bear hardship. Here is a lesson I've learned. There is no glory in pure backbreaking labor.

Frank would agree. He is wide like his log truck and thick-skinned as a yellow pine, and believes neighbors should be friendly. At five o'clock sharp each workday, on his last run, he would stop at my blue gate and yell, "Call off your beasts," and I would stop whatever I was doing and go down for our friendly chat.

"How can you stand it?" I'd say, referring to the cutting of trees.

"It's a pinprick on the skin of the earth," replies Frank.

"God doesn't know the difference."

"Well, I'm not God," I say. "Not on my place. Never."

So Frank would switch to safer topics such as new people moving in like knapweed, or where to find morels, or how the junior-high basketball team was doing. One day in October, when red-tails screamed and hoarfrost tipped the meadow grass, the world gone crystal and glowing, he asked could I use some firewood.

"A person can always use firewood," I snapped.

The next day, when I came home from teaching, there was a pickup load by the woodshed—larch and fir, cut to stove size and split.

"Taking care of the widow," Frank grinned when I tried to thank him. I laughed, but that is exactly what he was up to. In this part of the country, a man still takes pains.

WHEN I FIRST CAME TO Montana I was slim as a fashion model and my hair was black and curly. I had met my husband, Caleb, at the University of Chicago, where a city girl and a raw ranch boy could be equally enthralled by Gothic halls, the great libraries, and gray old Nobel laureates who gathered in the Faculty Club, where no student dared enter.

But after our first two sons were born, after the disillusionments of Vietnam and the cloistered grind of academic life, we decided to break away from Chicago and a life of mind preeminent, and we came to live on the quarter section of land Caleb had inherited from his Swedish grandmother. We would make a new start by raising purebred quarter horses.

For Caleb it was coming home. He had grown up in Sunset, forty miles northeast of Missoula, on his family's homestead ranch. For me it was romance. Caleb had carried the romance of the West for me in the way he walked on high-heeled cowboy boots, and the world he told stories about. It was a world I had imagined from books and movies, a paradise, of the shining mountains, clean rivers, and running horses.

I loved the idea of horses. In grade school, I sketched black stallions, white mares, rainbow-spotted appaloosas. My bedroom was hung with horses running, horses jumping, horses rolling in clover. At thirteen I hung around the stable in Lincoln Park and flirted with the stable boys, hoping to charm them into riding lessons my mother could not afford. Sometimes it worked, and I would bounce down the bridle path, free as a princess, never thinking of the payoff that would come at dusk. Pimply-faced boys. Groping and French kisses behind the dark barn that reeked of manure.

For Caleb horses meant honorable outdoor work and a way to make money, work being the prime factor. Horses were history to be reclaimed, identity. It was my turn to bring in the monthly check, so I began teaching at the Sunset school as a stopgap measure to keep our family solvent until the horse-business dream paid off. I am still filling that gap.

We rebuilt the log barn and the corrals, and cross-fenced our one hundred acres of cleared meadowland. I loved my upland meadow from the first day. As I walked through tall grasses heavy with seed, they moved to the wind, and the undulations were not unlike water. Now, when I look down from our cliffs, I see the meadow as a handmade thing – a rolling swatch of green hemmed with a stitchery of rocks and trees. The old Swedes who were Caleb's ancestors cleared that meadow with axes and crosscut saws, and I still trip over sawed-off stumps of virgin larch, sawed level to the ground, too large to pull out with a team of horses – decaying, but not yet dirt.

We knew land was a way to save your life. Leave the city and city ambitions, and get back to basics. Roots and dirt and horse pucky (Caleb's word for horseshit). Bob Dylan and the rest were all singing about the land, and every stoned, long-haired mother's child was heading for country.

My poor mother, with her Hungarian dreams and Hebrew upbringing, would turn in her grave to know I'm still teaching in a three-room school with no library or gymnasium, Caleb ten years dead, our youngest boy packed off to the state university, the ranch not even paying its taxes, and me, her only child, keeping company with a two-hundred-and-thirty-pound logger who lives in a trailer.

"Marry a doctor," she used to say, "or better, a concert pianist," and she was not joking. She invented middle-class stories for me from our walk-up flat on the South Side of Chicago: I would live in a white house in the suburbs like she had always wanted; my neighbors would be rich and cultured; the air itself, fragrant with lilacs in May and heady with burning oak leaves in October, could lift us out of the city's grime right into her American dream. My mother would smile with secret intentions. "You will send your children to Harvard."

Frank's been married twice. "Twice-burned" is how he names it, and there are Bowman kids scattered up and down the Blackfoot Valley. Some of them are his. I met his first wife, Fay Dell, before I ever met Frank. That was eighteen years ago. It was Easter vacation, and I had taken two hundred dollars out of our meager savings to buy a horse for our brand-new herd. I remember the day clear as any picture. I remember mud and Blackfoot clay.

Fay Dell is standing in a pasture above Monture Creek. She wears faded brown Carhartt coveralls, as they do up here in the winters, and her irrigating boots are crusted with yellow mud. March runoff has every patch of bare ground spitting streams, trickles, and puddles of brackish water.

Two dozen horses circle around her. Their ears are laid back and they eye me, ready for flight. She calls them by name, her voice low, sugary as the carrots she holds in her rough hands.

"Take your pick," she says.

I stroke the velvet muzzle of a two-year-old sorrel, a pure-bred quarter horse with a white blaze on her forehead.

"Sweet Baby," she says. "You got an eye for the good ones."

"How much?"

"Sorry. That baby is promised."

I walk over to a long-legged bay. There's a smile on Fay Dell's lips, but her eyes give another message.

"Marigold," she says, rubbing the mare's swollen belly. "She's in foal. Can't sell my brood mare."

So I try my luck on a pint-sized roan with a high-flying tail. A good kids' horse. A dandy.

"You can't have Lollipop neither. I'm breaking her for my own little gal."

I can see we're not getting anywhere when she heads me in the direction of a pair of wild-eyed geldings.

"Twins," says Fay Dell proudly. "Ruckus and Buckus."

You can tell by the name of a thing if it's any good. These two were out of the question, coming four and never halter broke.

"Come on back in May." We walk toward the ranch house and a hot cup of coffee. "I'll have 'em tamed good as any sheepdog. Two for the price of one. Can't say that ain't a bargain!"

Her two-story frame house sat high above the creek, some Iowa farmer's dream of the West. The ground, brown with stubble of last year's grass, was littered with old tennis shoes, broken windshields, rusting cars, shards of aluminum siding. Cast-iron tractor parts emerged like mushrooms from soot-crusted heaps of melting snow. I wondered why Fay

Dell had posted that ad on the Sunset school bulletin board: "Good horses for sale. Real cheap." Why did she bother with such make-believe?

Eighteen years later I am sleeping with her ex-husband, and the question is answered.

"All my wages gone for hay," says Frank. "The kids in hand-me-downs... the house a goddamn mess. I'll tell you I had a bellyful!"

Frank had issued an ultimatum on Easter Sunday, determined never to be ashamed again of his bedraggled wife and children among the slicked-up families in the Blackfoot Community Church.

"Get rid of them two-year-olds," he warned, "or... "

No wonder it took Fay Dell so long to tell me no. What she was doing that runoff afternoon, seesawing back and forth, was making a choice between her horses and her husband. If Fay Dell had confessed to me that day, I would not have believed such choices are possible. Horses, no matter how well you loved them, seemed mere animal possessions to be bought and sold. I was so young then, a city girl with no roots at all. And I had grown up Jewish, where family seemed the only choice.

"Horse poor," Frank says. "That woman wouldn't get rid of her horses. Not for God Himself."

March in Montana is a desperate season. You have to know what you want, and hang on.

FRANK'S SECOND WIFE WAS tall, blond, and young. He won't talk about her much, just shakes his head when her name comes up and says, "Guess she couldn't stand the winters." I heard she ran away to San Luis Obispo with a long-haired carpenter named Ralph.

"Cleaned me out," Frank says, referring to his brand-new stereo and the golden retriever. She left the double-wide empty, and the only evidence she had been there at all was the white picket fence Frank built to make her feel safe. And a heap of green tomatoes in the weed thicket he calls a garden.

"I told her," he says with a wistful look, "I told that woman you can't grow red tomatoes in this climate."

As for me, I love winter. Maybe that's why Frank and I can stand each other. Maybe that's how come we've been keeping company for five years and marriage is a subject that has never crossed our lips except once. He's got his place near the highway, and I've got mine at the end of the dirt road, where the sign reads "County Maintenance Ends Here." To all eyes but our own, we have always been a queer, mismatched pair.

After we began neighboring, I would ask Frank in for a cup of coffee. Before long, it was a beer or two. Soon, my boys were taking the old McCulloch chain saw to Frank's to be sharpened, or he was teaching them how to tune up Caleb's ancient Case tractor. We kept our distance until one thirty-below evening in January when my Blazer wouldn't start, even though its oil-pan heater was plugged in. Frank came up to jump it.

The index finger on my right hand was frostbit from trying to turn the metal ignition key bare-handed. Frostbit is like getting burned, extreme cold acting like fire, and my finger was swollen along the third joint, just below its tip, growing the biggest blister I had ever seen.

"Dumb," Franks says, holding my hand between his large mitts and blowing on the blister. "Don't you have gloves?"

"Couldn't feel the key to turn it with gloves on."

He lifts my egg-size finger to his face and bows down, like a chevalier, to kiss it. I learn the meaning of dumbfounded. I feel the warmth of his lips tracing from my hand down through my privates. I like it. A widow begins to forget how good a man's warmth can be.

"I would like to take you dancing," says Frank.

"It's too damn cold."

"Tomorrow," he says, "the Big Sky Boys are playing at the Awful Burger Bar."

I suck at my finger.

"You're a fine dancer."

"How in God's name would you know?"

"Easy," Frank smiles. "I been watching your moves."

I admit I was scared. I felt like the little girl I had been, so long ago. A thumb-sucker. If I said yes, I knew there would be no saying no.

THE AWFUL BURGER BAR is like the Red Cross, you can go there for first aid. It is as great an institution as the Sunset school. The white bungalow sits alone just off the two-lane on a jack-pine flat facing south across irrigated hay meadows to where what's left of the town of Sunset clusters around the school. Friday evenings after Caleb passed away, when I felt too weary to cook and too jumpy to stand the silence of another Blackfoot night, I'd haul the boys up those five miles of asphalt and we'd eat Molly Fry's awful burgers, stacked high with Bermuda onions, lettuce and tomato, hot jo-jos on the side, Millers for me, root beer for them. That's how those kids came to be experts at shooting pool.

The ranching and logging families in this valley had no difficulty understanding why their schoolteacher hung out in a bar and passed the time with hired hands and old-timers. We were all alike in this one thing. Each was drawn from starvation farms in the rock and clay foothills or grassland ranches on the floodplain, down some winding dirt road to the red neon and yellow lights glowing at the dark edge of chance. You could call it home, as they do in the country-and-Western songs on the jukebox.

I came to know those songs like a second language. Most, it seemed, written just for me. I longed to sing them out loud, but God or genes or whatever determines what you

can be never gave me a singing voice. In my second life I will
be a white Billie Holiday with a gardenia stuck behind my
ear, belting out songs to make you dance and cry at the same
time.

My husband, Caleb, could sing like the choirboy he had
been before he went off to Chicago on a scholarship and lost
his religion. He taught himself to play harmonica and wrote
songs about lost lives. There's one I can't forget:

> *Scattered pieces, scattered pieces,*
> *Come apart for all the world to see.*
>
> *Scattered pieces, lonely pieces,*
> *That's how yours truly came to be.**

When he sang that song, my eyes filled with tears.

"How can you feel that way, and never tell me except in a
song?"

"There's lots I don't tell you," he said.

We didn't go to bars much, Caleb and me. First of all we
were poor. Then too busy building our log house, taking
care of the boys, tending horses. And finally, when the an-
gina pains struck, and the shortness of breath, and we knew
that at the age of thirty-seven Caleb had come down with an
inherited disease that would choke his arteries and starve
his heart, it was too sad, you know, having to sit out the jit-
terbugs and dance only to slow music. But even then, in
those worst of bad times, when the Big Sky Boys came
through, we'd hire a sitter and put on our good boots and
head for the Awful Burger.

There was one Fourth of July. All the regulars were
there, and families from the valley. Frank says he was there,
but I didn't know him. Kids were running in and out like
they do in Montana, where a country bar is your local com-

---

* Lyrics from "Scattered Pieces" by David J. Smith, 1973.

munity center. Firecrackers exploded in the gravel parking lot. Show-off college students from town were dancing cowboy boogie as if they knew what they were doing, and sunburned tourists exuding auras of camp fires and native cutthroat trout kept coming in from motor homes. This was a far way from Connecticut.

We were sitting up close to the band. Caleb was showing our boys how he could juggle peanuts in time to the music. The boys tried to copy him, and peanuts fell like confetti to be crunched under the boots of sweating dancers. The sun streamed in through open doors and windows, even though it was nine at night, and we were flushed from too many beers, too much sun and music.

"Stand up, Caleb. Stand up so's the rest of us can see."

That was our neighbor, Melvin Godfrey, calling from the next table. Then his wife, Stella, takes up the chant.

"Come on, Caleb. Give us the old one-two-three."

The next thing, Molly Fry is passing lemons from the kitchen where she cooks the awful burgers, and Caleb is standing in front of the Big Sky Boys, the dancers all stopped and watching. Caleb is juggling those lemons to the tune of "Mommas Don't Let Your Babies Grow Up to Be Cowboys," and he does not miss a beat.

It is a picture in my mind – framed in gold leaf – Caleb on that bandstand, legs straddled, deep-set eyes looking out at no one or nothing, the tip of his tongue between clenched teeth in some kind of frozen smile, his faded blue shirt stained in half-moons under the arms, and three bright yellow lemons rising and falling in perfect synchronicity. I see the picture in stop-action, like the end of a movie. Two shiny lemons in midair, the third in his palm. Caleb juggling.

It's been a long time coming, the crying. You think there's no pity left, but the sadness is waiting, like a barrel gathering rain, until one sunny day, out of the blue, it just boils over and you've got a flood on your hands. That's what happened one Saturday last January, when Frank took me to celebrate the fifth anniversary of our first night together. The Big Sky Boys were back, and we were at the Awful Burger Bar.

"Look," I say, first thing. "The lead guitar has lost his hair. Those boys are boys no longer."

Frank laughs and points to the bass man. Damned if he isn't wearing a corset to hold his beer belly inside those slick red-satin cowboy shirts the boys have worn all these years.

And Indian Willie is gone. He played steel guitar so blue it broke your heart. Gone back to Oklahoma.

"Heard Willie found Jesus in Tulsa," says Melvin Godfrey, who has joined us at the bar.

"They've replaced him with a child," I say, referring to the pimply, long-legged kid who must be someone's son. "He hits all the right keys, but he'll never break your heart."

We're sitting on high stools, and I'm all dressed up in the long burgundy skirt Frank gave me for Christmas. My frizzy gray hair is swept back in a chignon, and Mother's amethyst earrings catch the light from the revolving Budweiser clock. It is a new me, matronly and going to fat, a stranger I turn away from in the mirror above the bar.

When the band played "Waltz Across Texas" early in the night, Frank led me to the dance floor and we waltzed through to the end, swaying and dipping, laughing in each other's ears. But now he is downing his third Beam ditch and pays no attention to my tapping feet.

I watch the young people boogie. A plain fat girl with long red hair is dressed in worn denim overalls, but she moves like a queen among frogs. In the dim, multicolored light, she is delicate, delicious.

"Who is that girl?" I ask Frank.

"What girl?"

"The redhead."

"How should I know?" he says. "Besides, she's fat."

"Want to dance?"

Frank looks at me as if I was crazy. "You know I can't dance to this fast stuff. I'm too old to jump around and make a fool of myself. You want to dance, you got to find yourself another cowboy."

The attractive men have girls of their own or are looking to nab some hot young dish. Melvin is dancing with Stella, "showing off" as Frank would say, but to me they are a fine-tuned duo who know each move before they take it, like a team of matched circus ponies, or those fancy ice skaters in the Olympics. They dance only with each other, and they dance all night long.

I'm getting bored, tired of whiskey and talk about cows and spotted owls and who's gone broke this week. I can hear all that on the five o'clock news. I'm beginning to feel like a wallflower at a high-school sock hop (feelings I don't relish reliving). I'm making plans about going home when a tall, narrow-hipped old geezer in a flowered rayon cowboy shirt taps me on the shoulder.

"May I have this dance, ma'am?"

I look over to Frank, who is deep in conversation with Ed Snow, a logger from Seeley Lake.

"If your husband objects... "

"He's not my husband."

The old man is clearly drunk, but he has the courtly manner of an old-time cowboy, and he is a live and willing body.

"Sure," I say. As we head for the dance floor, I see Frank turn his head. He is watching me with a bemused and superior smile. "I'll show that bastard," I say to myself.

The loudspeaker crackles as the lead guitarist announces a medley—"A tribute to our old buddy, Ernest Tubb." The Big Sky Boys launch into "I'm Walking the Floor Over You," and the old man grabs me around the waist.

Our hands meet for the first time. I could die on the spot. If I hadn't been so mad, I would have run back to Frank because that old man's left hand was not a hand, but a claw—

all shriveled up from a stroke or some birth defect, the bones dry and brittle, frozen half-shut, the skin white, flaky, and surprisingly soft, like a baby's.

His good right arm is around my waist, guiding me light but firm and I respond as if it doesn't matter who's in the saddle. But my mind is on that hand. It twirls me and pulls me. We glide. We swing. He draws me close, and I come willingly. His whiskey breath tickles at my ear in a gasping wheeze. We spin one last time, and dip. I wonder if he will die on the spot, like Caleb. Die in mid-motion, alive one minute, dead the next.

I see Caleb in the kitchen that sunstruck evening in May, come in from irrigating the east meadow and washing his hands at the kitchen sink. Stew simmers on the stove, the littlest boys play with English toy soldiers, Mozart on the stereo, a soft breeze blowing through open windows, Caleb turns to me. I will always see him turning. A shadow crosses his face. "Oh dear," he says. And Caleb falls to the maple floor, in one motion a tree cut down. He does not put out his hands to break his fall. Gone. Blood dribbles from his broken nose.

THERE IS NO GOING back now. We dance two numbers, the old cowboy and me, each step smoother and more carefree. We are breathing hard, beginning to sweat. The clawhand holds me in fear and love. This high-stepping old boy is surely alive. He asks my name.

"Mady."

"Bob," he says. "Bob Beamer. They call me Old Beam." He laughs like this is a good joke. "Never knowed a Mady before. That's a new one on me."

"Hungarian," I say, wishing the subject had not come up, not mentioning the Jewish part for fear of complications. And I talk to Mother, as I do when feelings get too deep.

"Are you watching me now?" I say to the ghost of her. "It's

come to this, Momushka. Are you watching me now?"

It's odd how you can talk to the ghost of someone more casually and honestly than you ever communicated when they were alive. When I talk to Caleb's ghost it is usually about work or the boys or a glimpse of beauty in nature or books. I'll spot a bluebird hovering, or young elk playing tag where our meadow joins the woods, or horses running (I always talk to Caleb about any experience I have with horses), and the words leap from my mouth, simple as pie. But when I think of my deep ecology, as the environmentalists describe it, I speak only to Mother.

I never converse with my father. He is a faded memory of heavy eyebrows, Chesterfield straights, whiskery kisses. He was a sculptor and died when I was six. Mother was five-feet-one, compact and as full of energy as a firecracker. Every morning, in our Chicago apartment lined with books, she wove my tangled bush of black hair into French braids that pulled so tight my eyes seemed slanted. Every morning she tried to yank me into shape, and every morning I screamed so loud Mother was embarrassed to look our downstairs neighbors in the eyes.

"Be quiet," she commanded. "They will think I am a Nazi."

And there was Grandma, who lived with us and wouldn't learn English because it was a barbaric language. She would polish our upright Steinway until the piano shone like ebony. I remember endless piano lessons, Bach and Liszt. "A woman of culture," Mother said, sure of this one thing. "You will have everything."

"You sure dance American," the old cowboy says, and we are waltzing to the last dance, a song even older than my memories.

"I was in that war," he says. "Old Tubb must of been on the same troopship. We was steaming into New York and it was raining in front of us and full moon behind and I saw a rainbow at midnight like the song says, 'Out on the ocean blue!'"

Frank has moved to the edge of the floor. I see him out of the corner of my eye. We should be dancing this last one, I think, me and Frank and Old Beam. I close my eyes and all of us are dancing, like in the end of a Fellini movie – Stella and Marvin, the slick young men and blue-eyed girls, the fat redhead in her overalls, Mother, Caleb. Like Indians in a circle. Like Swede farmers, Hungarian gypsies.

Tears gather behind my closed lids. I open my eyes and rain is falling. The song goes on, sentimental and pointless. But the tears don't stop.

"It's not your fault," I say, trying to smile, choking and sputtering, laughing at the confounded way both these men are looking at me. "Thank you for a very nice dance."

I CRIED FOR MONTHS, off and on. The school board made me take sick leave and see a psychiatrist in Missoula. He gave me drugs. The pills put me to sleep and I could not think straight, just walked around like a zombie. I told the shrink I'd rather cry. "It's good for you," I said. "Cleans out the system."

I would think the spell was done and over, and then I'd see the first red-winged blackbird in February or snow melting off the meadow, or a silly tulip coming up before its time, and the water level in my head would rise, and I'd be at it again.

"Runoff fever" is what Frank calls it. The junk of your life is laid bare, locked in ice and muck, just where you left it before the first blizzard buried the whole damned mess under three feet of pure white. I can't tell you why the crying ended, but I can tell you precisely when. Perhaps one grief replaces another and the second grief is something you can fix. Or maybe it's just a change of internal weather.

Frank and I are walking along Bear Creek on a fine breezy day in April, grass coming green and thousands of the yellow glacier lilies we call dogtooth violets lighting the woods. I am picking a bouquet and bend to smell the flowers. Their scent is elusive, not sweet as roses or rank as marigolds, but a fine freshness you might want to drink. I breathe in the pleasure and suddenly I am weeping. A flash flood of tears.

Frank looks at me bewildered. He reaches for my hand. I pull away blindly, walking as fast as I can. He grabs my elbow.

"What the hell?" he says. I don't look at him.

"Would you like to get married?" He is almost shouting. "Is that what you want? Would that cure this goddamned crying?"

What can I say? I am amazed. Unaccountably frightened. "No," I blurt, shaking free of his grasp and preparing to run. "It's not you." I am sobbing now, gasping for breath.

Then he has hold of both my arms and is shaking me – a good-sized woman – as if I were a child. And that is how I feel, like a naughty girl. The yellow lilies fly from my hands.

"Stop it!" he yells. "Stop that damned bawling!"

Frank's eyes are wild. This is no proposal. I see my fear in his eyes and I am ashamed. Shame always makes me angry. I try to slap his face. He catches my hand and pulls me to his belly. It is warm. Big enough for the both of us. The anger has stopped my tears. The warmth has stopped my anger. When I raise my head to kiss Frank's mouth, I see his eyes brimming with salt.

I don't know why, but I am beginning to laugh through my tears. Laughing at last at myself.

"Will you marry me?" I stutter. "Will that cure you?"

Frank lets go of my arms. He is breathing hard and his face is flushed a deep red. He sits down on a log and wipes his eyes with the back of his sleeve. I rub at my arms.

"They're going to be black and blue."

"Sorry," he says.

I go over to Frank's log and sit at his feet, my head against his knees. He strokes my undone hair. "What about you?" he replies, question for question. "Do you want to do it?"

We are back to a form of discourse we both understand.

"I'm not sure."

"Me neither."

MAY HAS COME TO Montana with a high-intensity green so rich you can't believe it is natural. I've burned the trash pile and I am done with crying. I'm back with my fifth-graders and struggling through aerobics classes three nights a week. I stand in the locker room naked and exhausted, my hips splayed wide and belly sagging as if to proclaim, Yes, I've borne four children.

A pubescent girl, thin as a knife, studies me as if I were a creature from another planet, but I don't care because one of these winters Frank and I are going to Hawaii. When I step out on those white beaches I want to look good in my bathing suit.

Fay Dell still lives up on Monture Creek. I see her out in her horse pasture winter and summer as I drive over the pass to Great Falls for a teachers' meeting or ride the school bus to basketball games in the one-room school in Ovando. Her ranch house is gone to hell, unpainted, weathered gray, patched with tar paper. Her second husband left her, and the daughter she broke horses for is a beauty operator in Spokane. Still, there's over a dozen horses in the meadow and Fay Dell gone thin and unkempt in coveralls, tossing hay in February or fixing fence in May or just standing in the herd.

I imagine her low, sugary voice as if I were standing right by her. She is calling those horses by name. Names a child might invent.

"Sweet Baby."

"Marigold."

"Lollipop."

I want my meadow to be running with horses, as it was in the beginning—horses rolling in new grass, tails swatting at summer flies, huddled into a blizzard. I don't have to ride them. I just want their pea-brained beauty around me. I'm in the market for a quarter horse stallion and a couple of mares. I'll need to repair my fences and build a new corral with poles cut from the woods.

My stallion will be named Rainbow at Midnight. Frank laughs and says I should name him Beam, after my cowboy. For a minute I don't know what he's talking about, and then I remember the old man in the Awful Burger Bar. I think of Fay Dell and say, "Maybe I'll name him Frank."

Frank thinks Fay Dell is crazy as a loon. But Fay Dell knows our lives are delicate. Grief will come. Fay Dell knows you don't have to give in. Life is motion. Choose love. A person can fall in love with horses.

CHRISTOPHER TILGHMAN

Mary in the Mountains

SHE WROTE TO SAY THIS: *Send me a picture of the boy we never had, the one with blue eyes, big ears, and a smile that says, Nothing, so far, has hurt too bad.*

She wrote: *Yesterday, when I got your letter, I carried it with me like a dark bloom. I took it with me when I went swimming at the dam, and I lay down in the sun, gray-haired and white. A few feet away from me two high-school girls with long, thin bodies dove into the water without a ripple or splash. They wore black bathing suits stretched from hipbone to hipbone across their flat stomachs, and I touched your letter to make sure it was addressed to me.*

She wrote: *I think of you now when I look at the oak tree standing apart in the lower corner of my field. Last winter, against the snow, I saw your profile — it was your nose — in the branches. This summer there will be growth, and the deadwood that forms your eyebrows will not make it through the winter, but that is right: you were always leaving anyway. When I look at that tree, I think of you with your deep tangled roots and your fresh buds, but mostly I think of you alone.*

MARY RARELY LAUGHED; she was silent in groups and was content to pass unnoticed by anyone but Will through

his boisterous college days; she stuttered, often, on t's and
w's. She and Will were married in June 1958, in a white New
Hampshire church with high wooden trusses, under a cross
made of spruce that had twisted and checked. She wore her
grandmother's dress, petticoats, and lace, but as she came
down the aisle it was her black hair and white skin and green
eyes that people noticed. Will mumbled, but she repeated
her vows so clearly and slowly, with such conviction and determination, that husbands and wives all through the con-
gregation squirmed and avoided each other's eyes.

Will's friends, a week out of college, were disappointed by
the food, the lodging, Mary's bridesmaids, the lack of liquor
and late-night bars. Will had warned them to expect little,
just as he had tried to explain Mary to them for the past two
years. The ushers left the quiet reception as soon as Mary
and Will did, and reconvened that night in Boston for a
party they would all remember for the rest of their lives.
Years later Will heard about it and it hurt his feelings.

Will's mother never warmed to Mary—she had recognized, as few others ever had, that Mary was a mouse that
wasn't afraid to show its teeth—but Will loved her so much
he stayed awake at night counting the times she breathed.

They went to Europe for the Grand Tour. Will's mother
told everyone at the reception that at least the honeymoon
would be festive and gay, but they spent most of the first
month in cathedrals. Will listened in the gloomy shadows as
she explained the tympanum at Vézelay, the chancel at
Chartres, the altar and relics of Rouen. He wore Bermuda
shorts and black shoes and socks, a handsome face made
featureless by his sandy crew cut and heavy black glasses.
Even so, he worried what the Europeans would make of
Mary in her plain cotton shifts and wide-brimmed straw hat,
with her earnest look and stuttering French.

In their travels, they met, as planned, with three of his
ushers making a tour of nightclubs, cafés, and whore-
houses. As they drove off the following morning, Will
watched them go with the first stirring of regret. He said to

Mary, "Sweetheart, I'm getting a little tired of cathedrals."

"But I thought you liked them. I thought you said so."

"Of course, but aren't we here to see more? I really need to understand the French for my job." He added, "It's not as if you were a Catholic or anything."

So the itinerary changed, and they completed the circuit in the sweaty thunder of Tivoli Gardens and Place Pigalle. She loved the look of excitement on his face as they descended into the loud smoky music and steamy air; even as he shouted encouragement to her across a round table, she knew he longed for something unexpected, something that might save a little piece of himself for later.

On the night before their boat left, in a hotel in Le Havre, she surprised him with a leather box. Inside were tens of objects, pieces of ephemera from every region, every country, tourist bits like miniature landmarks and local crafts like clay figurines and fishing boats made of grass. All summer she had been collecting for this box.

She said, "It's so you remember. For your job."

SHE WROTE: *I am trying to bring back all the bedrooms I have ever lived in. Now that I have returned to my father's house for good, it seems time to see where I went. I bought a pad of graph paper, and a plastic square, and a box of hard pencils, and I am making a plan of each, a quarter inch to the foot. This is not as hard as it sounds because, of course, I have always had that same bed, a yardstick, but now it has your scratch across the headboard, a straight fissure through the curly maple like a road cut. Some of my bedrooms are very painful to remember, like the house in Wellesley. Other than that, I don't know what I expect to learn from charting my rooms, unless it is that wide windows have always been good for me.*

THEY LIVED IN CAMBRIDGE on the bottom floor of a brown-shingled two-family, not far from the consulting firm where Will analyzed international business trends. She researched butterflies and insects for *Horticulture* magazine, and on Friday afternoons, a few minutes before two, she would run across Massachusetts Avenue to stand in line for rush tickets at Symphony. Often she saw her mother-in-law arriving in her mink coat and yellow rubber boots, and occasionally curly-headed conservatory boys would ask her out for coffee.

Will looked forward to the day they would move out of their modest apartment with its too-friendly Italian landlord, but Mary loved that collection of small rooms, each one with a purpose, like jewelry boxes. They owned very little furniture, but there was a built-in hutch in the dining room, a small bookcase in the parlor, a window seat and mirror in the entrance hall, a linen closet outside the bedroom, and a line of brass clothes hooks in the bedroom. She covered the pantry shelves with paper and made orderly rows of bright cans and colored boxes, and each time she went in she would think of her father's garden.

On Sundays, they like to walk to the river, cross one bridge, then work down to the next, for a full circle that brought them home to hot tea. One Sunday, when spring had driven the last of the frost from the banks, Will said, "I just hope you're not getting bored. Don't you want to find something more to do? I don't know, ballet lessons?"

"But I'm never going to get bored. W-w-why do you ask that?"

"I just think someone as smart as you would want something more than that silly job."

The next Sunday, Mary went to church, alone. Inside the gray clapboard building there was order, and light, and flowers, and mystery, but still, she knew there would always be something missing from Will's life.

MARY KEPT GOING TO church, but Will moved them to Wellesley anyway. They drove into town one night to have dinner with two other couples; he thought it would cheer her after the latest miscarriage. Waiting for them, in a French spot decorated with Paris scenes made out of soldered tin, were the Billingses, who lived on Beacon Hill, and the Blooms, who were leaving, the very next day, for Selma.

"Tell the truth, Mort," said Will. "Aren't you scared?"

"They can't wipe out a whole bus. I don't think Sylvia should go but—"

Sylvia interrupted: "Kennedy *died* for this. No one has any *choice.*"

"But," said Will, "playing the devil's advocate here, isn't this a problem for the South itself to—"

Sylvia interrupted again: "The Jews that said that are all in *ovens.*"

Mary heard this with a start. Sylvia was right, she thought, but she hadn't realized the Blooms were Jewish. It was as if that gave them something to be, something to grow into. She looked at the Billingses, silent and distracted during the discussion, and wondered why they had been invited to this gathering. Then, as she had often done around Will's hearty friends, she wondered why she had been invited. Then, as he continued to debate, preparing his voice and hesitating every time he said the word *Jew* or *Negro,* she wondered why Will had been invited.

On the way home, driving out on Route 9, she could see Will chewing the inside of his cheek. Halfway, they came upon a car wreck, and there were police blinkers and the harsh light of ambulances with their doors open, and a man screaming for his wife. Mary felt empty and dark, a body that would bear no children, like their big stucco house in Wellesley, with hemlock hedges strangling every window. As they drove up the gravel driveway, Will announced, "I'm going to go. Mort and Syl are right. I'm going to Alabama."

After a few days, there was no more mention of Freedom Riding. Instead, he kept talking about that accident, the terrible arbitrariness of it, the momentary, mad collision of circumstance. For Will, the matter ended in a great black hole, but Mary, feeling the last hormones of her pregnancy forsaking her body, was not sure, not sure at all.

It probably shouldn't *surprise you to hear that however much I continue to grieve for you, which is illusory, I become more whole, which is fact. My life is a crab's life, the life of a scavenger content to hack at the pieces left behind. You're looking for the meaning of breath; I'm looking for a lost mitten. I have learned to envy your restless treasure hunt. I came to this conclusion the other day when I was working in my garden. I turned over a spade of sod that was dense with root, with seed and wildflower bulbs and tubers, and I saw a whole season of life laid out side to side, clumped and spaced, patient and forgiving. It was then I realized also how much I pitied you.*

Will, at last, had been transferred to the Paris office. The assassinations and the riots at Columbia had terrified him, but the barricades of that summer in Paris gave him the quickening heady sense of being there for history. He let his hair grow well over his collar and took to wearing tight shirts with epaulets, and salmon-colored trousers. Still, when he found them an apartment, it was on the Right Bank, a peaceful untouched neighborhood just off L'Etoile, a place with wrought-iron gates and cast-iron balconies, and high narrow doors and marble stairs.

Mary stayed behind for two months to wrap up her church committee work and to sell the Wellesley house to a family of seven.

When she joined Will in their new home in Paris, she found a pair of women's underpants hanging on a brass hook behind the bathroom door. They were beige, and American-made. She pressed them into her palm, where they burned like a hot coin, and she went dizzy staring at the black-and-white tiles on the walls and floor. She had no place of her own to hide them, so she put them in her pocketbook and carried them for weeks. She spent many days at the Louvre and kept wondering if she had made fun of the silly face he made when he kissed. When the underpants became gray in the pencils, ticket stubs, and loose change of her bag, she washed them and put them in her bureau. Every time she wore them she tried to picture her.

Will bought Mary a bright miniskirt and a see-through blouse at a boutique on the rue de Rivoli. She modeled them for him once, but never wore them outside. One day she went to lunch with a curator of Dutch paintings. He wore a cashmere suit and onyx cuff links; he seated her with a smooth assurance, ordered an aperitif with two ice cubes on the side, and snapped his long fingers at the waiter who forgot the condiments for his steak tartare. By dessert, all these stylish Continental ways had reduced her to a laughing fit, which she stifled into her napkin.

She took long train rides, slow locals to Avignon, Munich, and Amsterdam. She sat in compartments on worn seats of red velvet that smelled of babies and tarragon, and wrote thoughts in a journal. The words came out in unfamiliar voices, loaded with paradox and sudden turns she barely understood. Sometimes, when the door banged open and a businessman or a nun or a schoolgirl would slip in, she would look up in fright.

For their vacation, in the fall, they lived for a week on a canal boat, gliding in silence through vineyards and wheat fields. The captain's heavy wife served them fresh bread and chicken, and picked on Will. It was on the boat, while they were sitting in aluminum lawn chairs on the foredeck, heading into a red sun, that Will told her about trying LSD.

"In Cambridge. With Harvey and Monica. We knew you wouldn't be interested."

"W-w-when?"

"I told you. Last winter in Cambridge."

"No. When? Where was I? W-w-where was I? Was I sitting out in that prison in W-w-w... oh *shit*... in W-w-wellesley when you and Harvey and Monica all took LSD?"

"We did it a couple of times. Three times really. Harvey and I called in sick, and it was just stupid and infantile that we had to sneak around like that."

"Oh."

He waited for her to say more. When she didn't, he said, "You really can't believe what it's like."

Mary's eyes widened.

He persisted. "The thing is, what I remember most vividly, what I understood, for the first time really, truly, was you, and how much I –"

She stood up and slapped him across the face, so hard he began to whimper, and whimper, and he took off his glasses and wiped his eyes, and the color drained from his face except for the outline of her hand, which was blue.

WOULD IT PLEASE *you to know I'm seeing someone? I'm not in love with him, just seeing him, and how I love that way of saying it. Because as much as I loved you I'm not sure I ever saw you. My dog Arnold is seeing him too, with his nose; when he comes over Arnold samples his shoes, his crotch, his trousers, and then curls up in the corner of the floor. My friend does not talk very much, although I suspect he goes home worrying that he talked my ear off. So there the three of us sit, in that fussy parlor my mother thought so elegant, in the dark of late dusk, just seeing each other.*

THE BILLINGSES CAME TO dinner to look over the new Cambridge house, but they were so busy bickering at each other they had little appetite for the veal. Harvey sprawled in a loveseat with his hands tucked deep into his waistband and his feet stacked heel-to-toe, as if everyone was supposed to admire his shoes, and from time to time he would loll his head sideways to spew insults all over his wife.

Mary kept leaving the room, but each time she did, the conversation died, as if the three of them had so exhausted each other that the only fun left was to display it to the world.

"Oh yeah, Will. Did I tell you where Monica was that other night? I can't remember if I told you this one. Hey, Mary, hey wait, let me..."

After an hour of this Mary turned off the stove and went to her bedroom. She put on a nightgown, brushed out her hair, graying quickly now, and felt the promise of an early fall as it parted the curtains and passed over her bed.

THE MORNING OF HER forty-second birthday Will got up for work early and was gone by the time she came down. On the breakfast table he had set her place with a yellow place mat, and a folded yellow napkin, and a small blue box centered between the silver. She pushed the box aside and ate her breakfast, and all day long avoided the kitchen.

She opened it, finally, in the late afternoon. It was a string of pearls spaced with tiny gold balls, all strung on a fine golden chain. She stared at the pearls, cradled in satin, ran her fingertip down the line, and then burst into tears. Who could he have been thinking about when he bought those pearls for her? Around what young neck had he pictured them hanging?

YOU HAVE ASKED ME *if I forgive you, after all these years. You should know better than to ask a Christian that question. It's like asking a poet, Is the rain a symbol for death? If the truth were that simple, the answer would have been that simple. Forgiveness has nothing to do with time and nothing to do with me. Forgiveness is a*

high meadow, yellow grasses surrounded by the dense, sharp tangle
of spruce trees. It exists, I promise you, but it's not a place for me to
go, much as I would like to. It's a place for you to find, alone.

"WOULDN'T YOU LIKE to go away for a while? Maybe find
a place where you can think without me moping around?"

Mary jerked her head up, startled. She was reading in her
study, and from the corner of her eye the plumber's helper
Will was carrying looked like a club.

He repeated: "I've just been running it over and over.
And I suddenly realized how selfish I've been."

"Are you asking me to leave? Is that what you want me to
do?"

"No. Not at all. It's just that lately you've seemed so worn
out, and it's me, I know it's me doing this to you. So I
thought you'd have fun planning some kind of trip. To Europe maybe."

"I don't think I'd have much fun in Paris, even you can see
that."

"I did not mean France," he said curtly.

She reached her hand over to his hairy thigh. He was
wearing only his undershorts and watch. "Will. Sit down."
She gave him a slight push toward a chair. "Sit down and
talk to me."

"I really don't have time for this. I didn't want a big
thing."

"Is there anything wrong?"

"Wrong? I clogged the toilet." He held up the plumber's
helper for her to see.

"Is everything at work okay? Everything's all straightened
out?"

"What in God's name are you after? Everything's fine at
work. You know that."

"Do you want me to be your friend? Is someone treating
you badly? You can talk to me about it."

He blushed.

"Do you feel okay? You're not worried about any health things, are you?"

"No."

"Then there's nothing wrong," she said, and glanced back at her book.

"Well, Christ, Mary. Doesn't the world strike you as a bit peculiar? Just look out the window. Read the paper some- day. You get killed these days for having a fashionable pair of sunglasses. Reagan's going to win and then you can kiss it all goodbye. The Russians are moving missiles into East Germany, the Arabs have us by the balls, and the spics, from Mexico to Tierra del Fuego, are going to self-destruct, ex- cept they'll take us and our economy with them. I've never understood why all your church stuff makes you miss these little details. Next time you're on your knees I really wish you'd think about this."

"I have noticed that the world is not a kind or generous place. That's what I think about when, as you say, I'm on my knees."

"But you don't think about me, do you?"

"I thought you said nothing is wrong with you."

"Jesus, Mary. How can you be so cruel? You're just so goddamn *cruel.*" His mouth quivered and tears flooded his eyes.

She reached out again for his knees, but he bolted up and ran out into the hall, where he let out a yelp, like a dog. He was still carrying the plumber's helper, and a few minutes later Mary heard a great rush of water as the toilet ran free again.

ON WEDNESDAY, *or Thursday, if Wednesday is rainy or bitter cold, I take my neighbor Violet for a walk. She is not much past sev- enty, but she says living in the same house all her life has given her arthritis and she leans very heavily on me. She would like to go out more often, but I have to take a rest between outings. Violet has never been outside the state of New Hampshire, which is fine with her really, but she loves to hear about other places and wonders if she would have the courage to climb what she calls the Iffel Tour. As we walk, picking our way around tricky stones and across frozen ruts, so entwined it's hard to know which of the four legs are the bad ones, I tell her my stories. I'm sure by now most of what I say is plain fiction, but she doesn't care. When I repeat myself, she starts jabbing a deformed knuckle into my side to urge me to get on to the part she loves, about trains, and about people who fear for their souls. She sighs happily when I close out a chapter, as if there is now music, and sometimes, on the sad but replete close, Violet says, That was lovely. Along the way she has formed a very firm picture of you, and even though I have never told her anything severe, she tenses when you come on stage and gives you a villain's hiss. She is Catholic, though, and says rosaries for you. She wants me to convert so I can drive her to Mass. I tell her to go to hell and we both laugh, two ladies with the vague fear we're going there anyway.*

MARY'S FATHER DIED a few months after his eightieth birthday, and left the house to Mary. A few months later, she and Will packed most of her portable things into their cars, and they drove up from Boston into the mountains in a convoy. Will insisted they stop in Concord for a "nice lunch," and Mary sat in a renovated mill building and pictured them eating ice cream together, thirty years earlier. She could not understand why, with everything that had happened since, she didn't want this breakup.

After they had unloaded the cars she began to ache, a hollow tightness she hadn't felt in years. Will waited in the mudroom while she cried softly and briefly; then they kissed and he was gone. The old forester's woolen pants and mackintosh still hung on the pegs of the mudroom, with a sprig of fir stuck in one pocket. Six pairs of boots, one for each working day, stood in a line, and the last pair was still caked with mud.

The house smelled faintly of lavender and cedar, her mother's presence decades after her death, and of wood smoke and dogs, her father's. In the dark parlor, upholstered in English linen with camelbacks and ball-and-claw feet, she found the row of Staffordshire her mother had collected: the chimney sweep, the happy milkmaid, the sea captain home for good.

She walked into her father's study, with its rows of Kipling, Gibbon, and Tennyson, its Loeb Classics, its Zane Grey and Bret Harte. In the corner was a pile of Christmas novels, most from her and all, how it pleased her, unread. On the desk was the last manuscript of a forestry handbook that would never be published. She rubbed the desk surface and smelled her father's chalky forearms on her hands, and knelt down to kiss the permanent shape in the leather of his chair.

SHE WROTE: *It is a paradox I cannot escape that you, who believe the world has been so uniquely damaged by the modern age, are still capable of the deepest faith, while I, who find the Holy Ghost in even the most hideous and ardent acts, will always be among the children at the gates. Faith is the assurance of things hoped for, the conviction of things not seen. You, on your treasure hunt that has caused me such pain, have held hopes beyond madness, and you have stared at the unseen so long that your eyes are hollow. Your thirst, that sandy being I used to feel in bed with me, turning your blood to powder and your flesh to bone, will save you.*

She wrote: *If you send me a picture of your son I will put it on my bureau. It was kind of you to write and not just send an announcement, although an announcement is more than I would have expected. The joy, at your age, to have a child at last. But please don't think his picture will be alone on my bureau. Please don't think yours is the only face I see in the branches of oak trees. I've never lost anyone. That is what will save me. The memories are my grace, and all of you, as you can hear me say, are w-w-welcome in my heart.*

MOLLY BEST TINSLEY

Zoe

She liked to be the first to speak. It wasn't that she wanted to be nice, or put them at ease; it was her way of warning them not to be, of setting the tone she liked best: bemused, even ironic, but formal. She didn't want any of them thinking she was someone to cultivate. Whenever those voices, low and strained, interrupted her life downstairs, whether they came late at night from the front hall or mornings from the kitchen, she slipped into the one-piece camouflage suit she used as a bathrobe, wrapped the belt twice around her slim waist, and ascended to meet her mother's latest. She liked to catch him with breakfast in his mouth, or romance on his mind, and then before he could compose himself, announce, "I am Zoe, her daughter," offering a little bow and a graceful hand, limp as a spray of japonica.

It usually left him stammering, fumbling — this blend of childlike respect and self-possession. If he'd already begun to imagine her mother recharging his life with pleasure and purpose, Zoe's winsome presence made such visions more intense, then tipped them into unsettling. Though he'd never gone in for kids before, he might find himself thinking at first how agreeable it would be to have a delicate creature like her around, slender, long-legged, with pale freckles across her nose. These days she has her auburn hair bobbed at the ears so it curls up shorter in back above a softly fringed nape. But if he thought for a moment how much the child must know, her poise could seem ominous – all the things *he* didn't know, was hungry to find out, but might not want to hear.

"So what's it like, living with her?" one of them asked Zoe once, as if he expected soon to be sharing the experience, to be given exclusive credit for recognizing that her mother was an extraordinary woman. He reminded Zoe of a large rabbit – a confusion of timidity and helpless lust.

"There's never a dull moment," Zoe answered, sweet but nonchalant. "I meet a lot of interesting men." That was stretching things. Most were rabbits.

Often they felt called upon to tell Zoe, "Your mom's a great lady." Did they think Zoe was responsible for raising her mother and not the other way around? Or that she had a choice of mothers? Or that she couldn't guess what they meant, that her mother was something else in bed, that they'd never done it to a Sibelius symphony before?

Since the age of five when her parents split up, Zoe Cameron and her mother, Phyllis Rush, have lived beyond the D.C. Beltway in The Colonies of Virginia, clusters of townhouses subtly tucked into one hundred acres of rolling woods, whose inhabitants readily paid a little more to get aesthetic design and proximity to nature. Set against the ridge of a hill, with cathedral ceilings and an expanse of glass to the south, Zoe's mother's unit welcomes light, draws it in to challenge her work – heavy terra cotta, here and there a dull giant bronze – set off by white walls. Each piece has been given a woman's name, yet they are only parts of women, global buttocks and thighs, pairs of breasts larger than the heads mounted upon them – Leda, Electra, Helen, truncated. They are one reason Zoe stopped bringing home friends, who tended to stare about in stunned silence or whisper words like *gross* and *perverted*. Zoe has learned contempt for kids her own age, who cannot understand true art. Yet she hates her mother's women: fat, naked blobs. The bald definition of nipple or vulva makes her sick. There are more of them on exhibit in the local gallery her mother manages in The Commons. The public tends not to buy them, but Phyllis does enter them in shows and they have won awards, including a purchase prize at the Corcoran. After that, a man from the *Washington Post* came out to photograph Phyllis at home in her skylit studio. Zoe declined to be in any of his shots. He took her mother to dinner in Great Falls. When Zoe came up the next morning to leave for school, he was in the kitchen alone making raisin toast. He offered her a slice, trying to act as if he owned the place, but she drank her sixteen ounces of water as if he weren't there. It was easier than ever to resist that sweet yeasty aroma, tainted as it was by his male pride.

As far as Lucas is concerned, Zoe would give anything to go back and start over again with the moment she arrived home in the early afternoon to find his body sticking out from under the sink. Thinking her mother had finally called someone to fix the dishwasher, Zoe set her wide-brimmed hat down on the table and looked on absently as the body twisted and grunted with its efforts. Her hunger had been stubborn that day, conjuring extravagant food fantasies that almost sabotaged a test in precalculus. But she had conquered temptation, and now what she wanted was plenty of water and maybe a carrot to get through until dinner.

"Let me out of here," came a roar, all of a sudden, followed by bumping sounds and *great God*'s, and the upper part of the man extricated itself from the cabinet. His knuckles were smudged with black, his once-starched shirt was sharply wrinkled, and he rubbed the top of his head ruefully, but when he saw Zoe, his expression flexed in a smile. "Well, look at you," he said. "Don't you look out of this world!" And not expecting such a remark from a repairman, Zoe, who was known to become transfixed by her own image whenever she found it reflected, who that day was wearing one of her favorite suits – broadly padded shoulders over a short slim skirt, a blue that turned her eyes blue – could not bring herself to disagree, nor think of anything to say back. She did try her ironic geisha bow, but in the same instant noticed the roaches hurrying over the sill of the sink cabinet and out across the kitchen floor in a dark stream.

Before she knew it she had emitted a soft scream, more out of embarrassment than fear. She had certainly seen roaches in the kitchen before, those nights when she gave in to temptation and felt her way up the stairs in the dark. Thinking it was almost like sleepwalking, she was almost not responsible for what she was about to do: forage for food, cookies, bagels, leftover pasta, cinnamon raisin toast drenched in butter. When she turned on the light, there they always were, collected on some vertical surface in clusters of imperceptible activity, and she caught her breath in disgust, but went on to get what she had come for.

"They must have a nest under there," the man said, a little out of breath. He was somehow hopping and stooping at the same time, slapping at the creatures with one of his moccasins. "How about giving me a hand here?"

Zoe looked down helplessly at her clothes, her inch-high patent heels.

"How about insecticide, a spray or something?"

"If we have any, it's in there." She pointed to the cabinet from which they kept coming. The floor around him was awash with brown spots. Some had been hit and were finished moving. "Close the door," Zoe cried. When she realized the sense of her suggestion, she repeated it more calmly.

He smacked the door shut, and the stream was cut off. "Good thinking," he said.

She pursed her lips to hide her pleasure. Producing a fly-swatter from the closet in the front hall, she commenced ceremoniously to slap at the remaining roaches from the comfortable distance its handle allowed. "Mother," she called.

"She went to the store," the man said, rubbing his bare foot along his pants leg, then replacing his shoe. "I thought I'd keep myself busy until she got back."

That was when Zoe realized he wasn't a plumber and that she had been inexplicably foolish. Her mother, who scorned home maintenance, who refused to spend any time on fixing things when she could be making something new – why would her mother suddenly hire a plumber? "I am Zoe, her daughter," she said, with a final stroke of the swat-ter, but it was too late.

"I assumed as much," the man said. "From the side you're a dead ringer." He introduced himself: Lucas Washburn. He had light, almost frizzy hair and eyebrows, no cheek-bones to speak of, and his nose must have been broken once and never set straight. His skin was fissured from past acne, and his eyes were a flat, changeless gray. He was not hand-some, Zoe decided, but there was something about him. His hair was cropped short, his skin evenly tanned, his khaki pants creased. Clean – in spite of his disarray, he seemed oddly, utterly clean.

"I assumed you were the plumber." Zoe pulled the broom out from beside the refrigerator and began with dignity to sweep roach hulls into a pile.

"I can see why. I hear you're down to one bathtub."

Zoe stiffened at the forced intimacy, the hint of sympa-thy. She normally did not interfere in her mother's affairs, patiently allowing what Phyllis would call nature to take its course. But this man, with his long cheekless face, who had

poked around under their sink, discovered their roaches—
he was not at all her mother's type, and the sooner he was
history, the better. "And it happens to be my bathtub downstairs, which gets pretty inconvenient if you think about it.
One of her quote friends pulled the soap holder off the wall
in *her* tub and half the tiles came with it, and the guest tub
has a leak that drips into the front hall. Actually, the whole
house is a total wreck." She finished, and made herself
laugh, but in the silence that was his reply, she heard her
words echo like a blurted confession, false notes, as if something were playing in the background in a different key.
Blasé wasn't working.

"If I had my tools," Lucas said, "we could get this sink to
drain, and I could take a look at those tubs. Next time I'll
bring my tools."

That is a lot to assume, next time, Zoe thought, and to her surprise, that was what she said.

Lucas nodded solemnly, then turned his back on her and
began washing his hands. Should she explain that her
mother had very liberal views, that if men and women were
allowed to live naturally, without the inhibitions imposed by
society, they would choose to spend their nights in each
other's beds all the time, different other's beds as the impulse moved them, mornings parting, more often than not,
forever? And that was all right with her, Zoe, for it was
much worse when a man of her mother's showed up a second time, all twitchy and trembly, and suggested doing
something that included her, and her mother, seduced by
some transient vision of family, agreed.

"I appreciate the warning," Lucas said, drying his long
hands finger by finger. Then he added, "Maybe I've got
something in common with those guys in there"—he jerked
his head toward the roach settlement—"I'm pretty hard to
get rid of."

That night her mother and Lucas fixed strip streaks,
streamed artichokes, wild rice. As she often did, Phyllis set

up small folding tables on the balcony off the living room in view of the sunset, but Lucas moved the hibachi to the backyard below to comply with the county fire code. ("What fire code?" Phyllis asked. She had never heard of any fire code.) Zoe went downstairs to change into a faded denim jumpsuit, espadrilles. She rolled a fuchsia bandana into a headband and tied her curls down, Indian-style. She freshened the strip of pale blue shadow on her lower lids, all the while aware that Lucas was right beyond the glass door, the drapes that don't quite meet, calling arguments up to her mother in favor of well-done. Phyllis stuck to rare. Her face blank and impersonal, Zoe made a last appraisal in the full-length mirror. She pushed a fist into her sucked-in abdomen. *I hate my stomach,* she thought. You couldn't trust mirrors; they could be designed to make people look thinner. All the ones in stores were deceptive that way.

Lucas sawed off huge blocks of meat and swallowed them almost whole. Her mother plucked her artichoke, petal by petal, dragged each one through her lips slowly, her subtly silvered eyelids drooping with the pleasure. She had a strong jaw, and a wide mouth, with large teeth—but she knew how to recontour her face with light and shade, to make her eyes seem bigger, mysterious. Yes, Zoe had her nose, rising fine and straight from the brow, nostrils flared back, so that if you happened to have a cold or be cold, their moisture was open to view. Zoe had learned to carry her head tilted slightly forward, to make it hard for anyone to see into her nose.

To Lucas's credit he seemed not to be noticing Phyllis's sensual performance. He was expressing his suspicion that her clogged dishwasher and drain stemmed from a failure to scrape dirty dishes thoroughly; a small chicken bone in the trap, for example, was all it took to start an obstruction.

Phyllis threw her head back and laughed. "You sound like my mother," she said.

Lucas wasn't fazed. "You're talking to someone who's

trained to eliminate human error." Lucas flew for Pan Am; Phyllis had picked him out of the happy-hour crowd in the lounge at Dulles Airport after dropping off a friend.

Phyllis stroked his closest arm. "That's Mother all over again."

"Another word for it is *accident.*"

"It's only a dishwasher," Phyllis said, sullenly, and the fatalist in Zoe settled back with the vaguest sense of loss to watch this man ruin things with her mother long before he could get the bathtubs fixed.

In a steady, almost uninflected voice, he was talking improvements. He could see a brick patio in their backyard, and redwood planters and a hexagonal redwood picnic table. Zoe saw clumsy strategy, tinged with pathos. He frankly admitted he was tired of living on the tenth floor of a condo in Hunting Towers. Between his job and the apartments he unpacked in, he never had his feet on the ground. "It's about time I got my feet on the ground," he said. Phyllis suggested he sprinkle dirt in his socks.

She was being strangely tolerant; maybe he had touched off an attack of what she called her "passion for reality," when practical dailiness, what everyone else did, became the exotic object of curiosity and desire. Lucas was neither suave nor witty. If you sanded his face, he might be handsome. Zoe guessed he had what her mother would call a good body, though Zoe had trouble looking at a male body long enough to form a complete picture of one. She tended to focus on them piece by piece, and they stayed like that in her mind, a jumble of parts. Her mother often said it was an insult to women the way men let themselves go after a certain age, after they had good incomes. Phyllis kept her weight down by smoking and thought women should band together and hold men to the same physical standards everyone held women to.

"Why me?" Phyllis asked Lucas, and seemed genuinely to

wonder. "For how many years have you been tied to no place particular and been perfectly happy? Why pick on my place? Maybe I like it this way."

"Look at that," Lucas said, pointing above them at a strip of white streaks and blotches on the cedar stain. "Look at the mess those birds have made of your siding. Starlings. They must have a roost in the eaves. I'd have to take care of that before I'd put in a patio right under their flight lines!"

Phyllis pulled forward a lock of her thick dark hair. "I don't begrudge them that. It's nature." She gave a quick yank, then let the breeze lift an offending gray strand from her fingers.

"Like roaches under the sink."

Zoe held her breath as her mother lit a cigarette. Was he joking or criticizing? Either way he had no right; either way her mother would finally put him in his place. Then why was she stretching, smiling languidly at his rudeness? "Everyone has them," she said, blowing a plume of smoke. "They're a fact of life."

"You don't have to give in totally," Lucas persisted.

"It isn't in me to go around poisoning things."

Her mother's reasonableness was a puzzle to Zoe. *Why him?* she kept asking herself, until the answer came to her, all at once: it made her a little queasy. It was obviously something to do with sex that gave Lucas this power, this license. Wasn't her mother always declaring that everything came down to that? It must be something sexual he did to, or for, her mother that Zoe, for all her determined precocity, had not yet figured out. Then she felt very empty — empty as though she had failed an exam, empty because she didn't want to think of Lucas that way. In the back of her mind, she had been hoping he was different, and she didn't even know she was hoping until he turned out to be the same — just another male, who in the irresistible flux of life must soon disappear. Well, she couldn't care less.

THAT NIGHT ZOE ATE. Once dead silence told her that Lucas and her mother had settled down, she stole upstairs in the dark, removed from the freezer a half gallon of vanilla ice cream and went back down to her room. She sat on the bed, and, gazing at the photos of lithe models she had cut from her magazines, began to spoon ice cream into her mouth. Each mouthful hit her empty stomach like a cold stone. It made her feel a little crazy; she couldn't think straight anymore. She swung between defiance – when she agreed with herself that this was incomparable pleasure, no matter how high the price, this cool, bland sweetness, this private solitude – and despair. "Eat up," she heard her mother encouraging, as she had all evening, though never showing concern when Zoe didn't. "She eats like the proverbial bird," her mother told Lucas. And then Lucas had said, "Do you know how much a bird eats? One of those starlings, for example? They eat something like four times their body weight in one day."

Ah, Lucas, the way he looked at Zoe then, as if he knew that sometimes she forgot she must be thinner. She forgot the terrible burden of stomach and hateful thighs, which kept you from ever being wonderful, and she ate, and having forgotten, she ate more, to forget she forgot. One hand around the damp, softening box of ice cream, in the other the spoon, hands like bird claws, eating like a bird. Her stomach danced madly as if filled with birds. Her whole body felt in motion. She strutted across her own mind, plump-chested, preening; she opened her wings and took off, soared and swooped above the balcony where Lucas, the flier, watched captivated. And then the ice cream was gone, and all that motion froze, like someone caught in the act. She looked down at her denim thighs spreading against the bed; she could barely get both hands around one. Her stomach was monstrous, almost pregnant. She was losing her shape. She would turn into one of those crude female blobs of her mother's. The thought alone was all it took to convulse her, as, eyes closed above the toilet, she imagined all the birds escaping from the cage of her ribs.

Afterwards she would not allow herself to sleep. Awake burned more calories, burned flesh from bones. She held one hand to the hollow of her throat and felt her heart beating as fast and hot as a bird's.

THIS AFTERNOON ZOE found her mother nestled in the wine velvet cushions of the sofa, her legs drawn up under a long Indian cotton skirt, smoking with one hand, sipping maté tea with the other. From the dull puffiness of her mother's eyes, Zoe could tell she had been crying. *It is all right to cry,* Phyllis has always said. *It is a natural response of the body. Holding it back is harmful.* Zoe hates it when her mother cries, hates to see the pain, the rivulets of mascara, the surrender.

"The bus was a little late today," Zoe says, hitching the knees of her linen pants and perching on the chair opposite.

Her mother pulled herself upright, bare soles on the floor, began carefully to shift the position of everything around her—the huge pillows, ashtray, teapot, the extra cup, which she filled and handed to Zoe. "You're not happy," she told her daughter.

"I'm not?" Zoe asked, with a careful laugh.

"Oh, Zoe, you don't have to pretend. But why, when two people love each other, can't at least one of them be happy? You'd think they could pool their resources and work on one of them. Tell me something you want, Zoe, okay?"

"Kids my age just aren't very happy." Her mother was in one of her moods. "We grow out of it. It's no big deal."

"But what would make you happy? We could manage it."

"You must have had a bad day," Zoe said.

Phyllis took a long pull on her cigarette. "For six hours I

have tried to work." She didn't exhale but let the smoke seep out as she talked. "I felt like any minute my hands were going to do something no one has ever done before, but they never did. Nothing. I might as well have been kneading bread. At least I'd have something to show for my time."

"Let's go to the mall," Zoe suggested. She and her mother have always had a good time shopping for Zoe's clothes. When Zoe was small, her mother said, it was like having a doll. Now Zoe has her own ideas, and Phyllis, rather than objecting, seems able to guess almost infallibly what they are – sophisticated angular lines, in pastels or white and black, plenty of defining black; Phyllis combs the racks, and brings a steady supply of possibilities into the fitting room for Zoe to try. Phyllis has always shopped for herself alone and piecemeal, at craft fairs, antique markets, Episcopal church rummage sales in Leesburg, Fairfax. She's owned her favorite jacket for more than twenty years – brown leather with a sunrise appliquéd in faded patches and strips on the back.

"I'm going back to pots," Phyllis said dramatically. "Tomorrow I'm hooking up the wheel."

"Let's go to the mall." Zoe bounced twice in the chair to demonstrate eagerness. "I need summer things. That would make me happy."

Her mother paused, searched Zoe's face. "Lucas gets in at five," she said finally. "I think he'll be coming right over."

"Lucas?" Why the flare of panic? Zoe had not seen him since the afternoon of the roaches, assumed that, like one of her mother's moods, he had passed.

"That's what he said last week before he left. He had back-to-back European runs. He said he'd be carrying his tools in the trunk of his car." Her mother's voice quavered, as if she were afraid of something, too.

"What did *you* say?"

Her mother went into a prolonged shrug. "I said all right."

"Well, you must like him then," Zoe said dismissively, deciding it was all right with her, at least one of them would be happy.

"I don't know. I don't understand him. I don't know what he's after." She laughed nervously.

"Mother," Zoe said, stressing each syllable. This was no time for either one of them to act innocent.

"Do you know what he said to me? He said, 'Why do you women assume that's all you've got to offer?'" Phyllis shook her hair violently. "We shouldn't be talking like this."

"We always talk like this."

"I know, but . . . "

"Don't be weird, okay? You've got to tell me what's going on." That has been, after all, Zoe's main fare – knowing. "I can handle things."

"I was asking him to spend the night."

"So?" Zoe had handled that countless times. Then all at once question and answer came together in her mind. "He didn't spend the night?" A rush of feeling, worse than any amount of fear, washed away her strength. She fell back into the chair, crushing her linen blazer.

"He said, number one, it wasn't safe anymore and I should know better, and number two, that it didn't matter because he'd promised himself the next time he met a woman he liked he would wait to sleep with her for six months." Her mother spoke haltingly, as though his reasoning mortified her.

"He said he liked you anyway?"

"He said he'd been through enough relationships that began with great sex. He can't afford another."

Zoe pulled herself up straight again. "Did you tell him what you think, about tapping into the flow of nature, and creating the sensuous present?"

"I can't remember," her mother said faintly, then all at once roared angrily through her teeth. "Forget him," she said, bounding up, jabbing each foot into a thong. "Let's go. He's too damned controlled. Forget him."

"I don't mind staying here and waiting to see if he shows up." Zoe's voice was playing tricks on her, first whispering and then suddenly wanting to shout. "It would be nice to have the plumbing work."

LUCAS ARRIVED AROUND SEVEN, looking as if he'd never thought for a moment that he wouldn't. He was wearing fresh khakis and a white knit shirt, with the last of four neck buttons open. He had stopped somewhere to rent a giant ladder, which he had tied onto the ski rack of his perfectly restored Karman Ghia. If there was awkwardness in the rather formal greetings he received from mother and daughter in the front hall, he didn't seem to notice; he was more interested in introducing the two of them to his plumber's pliers, assorted wrenches, a drain snake, a staple gun, and a roll of six-inch-wide screening. He was ready to work.

"You must be hungry," Phyllis said. "I've got pastrami, Swiss cheese. A wonderful melon. Aren't you too tired for this? I mean, what time is it for you? It must be after midnight. You ought to sleep. I can make up the couch," she added quickly.

He wasn't ready to sleep. He'd spent all that time in the air dreaming of feet-on-the-ground work, making mental lists of things to do. He had promised to return the ladder the next morning, and the sun was already dropping into the trees in back. "First things first," he said, unlashing the ladder from his car. He took one end, Phyllis and Zoe the other, and he led them back into the house, down the front hall, miraculously through the living room, without bumping a life-sized bronze of staunchly planted legs and hips — the Arch of Triumph, he had dubbed it last week. Out on the balcony, he passed his end over the rail and took over theirs.

He dug the ladder firmly into the grass below, then produced a shoelace from his pocket and tied one end around the staple gun, the other around a belt loop. He slipped the roll of screen up his arm, swung a leg onto the ladder, and descended. When he reached the ground, he stamped his feet a few times as if to get used to it. "Come on down," he called back to them.

Zoe had never been on a ladder before – the whole thing made her think of burning buildings, great escapes – she scrambled over the edge, linen pants, Capezios and all, and breathing deep against the slight sway, carefully eased herself from rung to rung. She was afraid of losing it if she looked down, so turned her eyes on her mother's face, where she found the blank patient expression of someone lying low.

"I think I'll use the stairs," her mother said, and disappeared. By the time she slid open the glass door, Lucas had extended the ladder twice to the impossible height of three stories. "It's simple physics," he had told Zoe, waving away her offer to steady the bottom. "It can't go anywhere." He had one foot on the first rung.

"Wait a minute, wait a minute," Phyllis said.

Lucas froze, eyes front, hands in midair.

"What are you going to do?"

"I am going to staple this stuff over the vents in the soffit, to keep the birds from getting up under your eaves and building nests and shitting on your siding." It took great control for him to speak that slowly, clearly.

"And you have to do it right now? I mean, it must be two in the morning."

Lucas looked at his watch and then back at Phyllis, stared at her as if he were having trouble translating her language. He didn't want to sleep, he didn't want to stop and wait for sleep to overtake him, he wanted to push himself until he dropped – at least that was what Zoe recognized.

Phyllis clenched her jaw, swallowed visibly. "I don't know whether I'm being pushed around or cared for."

"Give it a while," Lucas said, "and you ought to be able to tell the difference." Unblinking, he watched her, as she appeared to consider this. Then her shoulders fell forward.

"I'll be inside," she said.

Lucas was on the ladder, his feet over Zoe's head, when she realized that she must love him. She wasn't sure why — maybe because he didn't belong to her mother, maybe because there was something so definite about him, but it wasn't a boyfriend sort of love. He didn't have to return it; in fact she would rather he didn't. He just had to stay there, in her life, and let her watch him while he fixed things, and she would privately love him. The ladder flexed in toward the house.

"You sure this will hold you?" she called up to him. "What if the three pieces came apart?"

"I checked everything out," he called from the higher rungs. "But thanks for your concern."

She pursed her mouth. He was pressing the strip of screen against the eaves with the fingertips of one hand. With the other he tried to bring the staple gun into range, but he couldn't get it there: the shoelace was too short. He cursed and then tugged again, but only managed to hike his pants up on the right side where he'd tied it. The ladder shuddered, and Zoe clutched it for all she was worth.

Then, resolutely, Lucas climbed up a rung, and then another, until his head and shoulders ran out of ladder, the tips of which had come to rest just below the gutters. He wrapped his legs around the top rungs, twisted his right hip toward the house, and blindly felt the screen into place, firing the staple gun along its edges, clunk, clunk. He wavered precariously at each recoil. She gaped up at him in wonder, and not just his body at that odd foreshortening angle, but his whole heroic being seemed clear to her, shining. She was still afraid he would fall, but just as sure that there was a way to fall, a way to land so you didn't get hurt, and Lucas would know what it was.

In a few minutes he was down, and without pausing to comment or change the arrangement with the inadequate shoelace, had moved the ladder and mounted it again. He did this three times, four. And Zoe remained dutifully at his foot, face upturned, holding him in place with her eyes.

At first she thought her ears had begun to ring from craning her neck so long. She covered and uncovered them — the noise was outside, she had never heard it start, and now it had grown in volume to something shrill and unpleasant. Beyond the cluster of townhouses to the south, a long cloud of black birds hung in the pale violet sky. They were their own fixed path, funneling in from the invisible distance, spreading to rest on the saved trees at the base of the back slope. The shrieking came from the trees; when you looked closely among the leaves, it was as if each branch was thick with black fruit. Zoe had never seen anything like it.

When Lucas came down to move the ladder for the last time, she said, "They don't like what we're doing." It did seem their shrieking was directed at the two of them. "Maybe they think you've caught one of their friends up there behind the screen," Zoe said, to be amusing, but Lucas said it was just what starlings did, gather for the night in communal roosts. They had probably been there every night since early spring, carrying on, making a mess. She had just never noticed it.

"I guess I'd rather sleep up under our eaves where I could get comfortable than have to balance all night on a tree branch," said Zoe.

"Starlings are the roaches of the bird world," Lucas called down meaningfully as he climbed one last time. A few minutes later he was finished, sliding the ladder back to carrying size with loud clanks.

"Could you see whether they've built any nests yet up there?" Zoe asked.

"Didn't look," Lucas said.

"Probably they haven't yet." She gazed skeptically at the streaks and blotches on the siding.

"Hard to say. It is that time of year. You know," Lucas went on, "being a pilot, there's no love lost between myself and birds. I could tell you a story or two about the accidents they've caused, hitting propellors, getting sucked into jet engines, gumming up the works. A couple months ago out of Kennedy a bunch of gulls sailed right up into one of my engines two minutes after takeoff."

"That's weird. What happened to them?"

"The point isn't what happened to them. The way a jet turbine works, it's got these finely balanced blades. A bird carcass gets in there and the engine chokes up." Zoe made a little gagging sound of revulsion. "Look," Lucas said, "that engine was ruined. I had to fly out over the Atlantic and dump 100,000 pounds of fuel before that jumbo was light enough to land minus an engine. That's good money down the drain, not to mention the danger. When you look at it that way, it's them or us."

Zoe could tell that she was being tested. She wasn't supposed to waste sympathy on the gulls, act squeamish at their fate. That was all right. She could see that a jumbo jet was more important than a handful of birds. Lucas was realistic. How much he knew about certain things—clear, definite knowledge. She searched her mind for something comparably definite to say, something to suggest she was in agreement with him on the issue of birds. But all that came to mind in that driving clamor of bird screams was a jumble of her mother's pronouncements, bitter and nebulous as a mouthful of smoke.

LUCAS HAS SHOWERED IN Zoe's tub and crashed on the sofa, which Phyllis fixed up for him. There was nothing for mother and daughter to do then but retire early to their own rooms upstairs and downstairs, leaving him the middle. Was it because Lucas was watching that Zoe hugged her mother before they parted, something she never did willingly, unless for a camera? And why her mother's body seemed so sadly appealing to her arms – her mother's odd scorched smell, so suddenly sweet – Zoe didn't know.

Zoe won't be able to eat tonight because she doesn't dare try to sneak by Lucas. That is all right. She would much rather know he is stationed there at the center of the house, a guardian of order. Stomach clenched around its treasured pain, she lies awake thinking about this man – his determination on the ladder, when he thanked her for her concern. She goes over and over these moments in her mind, savoring them. She imagines that she has emptied herself in order to be filled more purely and perfectly by his image. When she closes her eyes, he is all she sees, poised at the foot of the ladder, then at different stages of his ascent. *Give it a while,* he keeps telling her, and she knows that he does what he does because he cares.

He has climbed far above her now, and the ladder keeps lengthening. He is climbing far beyond the roof of the house, so far she can hardly see him. Her stomach begins to ache with worry. Then the dreadful noise begins – she knows even while it is dim and distant, it is dreadful. She tries to call a warning to Lucas, but he is too high to hear, and soon the noise is deafening, and the sky darkens with enemy starlings. Lucas is engulfed by a black cloud of them; Zoe screams as loud as she can, but nothing can be heard over that noise. Then as she looks up, something comes sliding down the ladder, something shapeless, shrunken lands at her feet. She wakes up in terror, the noise still in her ears.

She must calm herself. She is awake now. She is safe inside. There are no birds, they are all asleep in the trees, balancing somehow on their branches without falling.

But that noise still shrieks in her ears, and she must make sure. She turns on the light and stumbles to the window, pulls the drape aside, tries to peer beyond the glass, through the reflection of her own room, her own body, all arms and legs, wrapped in a large men's T-shirt. She is awake now, yet it seems the noise has filled her room, and she drags open the glass door to let it out. The night air flows in, chills her into alertness. The noise inside dissipates, met as it is by another sound from above, beyond the screen, softer, but as shrill and relentless, the sort of sound, like crickets, or running water, you could confuse with silence unless you had been warned it was there.

JOAN WICKERSHAM

Commuter Marriage

On the platform at Penn Station, at 6:30 on a Saturday morning, a young woman in a red sweater stood waiting for the Boston train to pull in. She was small and slim, with short light hair pulled back into a stubby ponytail. Two shiny pieces had slipped out to frame her face, which looked quite young, schoolgirlish, although she was twenty-seven. The childish look was heightened by the fact that she was wearing bright red lipstick and smoking a short smelly cigarette, and doing neither with much authority. On her bony forearm was an enormous man's watch on a black rubber strap; every few seconds she shook her arm until the watch flopped down around her wrist, and she frowned at it, with a crease down the center of her freckled forehead.

The train came in a little late, and very slowly, as though aware of its own charisma—a faraway circle of light moving in, growing bigger, pulsing a little in the dark air of the tunnel, and then behind it a lumbering line of coaches, big, gray, dusty, hooked together like elephants in the circus. She knew that they were full of people, but it was still a surprise when the train gave a sigh and the passengers started coming out: sudden clutter and commotion all over that still platform. I am a woman meeting her husband at a train, she thought, and it made her feel important, glamorous, like someone in a Forties movie. She looked into the faces of the men surging across the floor past her. How would I feel if he were my husband? Or he? And then she saw Jack, and tried to think of one objective moment: and what about this one? But he was pressing his arms around her and bringing his face down against hers. "Ow," she said after a minute. "Your suitcase."

He let go of her instantly and stepped backwards with the suitcase that had been pressing into her legs; then he looked down at it, frowning slightly, as though it were a child he had called into his study to scold, but now that he had it there he couldn't remember what it had done wrong or figure out how to punish it.

They checked the suitcase, leaving it in a dented metal locker. "Why can't we just go back to the apartment?" Jack said, his mouth against her ear.

She shrugged; he still seemed a little strange and foreign, his hair a different length from when she had seen him last: someone she had just met at a train. "Ed and Caterina are there."

"Toss 'em out," suggested Jack.

"We can't do that. It's their apartment. I thought we'd spend the day doing New York things, and then go home. They're going out to dinner tonight, Caterina said."

"That's tactful of them."

"Don't be so grouchy."

"How about if we check into a hotel for the day? Does that count as a 'New York thing'?"

She hesitated, then kissed him quickly and bent to lift the suitcase and heave it into the locker.

THE SIGHT OF MAISIE, as always, even after five years together, turned him shy. She was so pleasing to look at, so neat. When she got out of bed in the morning, the bed was made. Her small body, naked, was surprisingly voluptuous, yet neat: small brownish nipples centered on round breasts, a golden isosceles triangle suspended between small shining hips. Her clothes, folded in the drawer at home, were deceptively inanimate, like sleeping faces – stacks of black jeans, folded-flat sweaters, and T-shirts in all colors: aqua, fuchsia, lime, black. Then she put them on and they belonged to her, she inhabited them.

Marrying Maisie had surprised him, like having a strange cat come to sleep in his lap: the mystery of being singled out. Dreaming his way through graduate school, he had met her at a party one spring and walked her home, up the stairs, into a bare, cool apartment where they sat on the floor and talked until morning. He could not remember leaving; his life with Maisie stretched back to that dawn, a continuum, a filibuster: if one of them stopped talking, the whole thing would be over. Maisie seemed like a detour from the fate that really belonged to him, dull, safe; he felt as though he had mistakenly got on the wrong bus, to a much more thrilling destination; his sense of honor prodded him to tell the driver, but he knew that if he told, he'd be put off.

THEY HAD LIVED together before they were married, but not much after. When they met, Jack was in the middle of a Ph.D. in German literature. They lived in each other's apartments and then consolidated into one place, in a noisy student-filled apartment building on the Fenway in Boston. All night long the building shook with the bass notes of a hundred stereos. They had to put their clothes bureau in the living room; their bed completely filled the tiny bedroom. Maisie worked as a secretary in the Harvard natural history museum; she hadn't figured out yet what she wanted to do. She cooked dinners for friends and dragged Jack dancing every couple of months. On Sundays they went for long walks and drank wine by the river and ended up at a foreign movie. Then Jack's father died and left him a

French-fry factory up in Maine. That sobered them both, a bucket of cold water. Jack had to go, for a while at least, to untangle the threads of the business and find someone else to run it or buy it. Of course I'm coming, said Maisie. I'll be the boss's wife, and I'll give gracious dinner parties that will intimidate the hell out of your employees. They got married and moved north, to a little cottage in a wintry deserted beach community. Two rooms upstairs and two rooms downstairs, and a fireplace that didn't work.

Something was wrong with the heat in that house. No matter how high they turned the thermostat, the rooms were still icy; at night the sheets were stiff and painful. One morning the pipes froze. Jack, swearing, put on his coat and brought in shovelfuls of snow, filling the bathtub with it, so that when it melted they would have water. Three days later the snow was still there, frozen, in the tub. Night after night Maisie sat on the couch wrapped in a blanket, watching television. She watched comedies and Westerns and late-night reruns and the news, impassively. Her mother came to visit from Virginia for a few days and said she thought the house could be charming, if only Maisie would do something with it. Why didn't they take the car over to Calico Corners and pick out some nicer curtain fabric, and maybe make some cushions for the living room? Maisie shook her head; this question seemed to her unanswerable. Her mother and Jack looked at each other, worried; good, thought Maisie, good.

So when she said she wanted to try working in publishing, and that the only place to do that was New York, Jack was actually relieved. It was the first time she'd wanted to do anything since they'd moved to Maine. Caterina and Ed said they'd love to have her. ("Are you kidding?" said Caterina over the phone. "A built-in babysitter!") Maisie had read articles about husbands and wives pursuing careers in separate states, with enormous phone bills, hopping on and off planes. She saw herself arrive back in New York after a few days in Maine with Jack: a long tanned leg (they had spent the weekend sailing) thrusting out of a taxicab, followed by a briefcase bulging with manuscripts, and glowing Maisie saying "Keep the change" and tossing her hair back and running up the stairs two at a time to her top-floor brownstone apartment. When Jack came down she would let her answering service take all the calls, while she and Jack lay in bed before an enormous atelier window. Then she would get up naked and call in for her messages, impatiently writing them down with a silver pencil: call this agent and that agent, and this famous writer is stuck on his book and needs your advice, and can you fly out to California this week to discuss the movie rights for that horrible but phenomenally successful potboiler you pulled out of the slush pile last year?

WHEN THEY LEFT THE station, she took him to her office, which he had not seen in his two previous visits to her in New York. The Saturday darkness and emptiness stripped it of its importance. How could she make him see the bustle of the book-lined reception area, the flashing lights on the telephones, the sheets of paper curling out of typewriters and computer printers? On the other hand, the desertion of the place gave Maisie new power; she was free to stroll down the long halls pointing out the offices of editors, walking around conference tables and letting her hand trail along their gleaming surfaces. She stopped to show him the aquarium in her boss's office; he bent obediently to look through the glass at a tower of slow ascending bubbles, rainbow-skinned fish hanging still in greenish water. She did not tell him it was part of her job to feed them. Then on to her cubicle, where she had left the desk strewn with urgent-looking clutter: memos, three fat manuscripts, message slips, mailing envelopes stamped Priority, all put there in excitement the night before, knowing that the next time she saw them Jack would be with her, impressed. But he only glanced at the desktop. He lifted and dropped the cover of a thesaurus that lay on top of her filing cabinet, and looked at the topless walls and said, "It must be kind of distracting, working in here," and she could tell he was thinking, You left me alone up there to come work in a cubicle?

TO GET TO THE FACTORY, you drove north, north, north. You smelled it before you saw it, an oily fried smell breathing out of the pines along the road. It was cold where the factory was, always winter, but the building gave off a feverish yellow sweat, and the snow in the parking lot was slippery with grease. When you came away, you smelled of it. Jack's hair was cold and greasy, and his clothes; the first thing he did when he got home was take a shower. He went to the factory every day and sat in his father's old office overlooking a slippery ravine behind the building: graying grass-cloth walls, cans of old paper clips and pencil ends, manila folders, their ends softened and frayed, iron tiered trays with In and Out written on masking tape in his father's handwriting, faded and stuck on too long ago now to come off. A diagram on the wall proclaiming the respective merits of the Maine and Idaho potatoes, and adjudging the Maine superior; hidden in the desk a research report revealing that more consumers preferred Idaho. Under the rickety swivel chair a plastic T-shaped mat designed to protect the carpet; it was too late for the carpet, which was filthy and beaten down, but all day Jack swiveled the chair around on the mat: his island. He was the king in a parliamentary kingdom; there was nothing for him to do. The business ran itself: the potato buyers, truckers, peelers, cutters, oilers, packagers, shippers, and distributors were all in place, doing their jobs. At home in the first few months, he and Maisie had talked brightly about changes that would make the company more profitable and more attractive to a prospective buyer: new cuts, new packaging, new advertising, new incentives to make supermarkets carry the brand. But every day, when he came into the office, the heavy oily air sucked the ideas right out of him; he fell into the chair and swiveled, looking out the window, until it was time to go home. The things on the desk acquired the cachet of heirlooms, things his father had wanted him to have.

THEY WALKED AROUND on broad, mica-specked sidewalks. They stopped for brunch at a deli. They went to museums, where Maisie stopped intently in front of everything and Jack circled with his hands in his pockets and his jaw tight, willing the day to move along. They had coffee in a coffee shop, their elbows drooping on the scarred Formica tabletop. Being alone this way, in public, was exhausting; they had things to talk about, and the longer the things went unsaid, the bigger they loomed. The afternoon grew cooler; the sun went behind the buildings; and Fifth Avenue was suddenly, miraculously navigable, cleared of shoppers and people with cameras. "Can we go to the apartment yet?" said Jack, his feet dragging like a little boy's.

"Not yet," said Maisie, looking at her watch.

"It's not as though I don't know Caterina and Ed, or don't like them," said Jack. "I have no objection to sitting around and talking to them for a while."

"I want to be alone with you," Maisie said, and took him to walk around Tudor City.

Finally she let them get on a subway. There were free seats in the car, but someone had thrown up in one of them, and there was kitty litter sprinkled on top of it and around it. Maisie and Jack stood at the other end, hanging onto metal loops, with Jack's suitcase wedged between them. The trip took an hour. Jack said, "I can't believe you do this every day." Brooklyn, when they got there, was a dark, misty orange sky hanging over squat buildings packed with lamplit

windows. "I guess all those kitchens are full of families having Saturday night supper," Jack said. He imagined kids in
pajamas, after their baths, and a grandmother reading to
them or playing War with them, while the mother scrambled eggs. But Maisie said no, she thought the apartments
were full of people taking showers and putting on makeup
and getting dressed for dates.

Caterina and Ed's apartment was in a row of brown-
stones, some of which had carved wooden doors with bev-
eled glass panes, and chandeliers inside and glimpses of
living rooms painted dark green, with white shutters at the
windows and track lighting overhead; and some of which
had iron doors with metal grilles on them, and bedsheets
over the windows instead of curtains. They lived in a bed-
sheet building, up two flights on a black iron staircase that
hung off a shiny brown wall. Maisie turned keys in a series
of locks and at the last minute the door was pulled open by
Ed, who had wet hair and a faint mentholated shaving
cream smell. "Caterina's getting dressed," he said, shaking
hands with Jack. "How've you been?"

Maisie kept Jack and his suitcase in the kitchen until after
Ed and Caterina left, leaving the phone number of the restaurant where they would be. She wanted him to walk
through the apartment not as a guest, but as a possessor. Yet
following him through it, down the hall to her bedroom, she
felt a bit embarrassed, the way she had when her parents
came to visit her at college: two worlds, both loved, but best
kept apart.

His suitcase lay in the middle of her immaculate floor,
filled with a jumble of clothes he hadn't bothered to fold.
She thought of him in the little house in Maine the night before, bachelorlike, just throwing things in. And now it was as
though the pressure of some pent-up desire had burst the
suitcase open; socks and shirts had exploded all over the
room. The very messiness of it made her nervous. She had a
stately plan for this reunion: some wine, dinner in the

kitchen with candles and Caterina's linen napkins, a talk over coffee and cigarettes, and then a procession down the dark hall to bed. The sound of Jack splashing in the bathroom, the implacable hiss of the shower, filled her with dread; she felt as though something irreversible had been set in motion, a clock ticking steadily toward an hour. When he came out, red and shiny and scrubbed, she barely looked at him, ducked past him into the steamy bathroom, where she wiped off the mirror to look at her pale reflection and tried to remember how much she had missed him. His wet towel, crowding Caterina's on the towel rack, made the bathroom look sloppy; she took it and hung it on the back of the door. When she came out, she realized she had stayed in the bathroom too long; there was Jack, lying naked with the shades down. She wished he would not do that, take off his own clothes; it seemed so businesslike. But she could hardly ask him to get dressed again so that she could undress him. She untied her shoes and put them side by side next to the bed, and she lay down beside him.

Afterwards she was relieved: a responsibility discharged, the library books renewed and now you didn't have to worry about them for another two weeks. Relief made her lively; she threw back the covers and kissed him and told him not to move, she'd check on the baby and throw together some dinner. But he came after her anyway, slowly belting himself into his bathrobe. The baby was sleeping on her stomach, her head turned to the side, her mouth sucking softly and her tiny fists curling and uncurling. They stood on either side of her crib, looking down at her and then at each other, but neither of them said anything.

They had the dinner Maisie had planned: linguine with shrimp and vegetables. A salad. Raspberry sherbet. Jack ate and ate, plowing through what Maisie considered delicate food. She lit a cigarette and thought how this enthusiasm that should have gratified her instead irritated her. Didn't he understand how carefully she chose the tomatoes and zucchini at the farmers' market? How her hands itched after deveining the shrimp? How long it took to julienne everything?

"So," said Jack. "What do you think?"

"What do I think?"

"How's this going?"

"What do you mean?" said Maisie, putting her cigarette out in her plate.

"We said we'd try it for a while, and see how it worked."

"It's only been four months."

"So—"

"I can't exactly leave the job now. I mean, I like it, it's going well, and I've really only just started to learn. If I came back to Maine, we'd be right back where we started."

"I guess we could try living halfway in between. Boston—"

"Now that's crazy," said Maisie, pushing her chair back and carrying plates to the sink. "I'm not going to commute from Boston to New York every day."

"A couple of times a week."

"You'd be the first to tell me we can't afford it. Plane fares—"

"And what about Caterina and Ed?" said Jack. He was still sitting at the table, twisting to face her as she moved around, putting the food away.

"What about them?"

"You can't stay here forever, you know."

"Who said anything about forever? It's just temporary. Until I can afford my own apartment."

"Your own apartment? But that's so—"

"So what?"

"Definite."

She sighed, squirting dishwashing soap into the sink. Dennis, she thought, yes Dennis, the murder-and-crime editor at her publishing house, he would know how to handle this. They went out for drinks sometimes after work, to a little bar off First Avenue filled with solitary men and women in leather jackets. The tough look of the place at first thrilled Maisie, but nothing ever happened there. No one talked; they just wanted to drink. She and Dennis sat at a tippy little table in the back, Formica made to look like wood, and he told her about his marriage, made so his wife could get out of Russia. His wife was a painter who slept and drank when she was with him and went away for weeks at a time. It sounded very sophisticated to Maisie, this relationship that swung between politics and passion – after all, the wife didn't have to see him ever, they could have completely separate households, bound legally only until she established residency and could get a divorce. She imagined their home, Dennis's Village apartment, as sunlit and messy, empty glasses and vodka bottles, flattened paint tubes, old photographs of Russians stuck into the dusty mirror frame, a rumpled bed, a half-eaten sandwich. Dennis, she was sure, would not get entangled in the logistics of separate households; he would not go trundling back and forth in a sleeping car; he would not ask her in a timid, little-boy voice how long this might go on. He would accept the arrangement grandly, or reject it grandly. But Jack – in these discussions with him she always knew what he should say, but he never said it; and so, although she knew better, she was forced to proceed on what was explicit between them, like a minister who, knowing perfectly well why two people should not be married but receiving no answer to his "speak now or forever hold your peace" line, has no choice but to go on with the ceremony.

CATERINA WAS SITTING in a white wicker rocking chair, holding the baby on her lap. "Trot trot to Boston," she said to it. "Trot trot to Lynn. Be careful, be careful, Ellie doesn't fall" – and here she opened her eyes very wide, and her mouth, and the baby looked blandly back, and Caterina said, "IN!" and opened her knees so that the baby dipped briefly between them and came up again, looking surprised. Maisie stood at the window, pulling apart a begonia leaf along its veins. It came apart very neatly, as though the veins were deliberate perforations, put there by some considerate manufacturer. It had rained twice already that morning, but now the sun had come out, outlining the raindrops on the windowpanes in white. A strange overexcited brightness was in the room. "Doesn't it make you feel weird to know that no matter what you do with the baby today, she won't remember it?" she said.

"I don't think of it that way," said Caterina, hoisting the baby straight up in the air so its baggy yellow pajama-feet dangled. "Because, all right, maybe she won't remember this specific moment, but she's got to store up all these good days in her subconscious somewhere. And anyway, you never know when things really start to count."

Maisie dropped the pieces of the leaf she was holding and plucked off another one. "I read in a magazine that kids who are treated badly at an early age remember it."

Caterina gazed into the baby's face. "How could anyone treat that badly?" she said. "Look at those little cheeks. Don't you just want to bite them?"

Maisie looked at the baby. She was its godmother; so far this had produced nothing in her but an uncomfortable sense that she was letting the baby down. She had known Caterina for years; they had lived together in college, and seen each other through exams, lovers, jobs, and weddings; but seeing Caterina with the baby made her want to back away, as though she had come too close to the fire. She wanted to ask Caterina sometimes whether she felt trapped, but she knew what Caterina would say: Of course not. Nobody made me have a baby. It was my choice. Everything always seemed so clear to Caterina. Such a simplified idea of morality: this was right, and that was wrong. You did right even when it was unpleasant, and you shunned wrong even when you suspected it might be very pleasant indeed. The most infuriating thing was that so far it had all worked: here was Caterina sitting in her pristine blue and white living room, so milky, so serene, holding her baby aloft in the sunlight. Much as she loved Caterina, Maisie sometimes longed for the day when the moral system messed up, when Ed had an affair or the baby grew up and did cocaine. Then Caterina would come to her for advice for a change; and Maisie would listen sympathetically and then give the answer, which, she was becoming convinced, was the only true, compassionate one possible: I don't know. It's not fair. Sometimes you do the best you know how, and things go wrong anyway.

"So how are things with Jack?" Caterina asked, rocking in the chair.

"OK," Maisie said. She didn't want to talk about it, and she hoped Jack and Ed would get back soon with the Sunday papers. She was itching to light a cigarette, but Caterina didn't like people to smoke around the baby.

"Oh, well, it'll be easier when you go home for your vacation," said Caterina. "Then you'll have more time, and more privacy."

"The awful thing is I don't really feel like that's my home," Maisie said, and instantly regretted it. This was what always happened when she let herself be seduced into a conversation with Caterina: she would swear in advance to keep things on a light level, to keep herself under control, and somehow the lid always came up off the box and all her troubles came swarming out. I am Caterina's screwed-up friend, she thought; she could imagine Caterina and Ed lying side by side in bed at night, sighing and whispering to each other that they hoped everything worked out all right for Maisie. But the truth was that she did feel at home here, where she had her own room with an unfolded old sleep sofa that had once stood on Caterina's parents' sunporch. Right now the baby was sleeping in a narrow dressing room off Caterina and Ed's room, but Maisie knew that the room she occupied was the apartment's real child room, and eventually she would have to get out so that Ellie could get in. "I could always get my own apartment, I guess," she said aloud.

"And have Jack move down here?" Caterina said, wiping the baby's face with the diaper she always had slung over her shoulder.

"I don't know," Maisie hedged. "I don't think I can really ask him to do that."

"Why not?" said Caterina briskly, the words coming out in a rush, as though she had wanted to say them for a long time. "Frankly, I've never understood why he and Maine have to be a package deal. Let him get someone else to run the place, and move down here."

"I can't," Maisie said again.

"Why not? If he cares about the marriage, he should put you first."

"Yes," said Maisie, pulling off another leaf, "but what if I ask him to move down here, and it doesn't work out?"

Caterina was silent, rocking with the baby, who had begun to whimper. If she starts nursing now, I'll scream, Maisie thought, but Caterina just kept rocking. After a moment Maisie went ahead and lit a cigarette anyway, because her hands were shaking and she knew that Caterina would not rebuke her now; and she thought again how much she hated Caterina when she was unfolding her problems before her this way, like describing the symptoms of some embarrassing infection to the doctor in detail because you know it is your only chance of proper diagnosis and cure. But Caterina couldn't cure anything; she could only anesthetize. Maisie remembered the day before her wedding, driving all over Boston with Caterina, saying, "I don't want to get married." And Caterina soothing, "It's all right, everybody feels like that right before, I felt like that, don't worry." And she had let those words coax her to the altar, like a cat coaxed down from a tree. Caterina knew something about love and safety that she, Maisie, didn't know; but she would let Caterina's words guide her there.

In the dark, in bed, something was waiting to happen. Come on, come on, it said to Maisie, and she knew she ought to ignore it, but there was this immense silence that needed to be filled with something immense, so childishly she put her small hand into its big one and let it pull her along. "You don't love me," she began in a soft voice, as though testing a microphone.

"What?" said Jack, not so much as if he hadn't heard right but as if he wanted to give her a chance to change her mind: are you sure you want to say this?

"You treat me like a chum."

"Oh, come on."

"Yes," she said, her voice shaking now and gaining volume. "I feel like we're hiking up the mountain single-file, wearing lederhosen and *whistling*."

He had the sense not to laugh, or perhaps he was too alarmed to be amused. He pulled himself up on his elbow. "That's not how you feel when we're in bed together."

"Oh, yes it is. That's how you make me feel."

The words lay in the darkness between them, out there with no way to get them back, like a letter dropped into the mail chute. Maisie wished them unsaid, but there was a strange exhilarating sense of having set something going. She had never known before that making trouble could be a palpable physical sensation, like splashing in a still pond or bicycling downhill. I'm making trouble, she thought, and there was a reckless creative urge to make more. She pushed off the covers and got out of bed. Jack's discarded shirt was the first garment she came to, and she pulled it on and went to stand by the window. This discussion seemed to her historic, but it had not happened yet; she felt that she should speak carefully, for posterity, but there was also an itch to get on with it already, like standing backstage before a play and watching the audience trickle in, so slowly, so casually. She said, "You don't love me in a sexy way."

"Of course I do. All weekend I've wanted –"

"That's not what I mean. Your wants are so *healthy*. It's like wanting to exercise, or wanting to eat. It comes from the same part of you that likes to read, or see friends, or pet the cat."

"Maisie, what do you want?"

"I want it to be *dark*," she said. "I want it to be involuntary, to come out of *need*, not affection. I feel like we're so damned *affectionate* all the time. Why can't you ever get angry at me?"

"Keep talking this way and I'll get there."

"You see? You see? You're so rational all the time. You're so good-humored. Don't you know I'm saying horrible things to you? Don't you know we're in trouble? Why don't you stop me?"

But he stayed propped on his elbow looking at her, as though she were a messenger riding wildly ahead of a cyclone, and he was torn between believing her warnings and looking at the blue sky and the safe, quiet countryside all around them.

JACK DID NOT HAVE to catch a train back until Monday afternoon, but Maisie had to work. She had a meeting at lunchtime, she said, so she could not see him then, and she felt terrible about it. She really did seem to feel terrible; she put her arms around his neck and cried, and said she was sorry that things had not gone well. "It's just that we didn't have enough *time*," she sobbed. Jack said it was all right, they couldn't expect things to be perfect every time they saw each other. "But don't let this one become indelible, OK?" said Maisie. "Because we won't see each other for a while, so please just don't think about this too much – " He promised that he wouldn't, and that he would call her the following night after work.

After she left, he went into the kitchen, where Caterina was ironing. She clearly had been taken into Maisie's confidence, and was trying to pretend she didn't know anything was wrong; she blushed, and offered him tea, and questioned him gently about his work, and then, when he complained about the factory, said suddenly, sharply, "So why don't you sell it?"

He went into the bedroom and packed his suitcase, told Caterina he was going to spend the day in New York, and thanked her for having him. "Don't be silly," she said, kissing him on the cheek, "Maisie's part of the family."

The lockers in the station were full, so he left the bag in a checkroom and went out walking. In his head as he walked, he had a conversation with Maisie. I don't own you, he said. I want you to be happy. If it makes you happy to be in New York, then that's what I want.

And she said, If you don't love me enough to do something about it, then why should I give up everything to come live with you in that terrible lonely place?

All right, then, I do miss you. Get back here now.

And she said, You don't own me.

When he was tired he went back to the station to get his suitcase, but rummaging in his pockets he couldn't come up with the claim check. "Sorry," said the clerk. "I can't let you have it without the token."

"But I can see it," said Jack, leaning over the counter and pointing. "It's that green leather one right over there."

"Sorry."

"Wait. What am I supposed to do?"

"After thirty days it goes over to lost and found. You can claim it there."

"That's stupid. Why should I wait thirty days when I'm here, now."

They wouldn't give it back to him. So he sat on a bench fingering his return ticket and waiting for them to call the next train. As he sat there, he began to get an idea. What if he got a taxi and went over to Brooklyn and knocked on the door just like that, and said I'm staying. But he could hear voices on the other side of the door, talking and laughing and interrupting each other, stopped suddenly by his knock; and there he was, standing in the doorway, gazing in on the startled faces of his wife and the people she lived with.

TOBIAS WOLFF

Sanity

GETTING FROM SAN DIEGO to San Marco State Hospital
isn't easy unless you have a car, or a breakdown. That's what
happened to April's father, and they got him out there in no
time at all. The trip took longer for April and her stepmother: they had to catch three different buses, walk up a
long road from Pendleton Boulevard to the hospital
grounds, and then walk back again when the visit was over.
There were plenty of cars on the road, but nobody stopped
to offer a lift. April didn't blame them. They probably figured that she and Claire were patients – "fruitcakes," her
dad called them – out for a stroll. That's what April would
have thought, coming upon the two of them out here, on
foot and unaccountable. She would have taken one look and
kept going.

Claire was tall and erect. She was wearing her gray business suit and high heels and a wide brimmed black hat. She
carried herself a little stiffly because of the heels, but kept
up a purposeful, dignified pace. "Ship of State" – that was
what April's father called Claire when she felt summoned to
a demonstration of steadiness and resolve. April followed
along in loose order. She stopped now and then to catch her
breath and let some distance open up between herself and
Claire, then hurried to close that distance. April was a

short, muscular girl with a mannish stride. She was scowling in the hazy August light. Her hands were rough. She had on a sleeveless dress, yellow with black flowers, that she knew to be ugly and wore anyway because it made Claire intensely aware of her.

Cars kept going by, the tires making a wet sound on the hot asphalt. April's father had sold the Buick for almost nothing a few days before he went into the hospital, and Claire hadn't even looked at anything else. She was saving her money for a trip to Boston before April's father came home.

Claire had been quiet through most of the visit, quiet and edgy, and now that it was over she did not try to hide her relief. She wanted to walk. She said that the doctor they'd spoken with reminded her of Walt Darsh, her husband during the last ice age. That was how she located whatever had happened to her in the past—"during the last ice age." April knew that Claire wanted to be told that she still looked good, and it wouldn't have been a lie to say so, but April never did.

April had heard about Walt Darsh before, his faithlessness and cruelty. The stories Claire told were interesting, but they left April troubled and quickened, strange to herself. Now Claire was starting again, and April said, "If he was so bad, how come you married him?"

Claire didn't answer right away. She walked more slowly, and inclined her long neck at a meditative angle. She gave every sign of being occupied with a new and demanding question. After a time she turned her head and looked at April, and then looked away again. "Sex," she said.

April could see the glitter of windshields in the distance. There was a bench at the bus stop; when they got there, she was going to lie down and close her eyes and pretend to sleep.

"It's hard to explain," Claire said, cautiously, as if April had pressed her. "It wasn't his looks; Darsh isn't really what you'd call handsome. He has a sly, pointy kind of face...

like a fox. You know what I mean? It isn't just the shape, it's the way he watches you, grinning, like he's got the goods on you." Claire stopped in the shade of a tree. She took off her hat, smoothed back her hair, curled some loose strands behind her ears, and then put her hat back on and set it just so across her forehead. She found a Kleenex in her purse and dabbed the corner of one eye where a thin line of mascara had run. Claire had the gift, mysterious to April, of knowing what she looked like even without a mirror. April's face was always a surprise to her, always somehow different from how she'd imagined it.

"Of course, that can be attractive, too," Claire said, "being looked at in that way. Most of the time it's annoying, but not always. With Darsh it was attractive. So I suppose you could say that it *was* his looks, in the literal sense of 'looks.' If you see the distinction."

April saw the distinction, also Claire's pleasure in having made it. She was unhappy with this line of talk. But she couldn't do anything about it, because it was her own fault that Claire believed she was ripe for unrestrained discussion of these matters. Over the past few months Claire had decided that April was sleeping with Stuart, the boy she went out with. This was not the case. Stuart dropped hints now and then, in his polite, witty, hopeless way, but he wasn't serious and April wasn't interested. She hadn't told Claire the truth because in the beginning it had given her satisfaction to be seen as a woman of experience. Claire was a snob about knowing the ways of the world; April wanted to crowd her turf a little. Claire never asked anything anyway, she just assumed, and once the assumption took hold there was no way to straighten things out.

The brim of Claire's hat waved up and down. She seemed to be having an idea she agreed with. "Looks are part of it," she said, "definitely part of it. But not the whole story. It never is with sex, is it? Just one thing. Like technique." Claire turned and started down the road again, head still pensively bent. April could feel a lecture coming. Claire taught sociology at the same junior college where April's father used to teach history, and like him, she was quick to mount the podium.

"People write about technique," she said, "as if it's the whole ball game, which is a complete joke. You know who's really getting off on technique? Book publishers, that's who. Because they can turn it into a commodity. They can merchandise it as know-how, like traveling in Mexico or building a redwood deck. The only problem is, it doesn't work. You know why? It turns sex into a literary experience."

April laughed.

"I'm serious," Claire said. "You can tell right away that it's coming out of some book. You start seeing yourself in one of those little squiggly drawings, with your zones all marked out and some earnest little cartoon man working his way through them, being really considerate."

Claire stopped again and gazed out over the fields that lined the road, one hand resting in a friendly way on top of a fence post. Back in the old days, according to April's father, the fruitcakes used to raise things in these fields. Now the fields were overgrown with scrub pine and tall yellow grass. Insects shrilled loudly. April felt a strong hidden rhythm in the sound.

"That's another reason those books are worthless," Claire said. "They're all about sharing, being tender, anticipating your partner's needs, et cetera, et cetera. It's like Sunday school in bed. I'm not kidding, April, that's what it's all about, all this technique stuff. It's Victorian. It's trying to put clothes on monkeys. You know what I mean?"

"I guess," April said. Her voice came out dry, almost a croak.

"We're talking about a very basic transaction," Claire said. "A lot more basic than lending money to a friend. Think about it. Lending is a highly evolved activity. Other species don't do it, only us. Just look at all the things that go into lending money. Trust. Generosity. Imagining yourself in the other person's place. It's incredibly advanced, incredibly civilized. I'm all for it. My point is, sex comes from another place. Sex isn't civilized. It isn't about giving. It's about taking."

A pickup truck went past. April looked after it and then back at Claire, who was still staring out over the field. April saw the line of her profile in the shadow of the hat, saw how dry and cool her skin was, saw the composure of her smile. April saw these things and felt her own sticky, worried, incomplete condition. "We ought to get going," she said.

"To tell the truth," Claire said, "that was one of the things that attracted me to Darsh. He was a taker. Totally selfish, totally out to please himself. That gave him a certain heat. A certain power. The libbers would kill me for saying this, but it's true. Did I ever tell you about our honeymoon?"

"No." April made her voice flat and grudging, though she was curious.

"Or the maid thing? Did I ever tell you about Darsh's maid thing?"

"No," April said again. "What about the honeymoon?"

Claire said, "That's a long story. I'll tell you about the maid thing."

"You don't have to tell me anything," April said.

Claire went on smiling to herself. "Back when Darsh was a kid, his mother took him on a trip to Europe. The grand tour. He was thirteen, fourteen at the time – that age. By the time they got to Amsterdam, he was sick of museums, he never wanted to see another painting in his life. That's the trouble with pushing culture at children – they end up hating it. It's better to let them come to it on their own, don't you think?"

April shrugged.

"Take Jane Austen, for example. They were throwing Jane Austen at me when I was in the eighth grade. *Pride and Prejudice*. Of course I absolutely loathed it, because I couldn't see what was really going on, all the sexual energy behind the manners. I hadn't *lived*. You have to have some life under your belt before you can make any sense of a book like that.

"Anyway, when they got to Amsterdam, Darsh dug in his heels. He wouldn't budge. He stayed in the hotel room all day, reading mysteries and ordering stuff from room service, while his mother went out and looked at paintings. One afternoon a maid came up to the room to polish the chandelier. She had a stepladder, and from where Darsh was sitting, he couldn't help seeing up her dress. All the way up, okay? And she knew it. He knew she knew, because after a while he didn't even try to hide it, he just stared. She didn't say ˀ word. Not one. She took her sweet time up there, polishing every pendant, cool as a cucumber. Darsh said it went on for a couple of hours, which probably means an hour, which is a pretty long time, if you think about it."

"Then what happened?"

"Nothing. Nothing happened. That's the whole point, April. If something had happened, it would have broken the spell. It would have let all that incredible energy out. But it stayed locked in. It's always there, boiling away at this insane fourteen-year-old level, just waiting to explode. It's one of Darsh's real hot spots. He bought me the whole outfit; in fact, he probably still has it—you know, frilly white blouse, black skirt, black nylons with all the little snaps."

"He made you wear that? And stand on things?"

April saw Claire freeze at her words, as if she had said something hurtful and low. Claire straightened up and slowly started walking again. April hung back, and then followed a few steps behind until Claire waited for her to catch up. After a time Claire said, "No, dear. He didn't make me do anything. It's exciting when somebody wants something that much, it turns you to butter. You should have seen the way he looked at me. Pure hunger, like he wanted to eat me alive. But innocent, too.

"Maybe it sounds cheap, but I liked it. It's hard to describe."

Claire was quiet then, and so was April. She did not feel any need for description. She thought she could imagine the look Darsh had given Claire – in fact, she could see it perfectly, though no one had ever looked at her that way. Definitely not Stuart. He never would, either; he was too respectful and refined. She felt safe with him. Safe and sleepy. Nobody like Stuart would ever make her careless and willing, as Darsh did through the stories Claire told about him, even the worst stories. It seemed to April that she already knew Darsh, and that he knew her – as if he had sensed her at the margin of the stories, and was conscious of her interest. She understood that she would be at risk if she ever met anyone like him, as one day she knew she must.

They were almost at the road. April stopped and looked back, but the hospital buildings were out of sight now, behind the brow of the hill. She turned and walked on. She had one more of these trips to make, one more Sunday. The weekend after that her father would come home. He had the doctors eating out of his hand with that amused, I-don't-know-what-came-over-me act. It worked because he believed it himself. He'd been theatrically calm all through their visit. He sat by the window in an easy chair, feet propped up on an ottoman, a newspaper across his lap. He was wearing slippers and a cardigan sweater. All he needed was a pipe. He seemed fine, the very picture of health, but that was all it was: a picture. At home he never read the paper. He didn't sit down much either. The last time April had seen him, six days earlier, he had been under restraint in their landlord's apartment, where he had gone to complain about the shower. He'd been kicking and yelling. His glasses were hanging from one ear. He was shouting at her to call the police, and one of the policemen holding him down was laughing helplessly.

He hadn't crashed yet. He was still flying. April had seen

it in his eyes behind the lithium or whatever they were giving him, and she was sure that Claire had seen it, too. Claire didn't say anything, but April had been through this with Ellen, her first stepmother, and she'd developed an instinct. She was afraid that Claire had had enough, that she wasn't going to come back from Boston, or that if she did come back, it wouldn't be to live with them. Not that Claire was planning any of this. It wouldn't happen that way, it would just happen. April didn't want it to, especially not now. She needed another year. Not even a year – ten months, until she finished school and got into college somewhere. If she could cross that line, she was sure she could handle whatever came after.

She didn't want Claire to go. Claire had her ways, but she had been good to April, especially in the beginning, when April was always finding fault with her. Claire had put up with it. She'd been patient, and let April come to her in her own time. April used to lean against her when they were sitting on the couch, and Claire would give and press back at the same time. They could sit for hours like that, reading. Claire thought about things. She had talked to April, honestly but with a certain decorum. Now the decorum was gone. Ever since she got the idea that April had lost her virginity, Claire had withdrawn the protections of ceremony and tact, as she would soon withdraw the protection of her own self.

There was no way to change things back. And even if there were, even if by saying "I'm a virgin" she could turn Claire into some kind of perfect mother, April wouldn't do it. It would sound ridiculous, untrue. And it wasn't true, except as a fact about her body. But April did not see virginity as residing in the body. To her it was a quality of the spirit, and something you could surrender only in the spirit. She had done this; she didn't know exactly when or how, but she knew that she had done this and she did not regret it. She did not want to be a virgin and she would not pretend to be one, not for anything. When she thought of a virgin, she saw someone half naked, with dumb trusting eyes and flowers woven into her hair, a clearing in the jungle, and in the clearing an altar.

THEY'D MISSED THEIR BUS. Because it was Sunday, they had a long wait until the next one. Claire settled on the bench and started reading a book. April had forgotten hers. She sat with Claire for a while and then got up and paced the street when Claire's serenity became intolerable. She walked with her arms crossed and her head bent forward, frowning, scuffing her shoes. Cars rushed past, each in its own blare of music, a big sailboat on a trailer, a long slow convoy of military trucks, soldiers swaying in back. The air was blue with exhaust. April, passing a tire store, looked at the window and saw herself. She squared her shoulders and dropped her arms to her sides, and kept them there by an effort of will as she walked farther up the boulevard to where a line of plastic pennants fluttered over a car lot. A man in a creamy suit was standing in the showroom window, watching the traffic. He had high cheekbones, black hair combed straight back from his forehead, a big clean blade of a nose. He looked like a gambler, or maybe a hit man. April knew that he was aware of her, but he never bothered to look in her direction. She wandered among the cars, all Toyotas, and then went back to the bus stop and slumped down on the bench.

"I'm bored," she said.

Claire didn't answer.

"Aren't you bored?"

"Not especially," Claire said. "The bus should be here pretty soon."

"Sure, in about two weeks." April stuck her legs out and knocked the sides of her shoes together. "Let's take a walk," she said.

"I'm all walked out. But you go ahead. Just don't get too far away."

"Not *alone,* Claire, I didn't mean alone. Come on, this is boring." April hated the sound of her voice, and she could see that Claire didn't like it either. Claire closed her book. She sat without moving and then said, coldly, "I guess I don't have any choice."

April rocked to her feet. She moved a little way up the sidewalk and waited as Claire put the book in her purse, stood, ran her hands down the front of her skirt, and came slowly toward her.

"We'll just stretch our legs," April said. She kept chattering until they reached the car lot, where she left the sidewalk and began circling a red Celica convertible.

"I thought you wanted to walk," Claire said.

"Right, just a minute," April said. Then the side door of the showroom swung open and the man in the suit came out. At first he seemed not to know they were there. He knelt beside a station wagon and wrote something down on a clipboard. He got up and peered at the sticker on the windshield and wrote something else down. Only then did he take any notice of them. He looked their way, and after he'd had a good long look, he told them to let him know if they needed anything. His voice had a studied, almost insolent lack of concern.

"We're just waiting for a bus," Claire said.

"How does this car stack up against the RX-7?" April asked.

"You surely jest." He made his way toward them through the cars. "I could sell against Mazda any day of the week. If I were selling."

April said, "You're not a salesman?"

He stopped in front of the Celica. "We don't have salesmen here. We just collect money and try to keep the crowds friendly."

Claire laughed. She said, "April."

"That's a year old," he said. "Got it in this morning on a repossession. It'll be gone this time tomorrow. Look at the odometer, sweet pea. What does the odometer say?"

April opened the door and leaned inside. "Four thousand," she said. She sat in the driver's seat and worked the gearshift.

"Exactly. Four K. Still on its first tank of gas."

"Little old lady owned it, right?" Claire said.

He looked at her for a time before answering. "Little old Marine. Got shipped out and didn't keep up his payments. I'll get the keys."

"We're just—"

"I know, you're waiting for a bus. So kill some time."

April got out of the car but left the door open. "Claire, you have to try this seat," she said.

"We should go," Claire said.

"Claire, you just have to. Come on," April said. "Come on, Claire."

The man walked over to the open door and held out his hand. "Madame," he said. Claire stood her ground. "Claire, *get in*," April said. She had never spoken to her in this way, and did not know what Claire would do.

Claire walked up to the car. "We really should go," she said. She sat sideways on the seat and swung her legs inside, all in one motion. She nodded at the man and he closed the door. "Yes," he said, "just as I thought," He walked to the front of the car. "Exactly as I thought. The designer was a close friend of yours. This car was obviously built with you in mind."

"You look great," April said. It was true, and she could see that Claire was in possession of that truth. The knowledge was in the set of her mouth, the way her hands came to rest on the wheel.

"There's something missing," the man said. He studied her. "Sunglasses," he said. "A beautiful woman in a convertible has to be wearing sunglasses."

"Put on your sunglasses," April said.

ABOUT THE AUTHORS

RICHARD BAUSCH's "What Feels Like the World" won the O. Henry Award and was published in *Spirits,* his collection of short stories. He is also the author of several fine novels, and lives in Virginia with his wife and two children.

CHARLES BAXTER's three books of stories include *Through the Safety Net, Harmony of the World,* and *A Relative Stranger.* He is also the author of *First Light,* a novel. He lives in Ann Arbor, Michigan, where he teaches at the University of Michigan.

KATE BRAVERMAN is a poet, short-story writer, novelist, and single mother who lives in Los Angeles. "Temporary Light" is from her first collection of stories, *Squandering the Blue.* Her novels are *Lithium for Medea* and *Palm Latitudes.*

KAREN BROWN's story "Destiny" was her first published fiction. Born and reared in Hartford, Connecticut, she currently lives in Tampa. She has a B.A. in creative writing from the University of South Florida.

DOROTHY BRYANT is the author of eight novels, a collection of stories and essays called *Myths to Lie By,* and a celebrated and widely used textbook, *Writing a Novel.* She lives in California.

KATHLEEN CAMBOR received a master's degree in creative writing from the University of Houston. She lives in Houston with her husband and two children, and is completing work on a novel.

ELLEN HUNNICUTT's collection of short stories, *In the Music Library,* won the Drue Heinz Literature Prize in 1987. She now writes and teaches in Big Bend, Wisconsin, and has also written a novel, *Suite for Calliope.*

MAURICE KENNY is a celebrated Native American poet and writer. Winner of the 1984 American Book Award, he is currently the editor/publisher of Strawberry Press and teaches at the college level.

NANCI KINCAID's stories have been published in literary magazines, as well as anthologies. She is working toward an MFA degree from the University of Alabama, and lives in Tuscaloosa.

MAXINE KUMIN has published several books of poetry, four novels, a collection of short stories, and two books of essays. Her most recent works are *Nurture,* a book of poems, and *In Deep: Country Essays.*

COLLEEN J. MCELROY is a professor of English and Creative Writing at the University of Washington in Seattle. She has written six books of poetry and two short-story collections.

DENNIS MCFARLAND's stories have appeared in the *New Yorker,* and his very fine novel, *The Music Room,* was published last year. He has been a Wallace Stegner Fellow at Stanford University. He currently lives near Boston with his wife and two children.

DEBORAH ROSE O'NEAL's stories have been published in a wide variety of literary and general magazines, and have won her recognition with a PEN Syndicated Fiction Project award. She lives in Connecticut with her husband, two stepdaughters, and three sons.

PAMELA PAINTER has published stories in many literary magazines and is the author of a story collection entitled *Getting to Know the Weather.* Winner of the 1986 Great Lakes College Association Award for First Fiction, she is a founding editor of *Storyquarterly* and lives in Boston.

ANNICK SMITH's "It's Come to This" is her first published story. She was executive producer of *Heartland,* a film about pioneer life on the Great Plains, and with William Kittredge co-edited *The Last Best Place: A Montana Anthology.* She lives in Western Montana.

CHRISTOPHER TILGHMAN's first book of stories, *In My Father's House,* was published to acclaim last year. He is a graduate of Yale, and lives outside of Boston with his wife and two sons.

Molly Best Tinsley's story "Zoe" was included in the anthology *New Stories from the South*. She lives outside of Washington, D.C., and teaches on the civilian faculty of the U.S. Naval Academy.

Joan Wickersham's story "Commuter Marriage" is her first published story, and it was included in *The Best American Stories 1990*. She now is working on a novel. She lives in the Boston area.

Tobias Wolff is a celebrated writer and participant in an "interesting family situation." He and his brother, Geoffrey, both wrote fine books about their childhood (*This Boy's Life* and *The Duke of Deception*), respectively. Tobias Wolff's novels and collections of short stories include *The Barracks Thief* and *Back in the World*. He lives in Syracuse and teaches at the University of Syracuse.

OTHER BOOKS IN
THE GRAYWOLF SHORT FICTION SERIES

This book was designed
by Tree Swenson
It was set in Baskerville
type by The Typeworks
and manufactured by
Edwards Brothers
on acid-free paper.